PENGUIN BOOKS

INVINCIBLE

'Perceptive and well-wrought . . . the inner workings
and passions of a top club and a famous team'
Sunday Times, Sports Books of the Year

'Riveting. My only complaint about the book is that
it had to end' Patrick Barclay

'Brilliant stories' *Today*, BBC Radio 4

'Engrossing read from start to finish. It paints a wonderful and
vivid picture of one of the greatest achievements in English
football history' John Cross, *Daily Mirror*

'This is a book that contains some of the most evocative
prose I have encountered in a book about football and without
doubt solidifies Lawrence's place in the very top tier of sports
writing in English. The story and characters are fascinating
enough, but it is how they come to life and dance in Lawrence's
writing that makes this book such a wonderful telling of an
incredible tale' *Huffington Post*

'The story of an amazing season wonderfully told through the
eyes of the men who made it happen. I can't recommend it highly
enough' Andrew Mangan, *Arseblog*

'I picked it up and couldn't put it down. Brilliantly
depicts a piece of football history'
David Dein, Arsenal Vice-Chairman (1983–2007)

'Many striking aspects' *The Times*

'Lawrence is a writer who will help the reader to appreciate the
football on the pitch with an understanding of how the game is
played few can match. At the same time she never fails to appreciate
the passion that makes us fans' *Morning Star*

'If you were there in 71 and/or 2004, buy the book. If only now do you appreciate that we probably had four of the six best payers on the planet back then, buy the book and read their words. Let me make it simple. If you are an Arsenal supporter, buy the book' *Goonerholic*

ABOUT THE AUTHOR

Amy Lawrence has watched football avidly since her first trip to Highbury at the age of six, and has written about it, mostly for the *Guardian* and the *Observer*, for twenty years. She lives in London. @amylawrence71

The Invincibles are:

1	Jens Lehmann	17	Edu
12	Lauren	15	Ray Parlour
23	Sol Campbell	18	Pascal Cygan
28	Kolo Touré	9	José Antonio Reyes
3	Ashley Cole	11	Sylvain Wiltord
8	Freddie Ljungberg	22	Gaël Clichy
4	Patrick Vieira	5	Martin Keown
19	Gilberto Silva	30	Jérémie Aliadière
7	Robert Pirès	25	Nwankwo Kanu
10	Dennis Bergkamp		
14	Thierry Henry		

Arsène Wenger

Invincible

Inside Arsenal's Unbeaten 2003–2004 Season

AMY LAWRENCE

PENGUIN BOOKS

PENGUIN BOOKS

UK | USA | Canada | Ireland | Australia
India | New Zealand | South Africa

Penguin Books is part of the Penguin Random House group of companies
whose addresses can be found at global.penguinrandomhouse.com.

Penguin
Random House
UK

First published by Viking 2014
Published in Penguin Books 2015
009

Copyright © Amy Lawrence, 2014

The moral right of the author has been asserted

Set in 11.16/13.90 pt Bembo Book MT Std
Typeset by Jouve (UK), Milton Keynes
Printed and bound in Great Britain by Clays Ltd, Elcograf S.p.A.

A CIP catalogue record for this book is available from the British Library

ISBN: 978-0-241-97049-2

www.greenpenguin.co.uk

MIX
Paper from
responsible sources
FSC® C018179

Penguin Random House is committed to a
sustainable future for our business, our readers
and our planet. This book is made from Forest
Stewardship Council® certified paper.

For Mum
Who doesn't like football, but is one of life's unbeatables

Contents

Contents

x

Foreword

by Arsène Wenger

I've been making teams since I was ten years old. I grew up above a pub in Duttlenheim which was the headquarters of the local football team. I assisted when the guys picked the team each Sunday. I looked like a little boy trying to be the manager – I already had my opinions. When you are a kid you are one hundred per cent convinced of them.

I knew I had a special team in 2003–04 at Arsenal. It had always been my dream to go through a season without losing, even though it is not a normal ambition. What made that aspiration so special is that I strive for perfection. I have always wanted to do my job as well as I can. At the end of each season I ask myself, have I done the maximum with this team? If you win the championship you can still think the guy who finished tenth in the league has done better than you, because he has taken the maximum of the maximum of the potential of his team. Nobody can truly measure that. Only you know deeply if there was any more to give. So I always admired this idea to win a championship without losing a game, because after that you cannot do much better. You think then you have been as close as you can get to doing your job in a perfect way. To win, taking every drop out of the team, and pushing them as far as they can, is the utmost achievement. That's why you can never release the concentration, focus or commitment.

The season before the Invincibles, I came out and said the ideal target was an unbeaten season. We had won the championship in 2002 without losing a game away from home. In 2003 we lost it. I was, of course, disappointed. During the pre-season of 2003–04 I had a meeting with the players and said to them, 'Let's analyse why we lost this championship.' Some of them, like Martin Keown, said to me, 'It's your fault.' I said, 'Yes. I am ready to take the blame, but why?' He said, 'You put too much pressure on us. The idea of winning the championship without losing a game was too much pressure to take. It's impossible.' I said, 'Look, I said that because I think you can do it. But you must really want it. It would be an unbelievable achievement to be the first team to do that.'

I felt everything was there in this group. We had technical talent, we had the intelligence and the mental aspect that goes with that, and we had the physical potential to do it. I remember one day a friend of mine from France came to the training ground, and he sat at the entrance and observed. I didn't ask him to do that. After the training session he came to me and said, 'I watched all of your players coming in. When they walk through the door in the morning these guys have a special charisma.' He was right. They had charisma individually – everyone was different – but together they were even more special.

They showed me that you can achieve things that you think are not achievable.

Prologue

'Hello?'

'Hi, Ames, it's Tom. Listen. Do you want one of the old press box desks from Highbury?'

'Er, yes.'

The Tom in question knew someone who had salvaged a couple of such items when the bulldozers were in the process of demolishing the place that meant more to me than anywhere else in the world. Frankly, the desks themselves are not outstanding artefacts: small rectangles of MDF encased in grey plastic, attached to square metal legs which are painted glossy black. My knees were achingly familiar with them; it was cramped in that old press box. Depending on which seat you were given, there was a reasonable chance one of the posts would require you to bob and weave throughout the game so as not to miss anything. But my goodness, posts and all it was beautiful, and the venue for some astonishing times.

Every time I walk over one of the enormous bridges onto the smooth concourse of the Emirates Stadium I stall for a moment. It is impossible not to long for the place that is, in mind and spirit, forever home. Dear old Highbury, which was not as spacious, not as modern, not as lucrative as Arsenal's current abode, but whose soul seeped into every wall, every corridor, every nook and cranny. Walking within, you could always hear the echo of footballing tales of old.

Being able to explore the different parts of Highbury over the years created a treasure trove of memories: taken to the West Upper with my best friend and some Wombles to play with in the 1970s. Grabbing pocket money and jumping on the bus to pay at the North Bank turnstiles to sway with the crowd in the 1980s. Moving across to the Clock End to be with friends in the 1990s. Taking position to work in the East Stand in the 2000s. It is all still so clear in my mind's eye. Up the ornate stairs, marshalled by the twinkle-eyed member of the ground staff, Paddy, who liked to stand guard over the Marble Halls. The grand door which led into the tunnel, with a little room known as the halfway house tucked away just off it. The Gunners Shop, in my youth run by former goalkeeper Jack Kelsey. Round the back and through the car park behind the Clock End to the offices and the players' lounge above the old JVC centre. In through the red door marked PRESS and up through the thin stairwell leading to the media area. Sometimes I would sneak out the far door and into the hallway above the Marble Halls. What a vantage point; the dark oak-panelled board-room to one side, the door through which the manager's office was located on the other, and straight ahead the light shone through the gateway to the Directors' Box overlooking that perfect pitch. The whole place was magical, in a way that new stadia in a high-financed age cannot replicate. We belonged to it, and it belonged to us.

As far as souvenirs are concerned, I have that desk from the old press box. When I look at it, of all the games I watched from that vantage point, the one that remains in its own way more unbeliev-able than any of the others was this one: Arsenal 2 Leicester City 1, 15 May 2004. It was one of those occasions where it was neces-sary to make the effort to consciously slow down time. There was a compulsion to attempt to take in what was happening. Don't miss any detail. Store it, with as much clarity as possible. High-bury was sunlit, the supporters were watching the best team they had ever seen, and history was unfolding right there in front of everyone as Arsenal went about completing an unbeaten season for the first time in the modern game. Endeavouring to find the right words to capture the essence of this story, and to somehow convey the atmosphere and meaning, felt like a weighty responsibility. It was a pressure but also a huge privilege.

Ten years later, revisiting that season in conversation with the protagonists was incredibly rewarding. The perspective of Arsène Wenger, his phenomenal players, and other club staff added such depth and detail to the narrative and the characters involved. The memories they so generously shared allows them to explain in their own words how a rare sporting achievement comes together, how a squad of players is constructed, how a style is formed, connections created and a spirit fortified. They developed exceptional resources to sail through the currents of a season – sometimes smoothly, other times knocked about on a storm – to cross a historic finishing line intact. It's their story, so there could be no better method than hearing them tell it. I decided to leave Wenger's impressions in pure, unadulterated form, so he could express them in his own words to conclude the book.

Searching for the framework to capture the spirit of the Invincible era, neither a chronological series of matches nor a set of player portraits felt quite right. The testimony of the people involved made it possible to explore various themes that came together to create the symphony of that season. It was necessary to delve into the background to understand how it evolved over time, rather than restricting the time span to one season. I have also reproduced excerpts from the articles I wrote for the *Observer* during 2003–04 to reflect the mood of the moment, which tends to pack a different punch to hindsight and reflection.

The unbeaten season was an extraordinary achievement, created by an even more extraordinary group of people. Having watched that team and, more recently, heard them recount what happened, makes me doubly grateful to the Invincibles.

Those were the days.

Amy Lawrence,
London, May 2014

PART ONE

JANUARY 1989 – NOVEMBER 2003

I

Fractions

Venice, as a holiday destination, is a dreamy enough place to escape from the thunderous pressure of professional football. Robert Pirès was enjoying his break, when he chanced upon a couple of English football fans who stopped him to engage in conversation. 'What are you doing here, Ruud?' they asked. 'Ruud?' replied a perplexed Pirès. The strangers paused, hesitated, inspected him up and down before realizing their mistake. 'You are not Ruud van Nistelrooy!' He shook his head. 'Oh merde,' thought Pirès.

We pause. We hold our collective breath. This crowd of 67,639 partisans is transfixed. There are multiple layers in this particular collision course: Ruud van Nistelrooy versus Jens Lehmann. Striker versus goalkeeper. Manchester United versus Arsenal. North versus South. Red versus yellow. Champion versus challenger. Sir Alex Ferguson versus Arsène Wenger. In the minds of the supporters, it even boils down to a tribal version of righteous versus enemy. Us versus Them. The stakes are oppressive, bearing down on one penalty kick in stoppage time during an ill-tempered game that has been – until now – tight, fraught, goalless.

Van Nistelrooy stands, hands on hips, almost casual. He wipes his face with his forearm. Lehmann is pacing. He stomps back and forth across his goal line, arms outstretched, to try to disturb his opponent's clean sightlines. The referee's whistle gives its piercing signal: Showtime.

The run-up is confident, the strike ferocious. Lehmann plunges to his left. The ball's trajectory flashes past the goalkeeper's right. Perhaps the most extraordinary thing is the noise that the ball makes as it hurtles against the frame of the goal. It is a percussive, explosive, smack. It is startling. It is violently loud.

Despite being assailed by a cacophony of gasps, wails and screeches cascading down from all four sides, that clunk sticks in the mind of Lehmann to this day. 'Of course you hear it,' he says. 'It is so close. In that moment the whole stadium is silent, for that split second. As a goalkeeper you know when you have a chance that the guy is missing. I saw the ball flying past and by the flight of the ball I said to myself, *Oh, I'm not sure that that's in*. And fortunately it hit the crossbar.'

Rarely in life are we aware that the seconds we see unfolding before our eyes are in some way momentous or historic. Mostly, that importance is only conferred with hindsight. Who knew at that precise moment, when the ball made the woodwork jolt – neither a fraction too high to miss it altogether, nor a fraction too low to skim beneath it and into the goal – the significance would reverberate for days, weeks, months to come? Who knew an Invincible season rode upon such a fine margin? Nobody. Nobody knew, because frankly nobody bothered wasting many thoughts on something as outlandish as completing an entire league season with an unblemished record.

It was hardly a regular ambition. At the start of a fresh campaign, it is reasonable to aspire to win a trophy, perhaps to break a club record. For a striker it's normal to hope to score a certain number of goals, or for a defender to concede fewer than before. A stalwart is allowed to yearn to top the appearances chart. The most naturally talented might wish for an individual garland – player of the month, the year, scorer of the most beautiful goal. An unbeaten season is simply not a normal thing to dream about.

'These things weren't in our heads,' insists Sol Campbell. 'You just think about winning more games than the other teams around you and that's it.'

Campbell was a couple of hundred miles south from this pivotal moment. He was on compassionate leave after the death of his father. He watched the game on television at home. What he saw from a distance only backs up his conviction that fate played a part in deciding the course for this group of players – for him and his friends, his workmates, the men he grew to rely on, who in turn relied on him. 'The moment chooses you,' he muses. 'You don't choose the moment. Because if he scores, it's finished. Going unbeaten all season – it's gone. You've got to have the right team and things like that, but the situation chooses you. I truly believe that.'

Centre stage at Old Trafford, consumed by feverish emotions in the aftermath of van Nistelrooy's penalty miss, not one of Arsenal's players thinks for a second about anything other than avoiding defeat for one game only. This was a team, a collection of players, who each brought his own obsession with winning to the party. Together, it created a communal loathing of defeat that became overpowering.

The game is remembered not only for its dramatic denouement, but also for the overheated reactions which spewed forth. A decade down the line, most of the players have a similar first response to a prompt about that infamous 0–0 at Old Trafford. The same knowing smile presents itself. It encompasses mischief, determination and also a twinge of embarrassment. 'The Martin Keown picture,' says Dennis Bergkamp, chuckling to himself. It is the image that pops instinctively into everybody's minds. Kolo Touré breaks into a low cartoon-villain laugh. Heh heh heh. Ray Parlour's eyes twinkle. Robert Pirès emits a Gallic 'oouf', pulling an expression that perfectly captures the astonishment widely felt at the time, and remembers 'the impression Martin wanted to kill him'. Gilberto Silva and Lauren seem slightly dubious about what feelings they should give away. They appreciate it isn't right to be overtly jubilant about what went on that September day. Arsenal did enough of that at the time with some fairly serious consequences.

The moment when Keown leapt, roaring, into van Nistelrooy and clumped him on the back of the head – causing the United striker to visibly cower – has become one of the iconic images for that season in that it reflects how profoundly this team could not accept losing and how they felt driven to stick up for one another. Keown was still smarting from the fact that Patrick Vieira, Arsenal's captain and heartbeat, had been sent off in the eighty-first minute. Van Nistelrooy had been implicated in that incident, having jumped clumsily into Vieira, who kicked out in retaliation. Although it wasn't even close to making contact – 'there were metres and metres between my legs and his body,' Vieira would later explain – van Nistelrooy jerked back, as if recoiling from a jab, and gestured plaintively at the referee. Vieira's smile was laced with heavy sarcasm as he was shown a red card. The incendiary device was duly planted.

The dressing room is a torturous place when you have been sent off. It is a form of solitary confinement. You are not just banished from the pitch, and merely unable to contribute, but you are isolated and sent far enough away that you are not even allowed to watch what is happening. Vieira is struggling to deal with a boiling mixture of frustration, disappointment and anger towards his nemesis on the day. 'At that moment, I hated him,' he says. 'Of course, because of him faking and all that stuff. I don't hate him now. But at that moment I hated him. Do you understand what I mean?'

That question, articulated ten years down the line from the event, is recognition of how strange it is for an intelligent person to feel revulsion for someone else in a sporting context. The head knows he should rise above but the raging heart, on that hot Manchester afternoon, was consuming.

'It's tough, especially in a big moment like that,' Vieira explains. 'The game was crazy – especially going down to ten men, and the penalty. You feel like you let the team down. You feel like if you lose it is going to be your fault. There are so many emotions going through your mind, and everything is negative. You feel really bad. I was thinking about what had happened and was hoping we would get the draw. But I was so mad about the red card.'

Keown can't let it go. Van Nistelrooy has a reputation already amongst Arsenal's players, which only adds to the knife-edge mood. Looking after Vieira is something he had taken on as his personal responsibility. 'I was Patrick Vieira's minder,' explains Keown. 'People used to target Patrick, and I vowed I've got to be the person who gets there to get in between. Because we can't have this, we're not going to win anything unless we've got Patrick on the pitch. People were quickly seeing that Patrick never started any problems, but he would finish them. He was the captain, everything would go through him, let's not forget. But this occasion, yet again, somebody had feigned injury from Patrick, and had gone over. It was that same character, too. I'd already had a few run-ins with him. Now he'd got my mate sent off.'

Parlour was equally frustrated. 'We said "You're a joke" to van Nistelrooy and gave him a bit of stick, because he did cheat. And Patrick's a very influential player in our team, so straight away the players are going mad, really.' The survival instinct had to kick in quickly, though, with United at an advantage. 'We thought, *We've got to deal with it*,' says Parlour. 'Look, we've done it before. Many occasions we've had ten men. Most training sessions when you've got eleven v ten you have to defend it, so we knew what we had to do to get the result.'

It takes considerable grit to concentrate on protecting a valuable away point with ten men against a streetwise rival. When Gary Neville slings in a cross during stoppage time, Diego Forlán tumbles with Keown in close attention, and the referee, Steve Bennett, points to the penalty spot, Arsenal's ultra-competitive centre half looks stunned, as if his world is about to implode. Problem piled on problem piled on problem. Defend Patrick. Van Nistelrooy under the skin. Red card. Penalty. Last minute. My challenge. Can't bear losing. Emotional combustion.

'It was quite a comfortable afternoon until Patrick got sent off, and then it was like the Alamo,' recalls Keown. 'And of course *he* was the player that had created all of this, in my eyes, and in the players' eyes. So when I gave away the penalty, it was that feeling that Man United win in the last minute and it's going to happen again. And shit, it's me, it's my fault. And when he misses, the relief, and feeling of *It's you again, you cheating* . . . was overwhelming.

'And that's where it happened. To be honest, there wasn't a lot of time from when the penalty miss happened to the end of the game, so it kind of carried on. People look at it and say, "Do you regret that?" It wasn't perfect behaviour for kids to follow, but it was pent-up years of frustration really. Man United won a lot of things, and in our eyes we were winners. I never realized that it would be such a vital miss, from that penalty to what we went on to achieve.'

For Thierry Henry, it was all part of what would become a growing feeling that the dice would roll well that season. 'Even though sometimes we needed that bit of luck to turn things our way, it usually did,' he muses.

Vieira knows about the penalty but there is no television in the dressing room. He relies on sound. Of course, he is metaphorically miles away from that crack of ball on wood that Lehmann hears, but the noise of the chorus suffices. 'I didn't hear the big roar,' he says, a broad smile creeping into his face. 'If they scored it would have sounded different.'

Keown might have been the lightning rod for this particular episode, but he is not the only one to wade into the melee sparked by the final whistle. A little gang of Arsenal's players bombard van Nistelrooy, hound him as he stumbles off the pitch. Parlour, Ashley Cole, even Lauren – gentle, unflappable Lauren – are afflicted by red mist. He, too, lashes out at van Nistelrooy. 'I am very calm, I am very polite, a nice person in general, but I make my mistakes like everyone else,' he now explains sheepishly. 'It's just when I go to the pitch I transform myself. I like the crowd and being on the pitch with 80,000 people watching. I love it. When I go to the pitch [he clicks his fingers] I become a different person. I just want to be my best, I just want to win. Maybe that is why I reacted in that way. We are helping each other like a family. If I see my brother in difficulty I try to help him. Everyone was thinking the same way.'

The level-headed Gilberto tries, belatedly, to cool the situation down. 'That game was tense, you know? My job was to try to calm down the tension. I was one of the peacemakers,' he says. Even if it is not his nature, he understands how it is when something explodes. 'When adrenaline gets very high you can get a big reaction. Some Man United players did too. I remember someone, I think it was Ronaldo, pushed somebody then ran away. It was quite funny. The image is not good – as a professional footballer you must give an example for the spectators – but I think people understood it was just the heat of the game. Of course we had to apologize.'

Oddly, one of the players who is notably cool in the face of this inferno is Roy Keane, Vieira's direct rival in that period, and a player who would later have no qualms in expressing how riled the London team generally made him feel. 'I had a lot of hatred for Arsenal,' he says. 'I can't think of any other word when I was getting ready to do battle with Arsenal. Hatred was the word. I don't remember liking anybody at Arsenal. I knew I had to be at my angriest against them. I didn't feel like that about any other team, but Arsenal brought out something different in me . . . I behaved myself that day and I regret it!'

The fury continues down the tunnel, where players row, threats are thrown, insults hurled and Wenger and Ferguson have what some might generously describe as a frank exchange of views. When the blood stops pumping and the heartbeat slows, the funny thing is that they probably both have a point. Ferguson feels incensed that Arsenal's players have ganged up on his striker.

Wenger is infuriated because he thinks van Nistelrooy has conned the referee. But such is the nature of the beast that defending one's own interests tends to overrule acceptance of anyone else's grievances, or admissions of guilt close to home.

Back in the dressing room, Lehmann is riveted by it all. He is soaking up a new experience. This is only his sixth match in English football, having joined in the summer from the Bundesliga in his native Germany to replace David Seaman. Arriving at Arsenal at the age of thirty-three, he feels comfortable enough in his own skin to try to enjoy all the new challenges and cultural changes that his new league has to offer. But the scale of this madness surprises him. His only previous excursion outside the Bundesliga had been a spell with AC Milan six years previously. It had not been a success and he'd left within six months, but he is relishing his new English adventure, and all the post-match fieriness strikes a strident chord. He looks around and can see in each of his teammates an overbearing will to win.

'Yes, I liked it. I loved it,' he enthuses. 'I think probably they and myself didn't know how much I actually appreciated this type of game. Arsène didn't know he'd picked a guy who was probably made for this game. I didn't know it either. I enjoyed the biggest clashes, where you had to show the opponents: *Are you stronger than us, or are we stronger than you?* In the game I was coming out sometimes for crosses and I had been punched and kicked and everything, and the ref never ever whistled. After the incident at the end of the game, I remember a couple of friends from Germany telling me, "It's great! People punching each other, shouting at the referee, and nobody's getting booked, nothing happens!" But five days later six were charged by the FA for Arsenal, and three for Man U . . . At the time, it was the best game in English football, and the biggest game. It was Wenger versus Ferguson. The nice-playing Londoners against the successful tough guys from Manchester. A lot happened in the tunnel afterwards.'

Freddie Ljungberg thinks the result, and to an extent the

reaction, sent a message to United. 'It sounds cocky to say that, but of course there's always a power struggle for a team to be the big dog.'

Vieira is still stewing. 'I had a few more arguments with van Nistelrooy again after taking a shower, in the tunnel. I was still really mad about it,' he says.

Tempers are up. Football managers are expected to give post-match television interviews to the host broadcaster, and Wenger and Ferguson oblige, but talking into a camera moments after being totally immersed in a high-octane match is a procedure more or less designed to catch people at their least reasonable. Both men wear expressions of thinly disguised disgust. Their answers are suitably spiky.

Wenger: 'I think van Nistelrooy doesn't help. Frankly, his attitude is always looking for provocation and diving. He looks a nice boy, but I think on the pitch he has not always fair behaviour.'

Sky reporter Clare Tomlinson: 'Is that a kind of cheating in your book?'

Wenger: 'Yes, I think so, because I believe again that Patrick maybe should not have reacted but, again, you punish more the consequence than the source of the problem.'

Ferguson: 'As far as I'm concerned, I can defend Ruud van Nistelrooy. I've heard Arsène's comments in your interview and I'm really disappointed to hear that, because Ruud van Nistelrooy had a foul on Patrick Vieira, like there were many fouls in the whole game – Patrick himself had some fouls. And he's reacted badly! Ruud has not dived, he's tried to get out of the road, he's looked at the referee – *What kind of behaviour is this?* – and the referee has no option . . . As for the behaviour at the end of the game, I think the FA will be doing that anyway, so I don't need to talk about Arsenal's discipline . . . I think my players have behaved properly.'

The agenda is taking shape. Arsenal's rage about van Nistelrooy's role in the affair gets lost in the overall wrath which backs Ferguson's critique of the bullying behaviour witnessed at the end of the game. Righteous indignation closes in from all sides. The media heap censure onto Wenger and his players, and the Football Association quickly charge Arsenal with 'failing to control their players', while Wenger is asked by the authorities to explain his remarks about an opposition player cheating. Headlines are predictably fierce. 'Hit These Thugs With Hefty Bans!' shouts the *Daily Mail*. 'Tribal Squabbling Scars Old Trafford' laments *The Times*. 'Arsenal's Paranoia Damages Reputation Of Proud Club' tuts the *Independent*. 'Arsenal Are Facing 20 Match Ban Over Shameful Sunday: Kiss Goodbye To The Title' lambasts the *Express*. The same words crop up in article after article – spite, menace, petulance, shame.

Ken Friar, a member of the Arsenal board who had been watching events unfold from the Directors' Box, braces himself for a visit to the Football Association. 'My role was to represent the best interests in the club, so yes, you go and fight your corner,' he says pointedly. The club view is to say as little as possible in public, defend the Arsenal position with the FA, accept the punishment, and get on with it as calmly as possible. Some journalists are, however, able to rely on the fact the chairman, Peter Hill-Wood, will politely accept their calls, and manage to draw him into expressing some public embarrassment. 'There are no excuses. We were guilty of stupid behaviour. I have spoken to manager Arsène Wenger many times about this because, yes, we have a problem,' he is reported to have said. 'It seems that whatever we tell the players, in the heat of the moment, they forget.'

After four days of relentless criticism, Wenger issues an apology, albeit one that gives the impression of a truculent child who isn't entirely sincere.

Wenger: 'I watched it again and we overreacted. We apologize for that. But I think there has been an overreaction to what happened. No one was hurt and I have seen in my time in England – dangerous tackles and challenges that could end careers. I've seen ten times worse than what happened on Sunday. But none of my players was guilty of anything that could damage careers or of dangerous tackles. I don't say what we did was right. I have spoken to the players about it. Martin Keown knows he shouldn't have done it. There was a campaign for us to be charged. We have to acknowledge we were out of order with our behaviour but there was really an overreaction to it as well.'

Journalist Steve Stammers: 'There has been a suggestion of a points deduction?'

Wenger: 'Why not put us in Division One? Even in pub teams worse happens than happened on Sunday.'

It takes several weeks for the Battle of Old Trafford, as it became known, to be forensically examined by the authorities and for the FA's disciplinary mechanism to finally reach its verdict. In the meantime Arsenal's players do their best to put blinkers on and concentrate on the football pitch. They put together a sequence of three narrow and meaningful Premier League wins: Arsenal 3 Newcastle 2; Liverpool 1 Arsenal 2; Arsenal 2 Chelsea 1. There is one goal in particular which stands out. Pirès's match-winner at Anfield is stunning. Back in the north-west, two weekends after Old Trafford, spotlight burning, critics on their backs, coming back from a losing position, Pirès cracks a bending shot from twenty-five yards into the top corner. As he peels away in celebration, his face is euphoric. His teammates rush to him. One by one they engulf him – Ashley Cole, Thierry Henry, Edu, Sol Campbell . . . Their communal, cathartic roar is picked up by the touchline microphones for TV broadcast. The chorus of pure, instinctive, elation loads the strike with importance.

'I remember that goal,' says Pirès, with an expression of nostalgic joy. 'It was a source of pride. That goal gave us victory. I wanted to share the goal with the supporters. That was an important moment for Arsenal, so it needed a certain communion between the supporters and the team.'

Gilberto has an interesting take on the effects of the Old Trafford game, which encouraged Arsenal to refocus on business. He believes it was a wake-up call of sorts, to remind them to be super-sharp. That, he reckons, allowed them to build a narrative different from the story of the previous season. The Brazilian had arrived in the summer of 2002, a freshly minted gold medal from the World Cup metaphorically around his neck. He didn't know a huge amount about Arsenal but he had respect for what he had heard about them. The feeling was mutual. Towards the end of his first season, 2002–03, Arsenal and Manchester United were vying for pole position in the Premier League run-in. But Arsenal choked.

'In football you are not allowed to lose your focus at any time,' Gilberto explains. 'You can't. In the previous season, my first season in England, the crucial moment was in Bolton when we threw away the game. We drew against them 2–2. After that we couldn't return to our best. It seemed like everyone forgot about playing football. But that game at Old Trafford showed a different character, as if we had learned from the recent past. We didn't want that to happen again.

'After that I thought, if you don't lose this kind of game, we become stronger than we were before. That game was great – even with the difficulty we had – because it showed us that if we miss our concentration even for one second it can be crucial for the whole season. It could cost us, as it cost us in the previous season.'

For all the furore, there was a value in how the fracas at Old Trafford pulled the team even closer together, and refreshed their sense of collective determination. Parlour, however, remembers it rather differently. 'I got fined ten grand for that!' he winces. 'The ex-wife wasn't happy.'

The punishments are delivered on 30 October, almost six weeks after the event. The fines total £275,000, the largest financial penalty for indiscipline in the history of English football. The bans shared around the offenders equal nine matches (Lauren is suspended for four games, Keown three, Parlour and Vieira one each.

Cole is merely warned about his future conduct, and Lehmann's 'improper conduct' charge is dropped).

Arsenal release an official statement of apology, perfectly worded by their legal team, which says all the right things. It includes one fascinating paragraph hidden in the middle: 'The players are instructed not to allow themselves to be provoked and are reminded that their triumphs have come when they have not allowed themselves to be distracted from the game.'

Message understood.

★

Not that context is in any way an excuse, but it is interesting to recall how Arsenal went into the match at Old Trafford not at their most relaxed. Their previous two games had not gone to plan and pressure was bubbling up. A Premier League draw at home with Portsmouth was a minor disappointment, and came with the added frisson of a dive controversy, as Pirès tumbled to win an equalizing penalty. 'Everyone thinks that I simulated,' he says, remembering the accusation years later. 'But no. It's frustrating, but what can you do? For a while when I got the ball you hear everyone whistle. My teammates helped me, they said I shouldn't listen.' Four days later, in the Champions League, Inter Milan visited Highbury and walloped Arsenal. Having been entirely outmanoeuvred, beaten 3–0, and somewhat shell-shocked, the trip to Old Trafford was underpinned by a need to steady the ship. In this case the pressure boiled over, but as the season developed, other complications were handled with more decorum.

Besides, there was a broader contest against United, beyond the confines of the eyeball-to-eyeball rendezvous. The wider context of the rivalry tells of two teams who had jostled each other at the top of English football for six successive seasons. The backdrop of mutual dislike, with occasional flare-ups, stretched back a couple of decades. United had become the dominant team of the 1990s.

Then a period of see-sawing developed. Arsenal won the title
(helped by a famous win at Old Trafford secured by Marc Overmars) in 1998. United bounced back to win three on the trot. Back
came Arsenal in 2002 (this time the league was actually sealed with
a triumph delivered by Sylvain Wiltord's goal on United's own
turf). United reclaimed the league in 2003. 'Playing against them
always presented special challenges that I burned many hours over
the years thinking about,' Ferguson mused evocatively.

Now, in the 2003–04 season, every sinew was shaking in this
monumental footballing tug of war.

Bergkamp remembers the feeling of the balance shifting in this
relationship during his early years with the club. 'It became clear
to me in my first season at Arsenal that Man United was the team
to beat. They were there [he reaches his hand up] and we were not
even close. And we got closer. Even in 1998 we won it, but I didn't
really have the feeling that we were competing with them, it was
like a one-off. But throughout the rest of my career at Arsenal, we
were closing the gap. And when we won in 2002 I felt that this was
the moment. For us – but for them as well – they realized that we
were the better team now. Therefore they would approach us as
more of a threat, and maybe as the ones to catch. They were always
the ones to beat, but then suddenly *we* were the team to beat. And
I think that was in everyone's mind, from their team as well.'

Was not losing at Old Trafford critical, then, even if at the time
it had no resonance in terms of an unbeaten season?

'Yeah. We needed to live up to expectations, people expected us
to get a result there. It's a feeling in the team: *We're not afraid of you
any more, we can beat you. We are at the same level, maybe we're better.*
It's a different feeling. You're not more arrogant but maybe more
confident. We can do this.'

2

Revolution

'Star of Stars' was the headline in La Gazzetta dello Sport, *in recognition of the 1995 World Player of the Year, George Weah. A beautiful, baroque ceremony in Milan was attended by the football world's glitterati, to acclaim the top three footballers of the time: Jürgen Klinsmann, Paolo Maldini and, in first place, Weah. Hearty applause greeted the Liberian, a player who combined grace, power and imagination so naturally, and then the atmosphere suddenly changed when he said he would prefer the award not to be for him. He wanted to give it to his mentor, and called a French manager who was working in Japan to the stage. Up strolled a slightly embarrassed but deeply moved Arsène Wenger. It was not an exaggeration to suggest a large number of people in the audience were not too sure who this lean, bespectacled figure was. 'He deserves this more than I do,' said Weah as he handed over the prize. 'Thanks Mr Coach for everything.'*

David Dein first met Wenger during the 1988–89 season. That was a momentous time for Arsenal. Under George Graham, a young, hungry team that brimmed with desire won the title in the most breathtaking fashion imaginable. In stoppage time of the very last game, against the outright favourites, who were in front of their home crowd at Anfield, Arsenal planted their flag at the summit of English football's Everest for the first time in eighteen years.

Graham, in his previous guise as 'the Stroller', had been a player the last time Arsenal had successfully completed that ascent. A languidly skilful midfielder in the 1971 Double-winning side, he carried himself with a certain style as, away from the pitch, he enjoyed the good life. As a manager, Graham returned with a mean streak, tirelessly drilling his players until they knew their roles back-to-front and inside-out, which set the tone for that iconic finale in 1989. He was respected enormously as the clasp connecting two eras – those league successes bookended a period that shuffled between mediocrity, unfulfilled promise, and a flurry of cup finals with mixed results. In bringing success as both a player and a manager, and in pressing home the qualities defined in the staff handbook by the famous maxim 'remember who you are, what you are, and what you represent', he had quite an aura. In some ways, it was difficult to imagine a more 'Arsenal' manager than George. A man so obsessed with the history he had a study at home filled with rare memorabilia, he seemed to define the club, and embody its character. The idea that someone might come along and turn all that on its head was absurd.

Graham represented a link between Arsenal's past and present. And there at Highbury, midway through the 1988–89 season – although nobody could have known it at the time – the future appeared.

Monday 2 January was North London derby day. Wenger was in transit from Istanbul back to Monaco. He had been scouting a Galatasaray match, and had a stopover in England. Naturally, the only thing that occurred to him was whether there was a football match to watch. He called Dennis Roach, an acquaintance who was the agent of one of his players, Glenn Hoddle. 'I asked him, "Can you find a ticket for me at an English game as I am travelling through London?" He said he had a ticket for Arsenal. It was my first visit to Highbury,' Wenger recalls.

Playing that day was a tall centre half called Steve Bould, who years later would become Wenger's assistant manager. That team also included a group he would eventually coach in the shape of Tony Adams, Nigel Winterburn and a scorer on the day, Paul Merson. Wenger witnessed a 2–0 derby win, crowned by a very late goal from Michael Thomas charging through the midfield to flick past the goalkeeper. The Frenchman's memories of the game?

He grins. 'You could see that the legs were tired,' he says, a classically Wengeresque observation. 'It was after Christmas and they had played many games and had many drinks – it was not the most exciting game to watch. I just remember there was a red-haired guy who came on and made the difference.' That just happened to be possibly the least Wenger-like player on the books back then: Perry Groves.

On match days at Highbury, the Cocktail Lounge, which was next door to the boardroom, hosted all female guests, as well as scouts, officials from other clubs, and VIPs. They were served drinks and could take refuge from the stands outside. It was a smart room just upstairs from the Marble Halls, with a Grecian statue complete with a symbolic laurel (affectionately known as Fred the Greek) on an art deco plinth as its centrepiece.

In those days there was a clear demarcation line between who was allowed in the boardroom on match days, and who wasn't (no women, for starters – directors' wives were annexed to the Ladies Room). Wenger found that funny, but in the event he was introduced to Barbara Dein, the wife of Arsenal's vice-chairman David. Perhaps the two men would not have crossed paths without Barbara sending a message to her husband that the manager of Monaco was at the match. Barbara, appreciating how David is naturally predisposed to be sociable and keen to network in football circles, knew he would be interested. Dein made his way to the Cocktail Lounge to seek out the visitor, spotted this tall man in a trench coat and rimless glasses and went to introduce himself. 'He looked very elegant, not like your normal football manager,' recalls Dein.

They chatted, instantly got along, and Dein's social skills over the course of that first meeting would be a catalyst for chapters still to be written in the chronicles of Arsenal. How long was he in town for? Just overnight. Did he have plans for later? Nothing. Would he care to join the Deins at a friend's house for dinner? Love to. That chance conversation, that spontaneous invitation, planted the seed of what would one day become the Invincibles.

'He was by himself and looked lonely,' recalls Dein. 'That was the start. I hijacked him. That evening we went to a friend's house for dinner. The friend happened to be in show business and at the end of the dinner we started playing charades. I said to Arsène in my best French – because his English wasn't great at that time – do you want to play? He said yes. Ten minutes later he was acting out *A Midsummer Night's Dream*. I thought, this is an unusual guy. That night I remember, almost as if it was a lightning flash, the words appeared in my mind. *Arsène for Arsenal*. It's going to happen. It's destiny. I really felt it.'

Wenger felt something a little different. 'When I travelled with them to Totteridge I never thought I would spend twenty years of my life in Totteridge. It looked like such a complicated name!' he recalls. At the end of the evening, once they had established the friendship, and a connection in that Dein was a regular visitor to the South of France, it felt like this rendezvous would not be a one-off. 'I said if you come down, call me, we can have dinner,' says Wenger. 'So from 1989 to 1996 we were always in touch.'

In 1989, Arsenal were delighted with Graham, and Wenger was content at Monaco, so Dein's *Arsène for Arsenal* prophesy was more of a sense of something fated to happen one day rather than a desire for sudden change. But Wenger had cast a lasting impression. The Arsenal vice-chairman had the kind of nature that loved looking ahead, trying new things, and even though English football was extremely parochial at the time, he felt he had stumbled upon someone special enough to break new ground.

Observing Wenger at work when he was invited to Monaco confirmed Dein's instinct that he had unusual managerial qualities. 'I used to see how he interacted with the players, with the board, with the press, with the fans. I thought this guy is just a class act. He's different. Arsène spoke five languages, had an economics degree, had studied medicine, and was clearly not the usual ex-player turned manager,' says Dein.

They kept in touch, even when Wenger left Monaco for Japan

to work at Grampus Eight. Because Dein had had this premonition that Wenger would one day manage Arsenal, he liked to keep him abreast of how the team were doing. He sent videos to Nagoya of the latest matches, and in the days before internet and mobile phones for the masses, they would communicate by fax. It was a regular source of amusement that Wenger's faxes would whir through with somebody else's name printed on the top, as the fax machine had been left behind by a well-known player who lived in the house before him. That name? Former Tottenham striker Gary Lineker.

Wenger had taken the bold step of leaving European football for an unusual outpost in Asia in January 1995. Timing being everything, one month later Graham was gone. Graham was sacked by Arsenal as a consequence of the 'bung' affair, having been caught accepting illegal payments from a Norwegian agent during the transfer of two Scandinavian players. Arsenal were floundering. Dein's thoughts turned immediately to Wenger.

He took his suggestion to the board but the majority of its members vetoed the appointment, not really having the appetite for a foreign manager. It was complicated. Wenger was under contract, and besides, it still felt like a leap into the unknown to appoint a manager with no experience of English football. There was no precedent for a foreign manager to succeed in this league.

Although English football had already begun to broaden its horizons, managers from overseas were a rarity. Aston Villa had endured a terrible experiment with the first foreign coach to try his hand in England – a Czech by the name of Dr Jozef Vengloš whose single season ended with a narrow escape from relegation – and that made a strong case to back up the widely held if jingoistic view that the British game was for British bosses. 'Island mentalities are historically mistrustful of foreign influences,' Wenger observed. This was uncharted territory.

Still, Dein's mind had been whirring on his footballing travels. He felt the game was in the midst of some massive brainstorming session. Dein was a major architect in the negotiations that prompted the breakaway of the Premier League from the old Football League. He witnessed the onset of Sky television and the money it would bring. He saw the old European Cup morphing into the Champions League. He noticed the sparks of what would become an explosive global market, with international players beginning to travel in greater numbers to new leagues. He could feel English football taking a new direction, gathering speed, and he wanted Arsenal to hurtle down the fast lane, with Wenger in the driving seat.

Arsenal made a polite inquiry. Wenger made it clear that, however tempting the offer might be, he would not break his contract. There was a suggestion that a deal could be done if a replacement acceptable to Grampus Eight could be found, but that wouldn't be easy: the Japanese club were quite taken by their man.

Ken Friar, not someone to suffer fools, recalls the time Wenger hit a sticky patch at Grampus Eight: 'They had lost two or three games, and the chairman sent for the manager and said, "Things are not going well. I am sorry, Arsène, I am going to have to make some changes." So they fired the interpreter. True story.'

In the summer of 1995, Wenger staying loyal to his contract, Arsenal hired Bruce Rioch to be their new manager. They also recruited Dennis Bergkamp, a landmark transfer which represented how profoundly Arsenal wanted to change. This was daring stuff, out of their comfort zone financially, and a player of such global repute that his new teammates would bow and swoon, semi-jokingly chanting, 'We are not worthy.'

Rioch had his admirers, but strained to gain enough authority to convince the board he was the long term answer. Come the summer of 1996, he was relieved of his duties after a messy dispute with the board. Arsenal decided that while missing out on Wenger once might be unfortunate, to do so twice would be careless. That said, his appointment was still a brave decision, even though Dein had such confidence in a man he had come to know well. More than five years after it was made, that *Arsène for Arsenal* prediction came true as, on 30 September 1996, Wenger was officially unveiled. He smiled for the cameras sporting his Arsenal club tie on the pitch at Highbury.

★

The Frenchman had been the subject of conjecture for a few weeks in the Arsenal dressing room. Who was this stranger? Was he any good? Did he speak English? Will he want to change everything? Bring in new people? Am I expendable? They had seen some clips on the television, some photographs in the newspapers, and Glenn Hoddle and Mark Hateley, two names well known in the English game who had worked with Wenger in Monaco, spoke well of him. Those with a broader knowledge might have known that Weah, the first African to be honoured as World Footballer of the Year in 1995, had dedicated his award to his formative coach. But apart from that, the players really had little idea what to expect. Japan? Africa? France? How would he blend in with Highbury's ways? Emotions were mixed. There was some scepticism about a man coming in from Asian football, which lacked the status to give either inspiration or reassurance. There was also some intrigue, to provoke a sense that they needed to sharpen up to make a good impression. And as always happens when there's a change, every player was wondering whether he would fit the new manager's plans.

A few of them turned to the two new French boys who had recently arrived on Wenger's recommendation. Patrick Vieira, a loping giant with potential to burn, had been prised from AC Milan, and Rémi Garde, an old hand who spoke English and would be able to help the kid adjust as well as offer midfield cover, had joined from Strasbourg. The trouble was, they were more or less in the dark, too. 'The others were really curious. They were asking a few questions about Arsène and trying to understand his philosophy, but we didn't have much information,' admits Vieira.

'The only thing was we knew him because he was French. But as for the way he was playing, or the way he was as a person, we didn't really know. So we were like the majority of the players; we had to wait and see what was going to happen. The guy arrived and he didn't look like a coach, he looked like a professor. There were a few questions about that.'

A dressing room which contained a core of experienced players who were old enough to be comfortable in their own skin and know their own minds might have represented a significant hurdle for Wenger. But the beauty of what happened is that those very qualities – the confidence and wisdom that come with having travelled round several blocks – actually helped, rather than hindered.

Lee Dixon vividly remembers his first meeting with Wenger in the flesh, outside in the fresh Hertfordshire air, close to the training pitches where Wenger is at his most comfortable. The team were on their way out for a session with Pat Rice, an Arsenal stalwart (and another veteran of that 1971 team Graham played in) who had been acting caretaker. Wenger walked over to introduce himself. Just as Dein had been in the Cocktail Lounge several years before, Dixon was struck by the first impression. This man had a presence. He was interesting. He was different.

'He came out with his leather elbow pads on his jacket and studious glasses, looking very geography teacher-ish, and I remember thinking, *Ah, this is what he looks like*,' recalls Dixon. 'He was taller than I imagined. He was quite an imposing figure. But he's got no meat on him at all so in the opposite way he was quite frail looking. It was a strange combination of being tall but not having a footballer stature. If you see him in his shorts in the summer he looks more like a 1500-metre runner. That was the first impression. A studious type that was more of a student of the game with his mind than somebody you could take an example from physically.'

Ian Wright was equally curious. 'When he came he just looked so dishevelled,' he says. 'His suit was massive, his glasses were massive. He looked like a headmaster. But once he started doing his stuff it rammed home the point he was a professor of football.'

The job of winning people over was made easier because the group included so many characters who were interested enough, and open minded enough, to be won over. One theme that carries consistently through Wenger's successful teams is that he likes to handpick players with enough intelligence to want to learn. Wenger is a man with an extraordinarily high intellect himself, and the dynamic between a convincing teacher and a keen student motivates him enormously.

'Basically his foundation of coaching is based on that – the intelligence of the player, and the willingness of the player,' explains Dixon. 'How he picks his players is that he goes for the type of person who can almost educate themselves from their surroundings. He puts players in environments that are conducive with success in his opinion, and he expects the player to learn from the players around him and the tools he has made available. He was looking round saying: this is what I can do for you. You can further your careers if you take these things on board. My view was, *I don't want to go anywhere from here. I'm in. Let's have a look.*'

Keown was equally intrigued. 'When the boss arrived he was very different to any manager that I'd experienced really. There was such a contrast with George that some of us were a little bit worried. Do nice guys win things? He shook your hand in the morning. He wanted that eye contact. There was a respect suddenly for you, that you hadn't necessarily thought was there before. There would be a word here and there, a very skilful word to virtually every player, without being seen by the other players, but some word of encouragement or some word of reassurance. It was quite refreshing.'

It was time for a radical new world. Almost every facet of Arsenal Football Club would be shaken up. Keown, whose relationship with the club predates Wenger's arrival by almost two decades, was astounded by the scale of the changes. He was steeped in its ways. Old Arsenal had been a part of him since his youth.

'The first game I ever went to, by pure chance, was at Arsenal. Brought up in Oxford, there wasn't many big teams around. QPR was maybe nearest, about an hour away. Arsenal were going through a dormant period, in the mid-1970s. We went along to watch them, and I remember turning a corner, through the streets of Highbury, and suddenly there was this sort of Tardis effect. Behind these terraced houses there was an incredible spotlight, with crowds of people and the team warming up before a big game. It was just unbelievable how they managed to fit this ground in behind all those terraced houses. There was something very special about the way the stadium linked from people's homes to their backyards. In my backyard we used to have a rec, and in their backyard they had Arsenal stadium. You came down the Avenell Road and you suddenly got a glimpse of what was behind the facade of the East Stand, and it was quite magical.'

He was taken aback when one of the Arsenal scouts, Terry Murphy, arrived at his house for talks with his parents. 'The crisp jacket he wore, with an Arsenal tie and badge, clean shaven – My God, this guy's from Arsenal!' recalls Keown. 'You could just see everything oozing class, and I was expected to live up to that thereafter.'

Going about their business with a touch of class had been a hallmark dating back to Herbert Chapman's grand team of the 1930s. Arsenal's class was traditional, but also stuck in a past that would soon become obsolete in terms of modern football methods. Class was in short supply when it came to the training facilities, for example.

★

If Wenger had been given a guided tour of Arsenal Football Club circa 1996 in the style of, say, an estate agent showing an interested buyer around a property, Wenger would have been entitled to look around at some of the time-worn aspects of the infrastructure and think only about how to modernize.

Mr Wenger, here is Highbury, the grand ancestral home. Regard the beautiful art deco features, the historic Marble Halls, the manicured pitch.

Yes, thinks Wenger. It's a wonderful old-fashioned English stadium full of character. But economically, there are restrictions here with the 38,000 capacity. It is too small compared to some of Europe's superclubs, and there is no room for expansion.

Let me take you through to the training ground at London Colney, Hertfordshire. Conveniently located near to the M25. Clean country air. Some pitches, only occasionally waterlogged. You can share the changing facilities with University College London – that's who owns it at the moment, a minor detail. They have first dibs on Wednesdays and Friday afternoons, but other than that, it's entirely at your disposal for a small rental sum.

Hmmm, ponders Wenger, too polite to express his inner disdain that a major club with lofty aspirations has to share with students, and make do with facilities that are modest, to say the least.

Consider the playing staff: fine, upstanding citizens. The defence has been around for a long time and is rock solid. Midfield could do with a little updating . . . but if you look further forward there's Ian Wright, Paul Merson, and Dennis Bergkamp, an unusually excellent feature.

Some interesting ingredients there, reckons Wenger. With some polishing and upgrades there is definite potential.

Look at this fine regime. Some small alcohol issues, and a sweet tooth or two, but they are fit, highly motivated and have experience of winning . . .

Time, Wenger plots, for some major refurbishment.

Keown remembers fielding a phone call not long after Wenger joined Arsenal to let the players know there was a sudden change of plan. News came through about a fire at the training ground. 'Somebody had left the bibs in the drying room. It was very windy and kicked up and burned down,' he recalls. 'I knew of Arsène's displeasure about the training ground. He had made that clear. He was a perfectionist and wanted more. I said, "What's happened there?" and the reply was, "It's arson." I said, "Well I knew he didn't like the training ground but I didn't think he'd burn it down . . ." They said, "No, you idiot, it's arson – although it could be Arsène." I knew that, I was joking. Was the boss there in the night with a box of matches?' Keown can't help himself and he affects the voice of a dastardly villain with a French accent. 'Ha ha, now I can get my new training ground.'

The coincidental timing was lost on nobody. But ultimately, a trigger was required to accelerate Arsenal's progress, and there was an undeniable silver lining to the clouds of smoke that engulfed the old facilities. Wenger had been distinctly unimpressed with everything from the imperfect pitches, which were an acceptable quality for student matches but not professionals, to the fact that you walked in and virtually tripped over a massage table as there was no proper reception. The changing rooms were tiny, the run-down décor hardly inspired a sense of elite conditions and the canteen building provided food reminiscent of school meals and plentiful chocolate bars. There was also no dedicated gym or conditioning area, no specialist space for medics and no particular concern for cleanliness and clear thinking.

Vieira, who had come from Milanello, the highly respected base for AC Milan, was unimpressed when he first arrived. 'It was a nightmare,' he says, pulling a face as if he had stepped in something revolting. 'That fire was the best thing they did. Everything was disgusting. The food wasn't good, the changing room was old and dirty. You felt like you just went there to train, finish, and then take your car to go home and have a shower. At this level you should want to spend a few hours after training there, having some treatment, looking after yourself.'

The biggest crime of all to Wenger's sensibilities was that

Arsenal were restricted as to when they could use the pitches. If he wanted to put on a double session, he couldn't. They had to be out of there by 1.30 p.m. sharpish, so the students could come to play.

Not that the players minded. 'We enjoyed getting Wednesdays off because we didn't have anywhere to change,' recalls Keown. 'On a Wednesday we couldn't use the building. It wasn't really professional. Basic showers, bath, no weight room, you couldn't do any conditioning; you had to wait until the summer before you could move the equipment outside.'

For a while they used Sopwell House, a hotel in the countryside outside St Albans, as a temporary measure. Guests were often surprised to find a phalanx of Premier League footballers working out in the gym, relaxing their muscles in the Jacuzzi, or merely strolling down the hotel corridor. Arsenal took some rooms to set up for the medical staff and masseurs, and hived off a section of the restaurant.

The Sopwell House arrangement was not ideal, but as they had to take a short bus trip to and from the pitches to train together, that daily commute as an ensemble was good for bonding. There was a famous episode when a moment of off-the-cuff vibrancy from Wright showed the new faces that, for all their professionalism, there was never a dull moment as he took control of the wheel and crashed the bus. 'The driver wasn't there,' he recalls. 'I remember we were all on the bus and I just started it up. Smashed it halfway up the road. All the guys were screaming, *WRIGHTY!* The French boys were looking like, *What the hell is going on?*'

Vieira actually looks back fondly at the period at Sopwell House, although he confesses it was strange sometimes to be in the locker room getting changed for training, when he would look up and catch the eye of Joe Bloggs pulling on swimming trunks to use the hotel pool. It made for a slightly self-conscious atmosphere, outside of the modern footballer's bubble. 'It was good,' he says. 'It was much better than what we had before. It was too public, but we never had any big issues. In some ways it was nice to exchange some talk with other people. You are seeing different people and talking about different things. I liked that period.'

Everyone was learning, adapting, adjusting and getting to grips with diverse behaviour and ideas. With so much new information to take in, it was at times odd, funny, challenging and rewarding.

For Bergkamp, seeing the horizons changing was almost a relief. He had joined Arsenal content to taste authentic English football, but had still been alarmed by how it functioned in a back-water in terms of preparation. 'During my first season a lot of times I was with my mouth open. *What is happening here?* This is a professional club. You've got players sometimes going home at noon, just after training, then apparently they went out to go drinking, or to do something else. The pre-match meal was unbelievable. What I saw there, I thought, *This is not happening.*'

Did you eat it?

'You had to. But most of the time I would make my own way through that. It was really surprising to me. I was only there for one season at that time, but you heard the stories, the style of play-ing as well. Boring Arsenal. One striker up front. One–nil up, everyone back in defence. I thought that this was not the idea of a top team. Of a European top team. The changes Arsène brought in, for me that was normal. It brought us to a higher level.'

The fundamental point of the Wenger methodology was his wish to introduce a new way of thinking about how a footballer treats the major tool of his trade – his body. Different stretching regimes were introduced, and paying attention to what exactly was going into their bodies (and even how it was going in) stimu-lated plenty of debate. To Wenger himself it is blindingly obvious. As he says by way of simple explanation, 'If you put diesel in a petrol car it doesn't go very far.'

Was it really so shocking to have such an upheaval in terms of cuisine?

'All the food changed,' says Keown. 'It became very low fat and plain. There was an emphasis on chewing to win. That became a slogan – chew to win. It was explained to us that when you eat your food sometimes you feel a bit tired because the blood rushes from your head to your stomach to churn up the food. That's using energy to do that. But if you chew, that doesn't happen as your stomach has to do less. The theory is, we don't want you burning up unnecessary energy on match day, so we want you to chew.' He demonstrates a camel-like slow and deliberate chomping. 'If you are hungry and scoffing food it doesn't help. If you didn't have a bottle of water in your hand he wasn't happy because he wanted you to keep sipping as well.'

Were some of the players peeved?

'Yeah. We weren't allowed to have ketchup. Teas and coffees started drying up as he thought that was dehydrating. We'd be having diabetic jams so there was no sugar. We negotiated tomato ketchup back in again. You want us to eat this plain food? We'd better have some ketchup. Before, with Bruce Rioch, it was jelly babies and all sorts of stuff in the dressing room. The likes of Merse, who had almost become addicted to this stuff, was saying, "My God, what do I have now? I'm hungry!" Players were complaining of being hungry before the game. There was no sugar in your diet until afterwards. I went with it and felt much better in games.'

Ian Wright, a picky eater at the best of times, struggled to come to terms with the new eating expectations. 'The food was very bland,' he winces. 'I was always starving. I used to try to wolf it. I'd grown up with West Indian food, where there is a lot of seasoning, and all of a sudden you have rice that tastes plain, chicken that tastes plain and all the vegetables very plain. It was food for fuel, not for enjoyment. I can't remember any time being with the team that I actually enjoyed what we ate. I complained a lot.' Wright would deliberately avoid eating beforehand to make himself feel hungry enough to get it down.

Sometimes during games he even felt so under-nourished, and

the physio Gary Lewin suggested he was also dehydrated, that his vision was affected. 'On a few occasions I couldn't see out of the corners of my eyes,' he says. 'It was blurred. We had to constantly talk about fuel and water, water, water.'

Dixon found the new stretching regimes a challenge initially. 'For old-fashioned footballers, as I was, you touched your toes a few times, stretched your groin, the big muscle groups, before you got out on the training pitch and smashed balls everywhere. But Arsène was good like that in as much as he didn't force it on anybody. He didn't come in and go, "We're doing this, and if you are not in you're out." It was left to your own intelligence.'

Food supplements and, controversially, Creatine, which is used to improve muscle mass, were left out in bowls. Vitamin injections were encouraged. The science behind it was explained, just as it was with the 'chew to win' philosophy and the suggestion that alcohol intake be reduced and water sipping encouraged. Wenger invited a specialist nutritionist from France, Yann Rouget, to talk to the players about the effects of how they did or didn't look after themselves. Bergkamp laughs as he imitates a phrase that stuck in his mind. 'No doping, gentlemen. It is not doping.'

It was up to the players to make their own minds up about what methods to buy into. 'Some players took everything on board, some didn't,' says Dixon. 'With the supplements, Creatine and everything that was recommended and put on the table before training every day, some of the players started off trying it because the nutritionist, Dr Rouget, would come in and say, "If you take this, this is what happens to your body." Some listened, some didn't. It was made available to us and quite a lot of the lads tried it, but didn't feel any different, so dropped it. Some lads are still on it today. Dennis Bergkamp didn't take Creatine so a few of the lads were like, *If Dennis isn't taking it, I'm not taking it. He's brilliant!*

'It would be wrong to say it was all plain sailing. Certainly in the early days everything Arsène introduced was completely different. There was the odd thing – the eight-o'clock-in-the-morning stretching on a match day, getting us all out of bed for a stretching session before we had even had breakfast – it was like, *What is that?* We are not playing until three o'clock. Player power soon put an end to that.' Dixon wonders whether it was part of a master plan, deliberately introducing a number of new ideas, knowing some would not be so easily accepted, and the spirit of compromise would be welcomed if some were dropped.

'Knowing how clever and intelligent Arsène is, there were probably things in there that he knew full well we might not all buy into. He was willing to let a couple of them go. Tony Adams went to see him to explain this was really the complete opposite of what we were used to. We used to have a lie-in on a Saturday if we needed to rest. That change wasn't really working. So he gave us that one back. We went for a walk instead. That was probably him winning us over in the psychological battle. There is a whole array of different mindsets and characters in a dressing room and Arsène wasn't brainwashing. He just made things available, and then explained what might happen if you took this, or stretched like that.'

For Keown, all these new discoveries made him feel noticeably different: 'So you are doing the stretching, taking the supplements – they would take blood tests and tell you that you are low in iron or zinc or magnesium so you start taking all these things – and suddenly cramp stops in the games. You feel much better. The difference in the training was shown in more intensity, and had a different emphasis. You are winning games. You wonder, is it one of those things? Or a collection of them? But you are starting to feel invincible. It all seems to be working. That creates a feeling that you can beat anyone.'

The experts coming in to work with the squad grew exponentially. The number of masseurs and fitness coaches multiplied. When the new training ground was complete it had state-of-the-art hydrotherapy pools for specialist recovery and preparation. Those in rehabilitation were often sent abroad to work under the watchful eye of Tiburce Darou, a specialist trainer. An osteopath from France, Philippe Boixel, whose healing hands left even sceptical players amazed, paid regular visits to London Colney. As Pirès says, 'Boixel is a body mechanic, and his years of experience have taught him how to diagnose and recognize what treatment is best suited to relieve each player's aches and pains.'

Wright needed some convincing. 'These French doctors came over and were doing things with your chakras and releasing your channels, the first time I'd ever heard of that kind of stuff. It was different. I was quite excited about it once I got used to it.'

Keown became a convert. 'Philippe Boixel was an absolute magician. When he first came, the boss wanted all of us to see him. I'd never had a massage. I didn't want some bloke crawling all over me.' Wenger was insistent that Boixel would help. 'I'm fine, Boss,' said Keown, brushing the idea off. 'I remember waking up one morning and my knee was quite swollen. It was the day that Philippe was there. "See him, you never know . . ." So I did and he kind of threw me all round the bed, cracking my knee, my back, everything. He was able to tell me where the pain was. When I woke up the next day the swelling had disappeared. It was incredible.'

Even Lehmann, who arrived well into his thirties feeling pretty knowledgeable about his own body, was impressed by the ideas he came across. 'Philippe Boixel was like a second father to me, because I went every week twice. He came on Thursday and Friday. And the fitness coach, Tony Colbert, had a different approach to fitness training which was fantastic: whole body exercises. He created some really great exercises. I was much fitter when I left Arsenal at the age of thirty-eight, than when I came at thirty-three.'

The attention to detail was extraordinary to try to make sure every aspect of physical preparation was given every chance to make a percentage point of difference. The temperature on the team bus was adjusted to keep muscles supple. The chairs in the restaurant at the training ground were ergonomically designed to be comfortable yet supportive. Some players were sent to the dentist to get to the bottom of leg pain that might have its origins in the teeth or jaw.

In years to come, Wenger would laugh at the fact that there was a revolt from the back of the team coach when he first halted the supply of chocolate more or less on day one. The chant 'We want our Mars Bars back' started up from the players on the way to London after Wenger's first game, a 2–0 victory at Blackburn Rovers. 'I was sat with him at the front of the bus, he found it funny, but he turned around and just shook his head,' recalls Dein.

For Bergkamp, the transformation from good old Arsenal to a modern superclub was well underway. 'We were probably one of the first teams with those ideas,' he says. 'I think I played a role in that of course, Arsène played a role in that, Patrick played a role in that and every other player that joined the club. Not just because we played good football but because we played for a reason as well. Arsène didn't buy silly players. He bought players who had an idea, the same idea, about professionalism.'

Bergkamp only tolerates silliness when there is a practical joke to be had. It was a little known skill of his outside the dressing room, in fact, this prankster's eye. On the pitch, in the zone, however, it was time to be serious. With Wenger instilling new ideas, and the players broadening their horizons, boring Arsenal zoomed into a thrilling future.

In 1996–97, towards the end of Wenger's first season, Bergkamp reflected on the changes he witnessed going on all around him and expressed his pride in the way that Arsenal's style was evolving into something more pleasing on the eye, more of a purist's version of football. 'So far,' he said at the time, 'we have changed something in the style. But it would be better if we won something. Then they can say Arsenal won the championship, or whatever, and they did it in a way different to 1989 or 1991. That would be nice.'

What portentous words. The very next season, with Bergkamp

at the heart of it as the Premier League's Player of the Year, Arsenal won the Double. Some themes that would become familiar under Wenger presented themselves. Arsenal were endeavouring to chase down Manchester United, and won a typically intense duel at Old Trafford through some Marc Overmars trickery. With that they suddenly hit fifth gear, and accelerated through a ten-match winning run and over the finishing line.

Dixon loves that team, and will argue any day that in his opinion it was the best of the lot. Better even than the Invincibles. 'It had the mixture,' he says. 'Settling in Petit and Vieira in front of the old back four. People knew about Marc Overmars, but they didn't have a clue about Anelka, who just ripped the league apart that year. We had a bit of everything. Old fogeys at the back who played like they were ten again. And those two animals in midfield breaking everything down and setting everything up. Marc with his pace and this guy up front. Anelka hardly spoke to anyone all season he was so quiet. He just went about his business putting the ball in the back of the net. It was incredible.

'We had been in the wilderness a bit towards the end of George's reign and we wanted that time back. You could almost feel it building. The way we did it, we were so far behind, and going on that run we almost became invincible. In my experience, although I have won a lot of stuff, those times are so few and far between. To be in a dressing room where you are literally not caring about anything other than you are excited because you know you are going to win, if you could bottle that feeling . . .'

3
Alchemy

Jens Lehmann took the short trip across the border from his homeland in Germany to meet his new Arsenal teammates for the first time. The venue was Bad Waltersdorf, the Austrian mountain retreat Wenger favoured as the oasis of tranquillity to start tuning the Arsenal engine for the season ahead. At Lehmann's first training session, the group went to a nearby spa. What he saw struck him immediately as bizarre. 'My first impression was that the people going to the sauna are wearing their undies, or their swimming pants,' he remembers, with an inscrutable smile. 'In Austria and Germany you go naked. The English had their speedos on. And I said "Ah that's strange." And they told me: "Are you mad, going naked in the sauna? Someone takes your picture and you're in the Sun *the next day."'*

Asking anyone involved in Arsenal's golden era of 1997–2004 for a favourite team is a little like expecting someone to pick out one of their children. Each of the three title-winning sides had its own characteristics and nuances. The 1998 side was startling, as Wenger's vision for football shook the Premier League with an amalgam of old wisdom and new shimmering speed. The 2002 team evolved from that, fusing the aesthetics of Thierry Henry and Robert Pirès into the mix, adding Freddie Ljungberg's killer runs, and integrating players of great athleticism into the defence. Come 2004, the team developed a new charisma, as they went into games exuding a rare level of super-confidence that just doesn't come along very often in the lives of people whose vocation demands they perform.

The unbeaten season did not come from nowhere. The team developed its identity over a series of seasons. Characters, and their characteristics, were added to the composition as a painter builds his picture, augments it with detail, gives depth to colour, embellishes with impasto.

By the time 2003–04 came along, the group consisted of a close-knit set of players who were, in the main, around their peak age, having amassed vast experience. Wenger had seen some exceptional players come and go. Replacements needed to be handpicked. Some didn't quite deliver. The select few – people with the right skills and personality to slot as comfortably into the dressing room as they fitted into the team's game plan – blended into the overall scheme beautifully.

The archetypal Wenger player of that vintage needed to tick a number of essential boxes: physical prowess, cultured technique, keen intelligence, generous team spirit, will to win. Somewhere along the line speed was important – either in body, mind, or both. Robert Pirès chooses the word casting as if the manager was studying an exhaustive list of people auditioning for a movie before settling on the person that seemed exactly right for each role.

The fact that players from different nations and backgrounds brought their own flavours, in addition to the fundamental components, only made the mélange even more interesting. 'When you make a dish you need ingredients,' expands Pirès. 'Arsène chose the players, and he wanted to make a nice meal. He took a Cameroonian, Brazilians, he took Frenchmen, he took a German, he took a Dutchman, and he kept the English. Then you mix them [he taps hands as if to add the flourish of a wand on a magician's black hat] and it makes a magnificent dish like that of 2003–04. But in all this, the most important person is Arsène Wenger.'

The cordon bleu?

'Exactly!' he chuckles. 'Very good.'

As Wenger was to quickly discover, almost as soon as he had built his first winning team at Highbury, maintaining the magic formula is almost as difficult as creating it in the first place. Two reasons: one, because the shifting mindset from chasing success to defending it is a complicated trick to pull off; and two, because squads change on a frustratingly regular basis. Once the euphoria had abated after Arsenal's Double in 1998, they realized there was a downside to success, an unexpected problem. All of a sudden, Europe's most powerful clubs had their eyes fixed on their players. Temptation was everywhere and fighting it off made for stressful summers.

For years, David Dein and Patrick Vieira knew what was coming when the end of the season was approaching. 'My first week of my annual holiday was chasing Patrick every year,' Dein recalls. 'At the end of the season I said, "Patrick, where are you going for your holiday this year?" He'd say Barbados. "Where are you going?" Dominican Republic. "Where are you going?" Guadeloupe. "I'll be there, don't worry . . ." I had to make sure that he re-signed his contract and I would always follow him out. We had a standing joke. End of every season I'd be there.'

The first hint of what became an annual headache took the form of Nicolas Anelka's brothers. Anelka had arrived at Arsenal as a seventeen-year-old in 1997, much to the displeasure of his boyhood club Paris Saint-Germain. He was a silent sensation. So incredible that Real Madrid put him on their shopping list. A summer of ferocious negotiating with Anelka's brothers, who acted as his agents and drove Arsenal to distraction, was finally concluded as he left for Spain. Arsenal had made a profit of roughly £23 million for a young talent that had exploded onto the Highbury scene yet was gone within two years.

Wenger regretted the sale, despite the fact it represented extremely lucrative business. Half of the Anelka money covered the new training complex, which was built to immaculate specifications and transformed the environment for the players. The other half was put towards a replacement, another young French whiz, a guy who funnily enough grew up with Anelka and the two were firm friends. That just happened to be a kid playing on the wing for Juventus called Thierry Henry.

A year later another Spanish giant, Barcelona, came along to scupper Wenger's plans again. The two clubs wrestled with each other over Emmanuel Petit, whose partnership with Vieira had been such a cornerstone, and Marc Overmars, whose sparky wing-play had so often been decisive. During that summer, as he fought to keep the team jigsaw intact, Wenger's face told a thousand words as he wearily explained he could write a book on the Overmars transfer pow-wows alone. Vieira was particularly sorry to lose Petit, a man who had been a true partner – in midfield these contrasting talents were joined like two sides of the same coin. 'We are still really close,' he says. 'I played with Manu the right time of my career and he helped me a lot. He was really mature, and a sweet, emotional boy. He looked sometimes like he didn't care, but no. Manu will kill for you, he will die for you, he will give you everything.' There are crucial teams within teams that manifest themselves in certain combinations – when a midfield pair, or a striking partnership, or a defensive unit clicks, it can be devilish to replace. Another player with quality might come in, but will not necessarily recreate the connection.

It took Wenger two years to find a new partner for Vieira who could revive the kind of bond and balance he shared with Petit. The Arsenal manager attended the 2002 World Cup, where a member of Brazil's winning side caught his eye. It wasn't one of the three Rs who dominated the limelight up front (Rivaldo, Ronaldo and Ronaldinho), but a tough midfielder with a gentle soul, a player blessed with smart defensive instincts, a cool ability to read the game and snuff out danger, and a sunny nature that would be welcome in any dressing room. Gilberto Silva, the son of a blacksmith, who grew up sharing a bedroom with his three sisters in a house built by his father, had shown huge determination to become a professional footballer. At one point he gave up youth football to try to earn some money for the family with real work. He spent some time doing carpentry, and working in a sweet factory, before having one last stab at a football career. He progressed steadily, but it wasn't until his mid-twenties that he really rose to prominence at Atlético Mineiro. Come the summer of 2002, Wenger dropped this particular name when he was in conversation with Dein. 'What do you reckon? Do we have a chance to get him?'

The story of Gilberto's move to Arsenal gives an insight into how the relationship between Wenger and Dein – in itself another hugely important clique inside the football club at the time – was the engine that powered the team-building process. 'Arsène would say, "I think this player will fit in nicely and this is where I envisage him playing." Then it was down to me to go and do the deal and bring the player back,' says Dein. He travelled to Belo Horizonte to seek talks with Atlético Mineiro. They had two vice-presidents at the time, neither of whom cared to entertain this visitor from London. Dein more or less camped out at the club headquarters. 'I was almost sleeping on their doorstep for three days to get them to engage with me,' he recalls. His persistence paid off, and once they started talking, it took a week of negotiations to convince them to strike a deal.

Dein called Wenger from Brazil. 'I have a little surprise for you,' he said. 'I am arriving tomorrow at the training ground and you will see what it is.' The following day, Dein arrived at the pre-season camp in Austria and introduced Wenger to Gilberto.

With only a smattering of English at the time (although he would become fluent), Gilberto leaned on another Brazilian midfielder at the club during that time for support. Edu was a stylish player, who had suffered some injuries which limited his opportunities to play, but he was also valued as a vital member of the squad and much loved for his effortless friendliness. Straight away, even though they were effectively competing for a place in Arsenal's midfield, Edu welcomed Gilberto, took him under his wing, and taught him everything he could about the team, the culture, and what was needed to strike up that crucial on-the-pitch understanding with Vieira – even if that might have been to his own professional detriment.

'The decision wasn't for me or Gilberto about who plays in the first team or not,' explains Edu. 'The decision was for Arsène Wenger. I had it very clear in my mind. Gilberto was such a nice guy, and I had a great experience to try to help him as much as possible. I wasn't thinking about if we played in the same position. It's in the Brazilian culture to try to help each other. Even before Gilberto arrived I spoke to Arsène Wenger about him many times and said he was fantastic. I knew if he signed for Arsenal he would help us as a team. That was what I was thinking at that moment. My heart told me to think that way, not in a bad way.'

Gilberto picks up the story, enthusing, 'Even though he's younger than me he behaved like a big brother. He was fantastic to me, the way he helped me, the way he showed me around in London. I didn't want to live too far away from him. Of course I didn't want to bother him, but if I needed something he made it easy to solve the problem.'

Gilberto and Vieira began to develop a rapport, which would become a central force in the Invincible season. 'When I arrived at Arsenal Edu helped me even in this way – about Patrick's personality, how he was, how strong he was but also what a good man he was and is,' says Gilberto. 'It was so easy for us to understand each other, the way we played. We understood very quickly how to synchronize the movements we did on the field. I knew when he went forward I had to stay, and if I went forward he stayed until I returned into position. We always spoke a lot on the field. If I was in the wrong position he talked to me, and I did the same to him. You exchange knowledge to help each other. This is the way it has to be.' Needless to say, Wenger was delighted that Dein's mission to Brazil had been accomplished.

The balancing act of strengthening the squad, while fending off the vultures who would weaken it, was such a big task for Wenger and Dein that sometimes it felt like the close season was even more demanding than the actual football. Operating in shark-infested waters, with agents and money men on the attack, is quite the challenge. Together, in tandem, Wenger and Dein felt well armed. The chemistry between the two men worked perfectly. Wenger had the football vision and Dein had the contacts book and negotiating tactics to take care of business.

It was Wenger's detailed knowledge of the global game that had been one of the prime attractions to Arsenal in the first place. 'Above all, he was highly intelligent and had this worldly knowledge – I could see the English game was going global – and it needed somebody who had far better vision than buying players from the lower divisions in England,' explains Dein. 'That was one of his great attributes, this extraordinary, encyclopedic knowledge of players overseas, quite apart from the ones in his own domain, which was really in France. Of course they were unknown over here so we had the edge on the market.'

Before long Wenger was beginning to gain a reputation as a master educator, and players knew that if he sent word that he was interested, the chance to work with someone with a speciality for improving talent was particularly exciting. For a young Swede with a punk haircut and a style that mixed tenacity with technique – who was being chased by numerous clubs – it was Wenger who struck a chord. Freddie Ljungberg had been on the big-club radar since he was sixteen. 'I'd said no, no, no,' he recalls. 'Until I felt ready. Then I had three clubs I was going to see. So I did some research, as most people do. Arsenal were the champions the year before, they had a great history, a special history according to what I could find out. I got to the club and then my main thing was Arsène, how he conducted himself. He did so with grace and respect. We talked about football, how we thought football should be played, and the culture he wanted to bring into the club. And that's why I signed, because of Arsène's attitude.'

Wenger was a catalyst not only to recruiting foreign players.

His image as a forward-thinking coach with a love for purist football was key to a significant signing on their doorstep in North London. When it came to the business of rebuilding a legendary defence, Wenger was keen to keep some English heart at its centre. The man who would tick all the boxes was closer to home than Wenger and Dein ever imagined possible.

Few transfers were quite so dramatic as when Sol Campbell eschewed the chance to go abroad to instead make the four-mile journey down the Seven Sisters Road from Tottenham. For all the complexities it would bring, the bottom line was that Campbell simply wanted to play for Wenger, and wanted to play in the kind of team he had created.

'I was at the stage where I needed someone like Arsène, really,' he says. 'Do you know what? I was at a level where I just needed players around me who were bloody good at their job, who had the fight in them, loved winning, hated losing, but were at the top of their game and gentlemen at the same time. I needed to be in that type of environment. I wanted to be in a stable environment as well. I wanted to challenge for honours. And that environment was, for me, with Arsène and all the players who were there. They weren't perfect, I wasn't perfect, Arsène wasn't perfect, but together, we were perfect. It was great, you know. We played some wonderful football and I had some wonderful years there. Yes, we had our ups and downs. Yes, we had our arguments and things like that. But, end of the day, we were passionate about the game and we were all fighters. Fighters but gentlemen at the same time. Football-wise, it was perfect.'

It wasn't quite so perfect from a personal point of view as Campbell was under no illusions about the delicacy of even considering a move from Tottenham to Arsenal. Inter-club transfers are rare in this particular heartland with good reason, such is the tension and mutual loathing. Campbell was coming to the end of his contract and his agent, Sky Andrew, was the intermediary who first mentioned something so extraordinary it had an aura of taboo. To general surprise, both parties declared an interest as tactfully as they could.

Campbell, who was paranoid about being spotted even talking to anyone from Arsenal, needed time to work up the trust to go through with a move that would inevitably come loaded with notoriety. He visited Dein's house under the cover of darkness. For hours the two men chatted – Arsenal vice-chairman and Tottenham captain – walking around the expanse of lawn in the garden of the Deins' Totteridge home.

'We would wander around and just shoot the breeze, just the two of us,' Dein recalls. 'Not necessarily about football, about life. Sol is a very deep character. I have a lot of respect for Sol because it was not an easy move. In fact it was tremendously difficult, emotionally. The easiest move for him would have been to have gone abroad, where they wanted him. He was prepared to come, and particularly to play for Arsène.'

One night, the pair who had gone to such lengths to keep their meetings secret were busted by none other than Dein's youngest son, Gavin, who returned from a nightclub at around 2 a.m. to find his dad chatting to a surprise guest. Gavin broke the awkwardness by asking if anyone fancied breakfast, and he duly cooked everyone some French toast. Given the flavour Wenger had brought to Arsenal, it was an excellent choice for a slightly surreal early morning snack for all concerned. But in some small way the encounter made everyone feel this crazy deal was rooted in something meaningful. 'I wanted Sol to trust me,' said Dein. 'It was about trust. It was about family. It was important to show he was joining not just a regular football club but he was going to be part of our family.'

Campbell echoes those sentiments. 'If I didn't really trust David, I don't think I would have gone,' he says. 'No chance. No way. He is a charismatic guy. One of the main things with David is he can talk to players, he can talk to presidents, he can talk to the cleaner, he can talk to anybody. He can talk to all the guys in

UEFA, or in FIFA, and it's perfect how he can transfer and communicate with all these kind of guys. Because that's a special talent.
In many ways, when you talk about the creation of this Invincibles
team that went on to have the success it did, everybody says Arsène
did everything, because he's the manager, he's the high-profile
guy. We have this cult of the manager nowadays. But it was a team.
David took care of the mechanicals. Making deals. Cutting deals.
Getting it done, which you need. If you haven't got someone who
can get that deal done, then Arsène can't get the players! They
were a fantastic team.'

Wenger remembers those days fondly, when he and Dein reaped
the rewards of this winning formula as they pieced this team
together. 'We had a good comprehensive understanding,' he says.
'We didn't need to talk to each other too much, even if we loved
to do it. It was exciting, talking to Sol Campbell at two o'clock in
the morning in David's garden. What was amazing compared to
today is when we called the press conference there were three
journalists there because they thought we were going to announce
a young boy. It was such a shock. Sol is a very interesting man. He
didn't say a word to anybody. He kept it secret for three months.
That can't happen any more. We had fantastic work, fantastic
togetherness, in the team behind the team.'

Ray Parlour remembers how even the players were amazed
when this familiar face crossed the divide and walked in. 'Everyone's eyebrows shot up,' he says. 'I would probably never have
gone to Tottenham in a million years. They could have offered me
two hundred grand a week, I just couldn't have done it. It was a
funny situation. I said, "You feeling all right, Sol? What are you
doing, coming to Arsenal?" But he just said to us, "I want to win
trophies and I want to be involved in your team."'

From the supporters' perspective, once they got over the shock,
Campbell's signing was something to celebrate. As the author Nick
Hornby points out, that is not a normal reaction when signing
defenders. 'Well, obviously it was very amusing,' he recalls. 'But it

was also exactly what we needed. We know that Arsène will never spend big money on a centre back or a goalkeeper, or a full back even. He only wants to buy inside forwards. It must have been so painful for Spurs fans, that Sol could see what was going on, and that he would absolutely win something with these amazing players. It's got to be the only time that any of us have ever been excited about a centre-back signing in the whole history of my watching Arsenal. There aren't many clubs who can make that an exciting signing anyway. Somebody who stops other people from doing things. But it was an unrepeatable set of circumstances.'

Come the summer of 2002, at the end of his maiden season in red and white, Sol Campbell won the Double. It was a substantial reward for taking the most complex of calls on his career. That season had been one of defensive transition, with Lauren playing more regularly than Dixon, and Campbell stamping his authority in what would be Tony Adams's last campaign. Gentle alchemy was required to find exactly the right substances to create a golden season. The older generation segued into the new. The baton was smoothly passed.

The manner in which Arsenal won the Double in 2002 made Wenger wonder whether an unbeaten season was possible. He more or less challenged his players there and then to plant the seed in their minds. Arsenal were undefeated away from home through-out the 2001–02 season, and in the run-in embarked on a long sequence of wins, which showed immense mental fortitude. The FA Cup was claimed with a pair of inspired goals, from Ray Parlour and Freddie Ljungberg, to swat aside Chelsea. A few days later, the title was claimed at Old Trafford – the venue that often seemed to vibrate with possibility. The signals were unmistakable.

'There was a process to get to the 2004 team,' explains Keown. 'In 2002 we won the last thirteen games of the season, we didn't lose away from home, and we had three goalkeepers who picked up a Premier League medal that year, so never before has a squad been used to that extreme. That's some effort. The 1998 group were pioneers. The 2002 group reinvented itself. We were starting to set records, scoring in every single game, not losing a single away game, unbeaten runs. I just feel that everything that went before helped the 2004 team.'

But setbacks were part of that process, too. The players were unable to forget that during the period between the two Doubles, from 1998–99 to 2000–01, for three successive seasons Arsenal suffered a prolonged and painful bout of seconditis. Runners-up in the Premier League each time, plus defeated finalists in the 2000 Uefa Cup and 2001 FA Cup; it was becoming an unbearable habit.

Ljungberg, who arrived just after Arsenal won the 1998 Double and experienced all those knocks before the team was able to triumph again, describes how that inner frustration was a motivating force. 'In Sweden we say, you clench your fist in your pocket so nobody can see it,' he says, pointedly. 'Maybe that's what made us after three years erupt and get better. We were not happy in any shape or form.'

Keown agrees. 'It hurt so much when we lost,' he reflects. 'I remember standing on that pitch in 2001 and saying this ain't gonna happen again, because Liverpool were so lucky that day. So actually to be back there again in 2002 against Chelsea, then to win the league, it showed the resolve. The nucleus of the team were growing some big balls really because of the disappointments of what had happened before. It almost became that if we didn't win something we were going to lose another player. You think, *Hold on, how can we beat another team without Anelka, Overmars, Petit?* It's quite hard to come to terms with. A team can grieve for players.'

Henry feels it was particularly important the 2002 title was claimed at Old Trafford. 'It was putting a statement out there. We won it at your place,' he says. 'Man United had been more than dominating for years. It was kind of boring.'

Arsenal felt ready to dominate themselves. They began the 2002–03 season in dazzling style. A sequence of ten wins and two draws, a masterclass of scintillating attacks and majestic power, they were on course for something special.

Enter, stage left, a seventeen-year-old Wayne Rooney.

Arsenal's serenity was shattered as a precocious prodigy from Merseyside hammered a ninetieth-minute goal to inflict a defeat at Everton that shocked Arsenal's system. It took them a while to regain their composure, and that spell off-kilter cost them the title. They had to reluctantly hand the trophy back to Manchester United. Robert Pirès's goal won them the FA Cup, but that did not shift the feeling they might have done better with their season's work.

Bergkamp could never quite work it out. 'That's the only thing that surprised me sometimes,' he muses. 'After a successful season, or a trophy, we found it difficult to make the next step. I don't know why, maybe we needed to get more players in after a trophy, maybe we had to step up a little bit, or maybe we weren't ready for the opponents to have a different idea about Arsenal. Yeah, that was strange. We didn't get stronger off a trophy, we didn't find that extra step. It should make you stronger, but it was a little bit the opposite.'

Is it really that hard to retain the title? 'Of course,' insists Vieira. 'We should have won the league three or four times in a row. Easy. When we won the league, the year after we didn't have the same concentration and determination. Maybe we didn't have the new player who will take us to a different level. United, every year, made a big signing to lift them. That was the strength of United. Maybe we didn't bring new players to bring us to a different level and bring competition between us.'

Belatedly, a new player came in ready to ruffle some feathers. He was the only embellishment to the 2003 team. Wenger evidently didn't think much was needed to fine-tune the squad back into title-winning mode. The only signing was an essential one, as David Seaman, an iconic goalkeeper at the club for thirteen years, moved on.

Willkommen, Herr Lehmann. Nobody inside the dressing room was quite sure what they were getting. But they soon would be. Wenger had found the recruitment of a new goalkeeper quite troublesome, before he settled on a German international with a reputation for being very much his own man. There was good sense in bringing in a personality who would not be so worried about the pressure of following in Seaman's footsteps, as he thrived on putting himself under an audacious level of pressure to perform anyway.

The player himself remembers the deal was tricky, involving 'an argument with Borussia Dortmund because they didn't want to let me go', but Lehmann and Arsenal were both keen on each other and Dortmund relented.

In recruiting a thirty-three-year-old, Wenger introduced a man (and a character) who was mature enough to have no qualms about impressing the other players. He was confident enough to walk into a team with a potent winning mentality ready to take on anyone in the competitive spirit stakes. Integration would not be a problem.

'I think my strength was that I didn't really care,' Lehmann says, 'because I was older than the others, apart from Martin Keown. I'd won a European trophy, which they hadn't, apart from Dennis Bergkamp. On the pitch they wanted me as I was. They didn't want to have a guy who adjusted, probably nice and smooth talking on the pitch. They didn't want to have that. On the pitch I was really aggressive. But I can say that I never had fear on the pitch, I couldn't afford to in my game. And not to have fear meant I had to put myself into a very aggressive mode. My game was rushing out.'

He used music to get into his zone. His choice was German techno. Kraftwerk might have been a new one to the likes of Keown, who wanted something slightly softer with his seasonal choice of Gabrielle's 'Dreams Can Come True', but Keown found the whole thing quite illuminating anyway. It was not often he came across a player in the dressing room who could get more extreme than he did.

'He was one of the few people that I thought was even more intense than I was,' Keown recalls, slightly wide-eyed. 'And I used to say to Jens, "Any chance of smiling just occasionally?" And he would look at me like, *Oh, I am preparing for the game*. He needed to be in a certain mindset to play well, he was very, very focused. Trained incredibly hard. Super fit. Another winner. A bloody good goalkeeper. We finally got him to loosen up a little bit towards the end of the year.'

Vieira actually credits Lehmann with upping the ante in terms of Arsenal's winning spirit. 'Jens was a nightmare sometimes,' he laughs. 'He was a nightmare but he brought something. Before, our winning mentality was there [he places a hand by his head] and when Jens came it was there [he reaches it higher]. It's true! Jens argued with every single player in training. Because he wants you to get concentrated, he wants you to work hard, he wants you to win. If you are in his team and you think, *OK, today I am just going to look after myself*. No! Jens will not accept a player giving seventy per cent or eighty per cent. He expects one hundred per cent. Jens brought us to a different level in terms of the winning mentality. He was never happy, always complaining, but he was a really good guy.'

Lehmann himself remembers provoking Thierry Henry in training one day. They were on the same team, and the goalkeeper felt the goalscorer was not pulling his weight. 'Thierry didn't run, and I told him,' Lehmann recalls. 'When I told him the second and third time, he was so upset he shouted back in English and French. But in the end I think everybody knew that the others were looking at them. *For Christ sake I have to run around, because now the others are looking at my reaction*. Sometimes it was a bit of fun, but for us playing a game in training meant you had to win it. That was probably one of the big secrets of the group. Because everybody was there in training to win. Not just to play, and then see what's coming in the afternoon – a nice coffee and nap. Training was there to play and to concentrate and to win. For me training was always important.'

Henry agrees that this strong German mentality was a powerful new ingredient. 'Jens arrived at Arsenal and he soon understood that he had to be like us *and more* if he was going to be one of us. Sometimes he was losing it, sometimes he wasn't losing it, but it was always for the good of the team. And he was having a go at anyone at any time because he wanted to win. That was the beauty of that team for me. Not only the pass-and-move, not only the goals and style of football, but we were always going to let each other know what time it was. If someone was going to step out of the line, those guys were going to let people know.'

The summer of 2003 was significant not just for Lehmann's arrival, and for the experiment which saw Kolo Touré tried out at centre back in pre-season and inspired Wenger to rethink his defence. Arsenal also persuaded Vieira, Pirès and Bergkamp to renegotiate their contracts. For all the complications holding on to coveted players, Arsenal were not as vulnerable as they might have been simply because they created an atmosphere that was boldly ambitious, yet retained the old-fashioned warmth of a family club. That was certainly something that was possible at Highbury, led by a board comprising lifelong fans. It's impossible to recreate that in a modern stadium with the club owned by overseas investors as part of their portfolio. Arsenal in 2003 had an environment where some outstanding talent felt so at home, so comfortable, so content, and also so motivated, they wanted to stay. They bought into the Arsenal style, and there was enough promise of success, of a team designed to be at the very least competitive and compelling, to get deeply under the skin.

A glance at the core team who played the most matches in the starting XI over the season is instructive (see table). Look at the blend of ages – mostly around their mid-twenties, with a couple of veterans. Look at when they joined Arsenal – seven of them had been there for at least three seasons, giving a base of stability, know-how and experience of what it takes to win (and how it feels to fall short) in Arsenal colours. Only Gilberto and Lehmann had not yet won a trophy for Arsenal, but they had both won honours overseas.

The core of the 2003–04 XI

Player	Age	Joined
Jens Lehmann	33	2003
Lauren	23	2000
Kolo Touré	22	2002
Sol Campbell	29	2001
Ashley Cole	22	1999★
Freddie Ljungberg	26	1998
Patrick Vieira	27	1996
Gilberto Silva	26	2002
Robert Pirès	29	2000
Dennis Bergkamp	34	1995
Thierry Henry	26	1999

★ Cole was at Arsenal as a schoolboy, date of debut

Arsenal began the Invincible season strongly. They were powerful enough to withstand a fright in their opening game against Everton at Highbury when Sol Campbell was sent off very early. In their next match, a trip to Middlesbrough, they played sunshine football. On a blazing day in a kit that nodded its head at Brazil's famous yellow, Gilberto sprinted up from midfield to score one of the four goals with a beautiful finish. A cluster of Arsenal players accelerating into the box, with more than one possible goalscorer for a provider to aim at, was classic Arsenal. That style was dizzying and demoralizing for the opposition. Attacking at speed and in numbers was Arsenal's signature move.

For Gilberto, it felt special. It felt different. 'What made us stronger was the previous season,' he says. 'That was very disappointing for us. It was very hard to think about what happened. How was it possible to let the season go like this? Especially when you look at the players we had in our team. That disappointment made us very strong for the next season. Everything came together, the team kept winning, no matter who was on the pitch.'

4
Improvisation

Patrick Vieira only remembers Arsène Wenger joining in training once. The occasion is seared in everybody's minds because of the unforgettable moment that the manager was clattered by a triallist. He was over from the Ivory Coast, a boy by the name of Kolo Touré. He had already steamed into Thierry Henry and Dennis Bergkamp, and the other players were incredulous to see this kid who was apparently intent on taking out Arsenal's best players. Still, Wenger was an unlikely next victim. 'I was on trial and was desperate to stay, and everything I could see I was ready to smash,' Touré says. 'The ball went out and Mr Wenger went to get the ball back. Instead of waiting, I was so keen to show how much I was ready to fight in this game, I just carried on running and made a big tackle on Mr Wenger.' The boss was in pain. The rest of the players couldn't contain their laughter. Touré was mortified, and worried his over-enthusiasm had wrecked his chances. Ray Parlour later saw Wenger nursing his ankle with an ice pack and, feeling sorry for Touré, suggested the lad didn't mean it. 'I know he didn't mean it,' replied Wenger. 'I like his desire. We sign him tomorrow.'

Flexibility is imperative when managing a collective over a season. A plan can be in place, and at any moment an unexpected problem can be thrown into the mix which necessitates a quick fix. The ability to juggle, tinker, use your imagination and take risks has to be part of a manager's make-up. With the possibility of being hit at any time by an injury, a red card, a suspension or an unexpected setback, it becomes routine to have to cope with regular conundrums.

The capacity to react, to reorganize, was needed from game one, at home to Everton, when Sol Campbell was sent off a mere twenty-five minutes into the season. Wenger withdrew a striker, Sylvain Wiltord, and introduced Martin Keown to slot into the back four. Within minutes, ten-man Arsenal had taken the lead and by the hour mark they were leading 2–0. 'I was pissed off,' says Campbell. 'I hated getting sent off. You know they've got to up their game. When other guys have gone off I've said, "Well, we've got one more space to fill, we've got to start running." It galvanizes a team. If you've got the right mentality in the team, the team just gets in and gets tougher.'

A month later, the consequences of the Battle of Old Trafford needed serious attention in terms of squad strength and using resources. It didn't help that a cluster of injuries afflicted key players at the same time. Lauren was out of the picture with a damaged knee for several weeks. There was a choice to be made about whether to promote a youngster in his position, or switch Kolo Touré from the middle to the right, and bring in a more experienced central defender, which would mean two changes to the back line, but add more know-how. Wenger went for the latter.

Just to add another complication, Patrick Vieira missed around six weeks after picking up a thigh strain in the game that followed the Manchester madness. Dennis Bergkamp's fear of flying brought a regular headache for European away trips. Reshuffling, and making use of the broader talents of the squad, could seem like an endless task. The search for what Wenger calls 'internal solutions' became a constant challenge.

It increases the need for solidarity in a group when there is an unwritten hierarchy. Everybody knows the main men will play, fitness permitting, and the others must retain concentration, sharpness and a relish to slot in when chances present themselves.

'They were helping and that was the strength of that team,' says Bergkamp. 'It was not eleven players. It was not twelve or fourteen. It was eighteen to twenty with a fantastic mix of young players, upcoming players and experienced players. You always get some who are disappointed. The task of the team is then to pull them in, to demand of everyone to stay focused. I always say – and Arsène mentioned this as well – you can have a strong eleven, but it's all about players twelve to sixteen, and if they are strong enough. Because in a season you always get injuries. It depends if it weakens the team if you bring those subs in, or will it bring something different? And that was our luck, we had good players on the bench.'

Maintaining a focused, upbeat squad is tricky not only for the manager but also for the players themselves. Lauren was impressed by how the personalities involved sparked in each other a high level of collective motivation and responsibility. 'Exactly,' he says firmly. 'Even the players on the bench had the same conviction, the same mentality. That's a key point. Sometimes, we lost Dennis Bergkamp or Sol Campbell, but the one who was on the bench was ready to come in and was determined to do well. That made a huge difference.'

Ray Parlour emphasizes how those who were more peripheral than they might have wished for handled it in an unusually grown-up way. 'Whoever Arsène Wenger picked, the team he picked, that was it, we were going to go with it,' he says. 'There was no bitchiness about *Oh, he should be playing and he shouldn't be playing*. There was none of that. You can get that in football. Somebody thinks, *Well, how's he back in the team when he didn't play that well last week? I'm playing well*. Maybe behind the scenes it happened, but I certainly didn't see it in training and team spirit is the most important thing, because you're all in the same boat. You all see each other every day, and if you haven't got team spirit, you've got no chance.'

Outside of the mainstays of the team – the eleven who played regularly enough to give the impression of being a first pick – a further nine players made the minimum ten appearances to earn a 2004 Premier League winner's medal. The elder statesman Martin

Keown, reserve centre back Pascal Cygan, and a youthful Gaël
Clichy provided defensive cover. Edu and Ray Parlour were fan-
tastically reliable and influential in midfield. There were two
experienced attackers coming to the end of their Arsenal days in
Nwankwo Kanu and Sylvain Wiltord, and two young hopefuls in
Jérémie Aliadière and later January's spectacular signing José
Antonio Reyes.

Vieira credits Wenger with creating an inclusive atmosphere.
Underused players had to feel vital. 'The manager has to make
them feel like they are as important as everyone else,' he stresses.
'How? To show them more attention. If you looked at the Arsenal
team from a few years ago you knew who was going to be in the
first eleven. So that means the players on the bench knew that too.
But Arsène managed it really well. As players too, the ones who
were playing showed everybody is part of the team by showing
them attention.'

Vieira stresses his relationship with Edu, who often had to pick
up where either he or Gilberto left off, as a case in point: 'I was
really close to Edu. He didn't play that often. We talked about
everything and nothing. I never showed him that I was here and he
was there. Arsène bought players who were really talented, but the
right people as well. How do we treat the guy sitting next to us?
That was something really important to Arsène. You can be really
good but you have to fit inside the dressing room. That's why we
never had players who complained they weren't playing. We didn't
have those issues because we had good people, intelligent people,
in our dressing room.'

Edu contemplates the idea that the Invincibles could never have
happened without him *and* Gilberto, even if missing out on a game
occasionally was tough to stomach. 'You are right!' he chuckles.

Is it hard to be ready and committed when you are not a guaranteed starter, fitness permitting?

'First of all you have to respect the guy who is playing in your
position,' he says. 'Arsène Wenger has to make the decision and

there are good players all over the squad. Of course you want to play as much as you can. It's very understandable. From my point of view what made a big difference at that time was the respect for each other to make sure everyone is focused on helping the club. Arsène Wenger knew how to speak to the players who were not playing a lot and look after them. He kept everybody happy. He treats everybody as a person. The way he looks after the players is to do with their whole life. Footballers are people. We have feelings. We have sadness and happiness. You have to understand what is going on with each player to keep everybody in the same direction. He knows. If you are shouting and complain around him, we have our problems as well. The way he always looked after the players was fantastic.'

Edu was a manager's dream in the 2003–04 season. Wenger knew he had a player of great refinement at his disposal. Had fate worked out differently he could have comfortably been a guaranteed first pick, and he was probably the next best thing. He had endured a terrible time when he first joined the club. There was a bungled passport fiasco, when invalid papers supplied by an agent led to his being turned away at Heathrow, even though he was eligible for legitimate documents. It would take six months for a new passport to be processed, a time blighted by harrowing news back home. His family were robbed at gunpoint, and no sooner had they recovered than his sister, Fabricia, was killed in a car crash. When he did eventually make it to Highbury, he was in no fit state to play football. Twenty minutes into his first appearance he limped off hamstrung, the first of a series of injuries. 'When I arrived I had so many problems, everything inside my head was broken,' he said.

He handled everything with dedication and charm. 'I was always driven to succeed,' he added. 'I kept telling myself: *You have to win this battle.*' A vivid picture that springs to mind when thinking of Edu in an Arsenal shirt is of this upright, elegant midfielder arriving in the box to stroke in a goal at the San Siro at the end of November, his contribution to a collection that made up one of the most extraordinary results of the campaign. He pulled off his jersey and jumped in bare-chested joy in front of the travelling supporters. Not so important? Not so admired? No way.

That game was a brilliant booster. Internazionale 1 Arsenal 5. There was layer upon layer of importance: It was a scoreline that caused shockwaves in Europe. It demonstrated how the team had a defiant streak to recover from the embarrassment of being tormented by the same opponent 0–3 at Highbury, and proved a Champions League mission that looked hopeless could be inspiring. It did wonders for Arsenal's belief. It invited Thierry Henry, who was unplayable on the night, to stake a claim to a wider audience that he was amongst the best players in the world. But equally importantly, as well as showcasing its star, it displayed the depth of Arsenal's squad at its absolute best.

Without Lauren, the defence was reshuffled with Touré moving to right back and Cygan coming into the centre. Without Vieira and Gilberto (on the subs bench), Edu and Ray Parlour struck up an excellent combination in the heart of midfield. Without Bergkamp, Kanu stepped in to support Henry, with a young Aliadière coming off the bench to create the last goal.

Parlour, who put in a captain's shift on the night, remembers it feeling momentous. 'It was me and Edu in centre midfield! An unbelievable performance. I mean probably one of the best performances I've been involved in. I was skipper that night as well, and I couldn't believe Patrick took his armband back when he was fit again,' he grins.

Henry felt the essence of the squad was on display. 'People always talk about the usual suspects at Arsenal. You need to have a Ray Parlour, you need to have an Edu, I know it's a name that people don't talk about, but Pascal Cygan played well that night,' he stresses. 'The usual suspects are great to be around, but we had a good squad. It's not always down to two, three, four, six or seven players. You need almost twenty-five competitors and winners to be able to do what we did that season.'

The *Gazzetta dello Sport* reflected Inter's nightmare by printing a picture of Edvard Munch's *The Scream* to illustrate their post-mortem. The Italians felt particularly bewildered because of the sharp contrast in ethos between the two clubs. The Italians had spent in the region of £350 million and gone through ten coaches in a troubling search for success over the eight years since their benevolent sugar daddy at the time, Massimo Moratti, took over. During a similar time frame, Arsenal had replaced Bruce Rioch with Wenger and spent a fraction of that sum.

It was a handy case study to show the benefits of stability and patient team-building. It also was interesting in that Arsenal's overstretched squad, which was supposed to be a weakness, actually ended up a strength. The squad was not bloated, which left Wenger gambling at times, but this streamlined operation meant everybody felt involved, and respected for what they could bring.

The original defeat against Inter had left a bad taste. The comedian and actor Alan Davies remembers some early internet Photoshop jokes going around as Arsenal's sponsor – O2 – had been amended to 0–3. 'Some smartarse got that up quickly,' he grimaces. The reaction came with a big feel-good factor. Ljungberg liked the way they clubbed together to respond to adversity. 'It's important, when you experience some doubts, to stick together and show what you are made of,' he says. 'If things are happy all the time you don't get to know your real teammates. That's what makes the team gel, and maybe this wouldn't have happened without losing 3–0 to Inter. We always play our best football when our backs are against the wall. We definitely have a special spirit, great faith in each other. Turning it around is a great thing.'

There was an amazing atmosphere within the team that night. By the end, as the goals poured down on Inter, Arsenal's players were laughing on the pitch they were having such a ridiculous amount of fun. They hugged each other like soulmates. They looked liberated from some of the pressures they had experienced in the season up to that point.

Back in the dressing room, as they soaked up the effects of this shot of happiness, Jens Lehmann asked for some quiet. He had some serious words to impart. When he had joined, he managed to avoid the initiation speech or song that is normally required of a newcomer, making do with a casual hello. On a wild, wet, Milan night, he suddenly felt compelled to have his say, to praise what he felt was the most bonded team spirit he had ever come across. 'Wenger was just about to say something when Jens stood up on his own, out of the blue,' Parlour remembers. 'He said, "I was in goal watching and it was absolutely fantastic. I've been involved in lots of big games and that was one of my proudest moments, to be involved in the team." Wenger had a smile on his face.'

Lehmann elaborates: 'I had introduced myself. But not properly,' he explains. 'After the game I said, "Sorry. Now it's my speech." I addressed the great camaraderie and team spirit of the team, which I hadn't experienced at such a high level. I'd experienced it before when I had played for Schalke, but the players weren't as good as the players here. These were exceptional, world-class players, and still the camaraderie and the team spirit was fantastic. That was my impression, not after one week, but after five months.'

As they left the San Siro, the players' body language was striking. They wore giant smiles and looked as if they had shrugged an irksome monkey off their backs; they had found an antidote to their European neurosis. They looked bigger. As Pirès says, 'When people saw Inter 1 Arsenal 5, at San Siro, people said, "Wow, watch out for Arsenal." That evening, in my opinion, we left an impression in Europe.'

Edu needs just one word to sum up how he feels about that game: 'Beautiful.'

★

Henry was the talk of Milan. He had a habit of giving a masterclass on Italian soil, which always created a frisson as he had been a youngster with Juventus whose stay was abruptly cut short when David Dein successfully opened negotiations with his Juve counterpart, Roberto Bettega, and swung one of Arsenal's most significant deals.

Henry was progressing well at Juve in his first season, but it's true to say his long-distance admiration for the scene Wenger had built at Arsenal had been on his mind for a while. Even during France 98 – that golden summer for his country as they conquered the World Cup, before he had even left Monaco for Juventus – he spoke warmly of Arsenal and hinted of his desire to play for the team that was flourishing with the French presence of Vieira, Petit, Anelka and, of course, Wenger. Henry was not unhappy at Juventus. He was not particularly seeking an exit. But when the opportunity presented itself, he jumped.

What might have been had Juventus been firmer and he'd stayed in Serie A? Who knows. But it is fair to consider the question of whether there might have been a slightly different career path had he not come back under the guidance of Wenger, the manager who gave him his debut as a teenager at Monaco.

Might Henry have remained an orthodox winger, a player with speed and finesse who operated for club and country on the left flank, for the rest of his footballing time? Possibly. But what is certain is that Wenger's intervention, to reprogramme him as a central forward at the age of twenty-two, proved a spectacular success.

The goal that transformed that tie at Inter is a classic example of his redefined craft, and the way he crowned his penchant for creating goals with an instinctive feel for brilliant finishing. The catchphrase *va-va-voom* evoked that sense of him switching on the afterburners – but the key was that at high speed he retained such clean control and craft. He even possessed the cool-headedness to make expert choices as he improvised while he was travelling faster than most of his opponents. It was an intoxicating mix of precision and pace.

INTERNAZIONALE 1–5 ARSENAL, 25 NOVEMBER 2003

Nobody could have anticipated what happened next, even though Henry's exceptional qualities are no great secret any more. From an Inter corner and fairly ludicrous penalty appeal when Marco Materazzi plunged to the ground as Sol Campbell hooked clear, Henry did what he does best. Gathering the ball in his own half, his red boots touched the ball seven times in nine seconds. Two touches carried play towards the opposition box, one flick teased his marker, Javier Zanetti, three taps helped him to spring past the Argentine, and then he switched feet to lash into the far corner with his left foot. It was the Frenchman's fortieth goal of 2003. At the other end, Lehmann stood over Materazzi, still writhing about, presumably to give his penalty claim a semblance of credibility. 'See?' yelled the German. 'We've scored, it's 3–1.'

Observer

The reinvention of Henry into the highest calibre centre forward was the perfect example of another of Wenger's means of improvising. His flexibility, in terms of his desire not to put players into boxes, was a forte that in the early phase of his Arsenal life was rewarded again and again. He had this capacity to reshape players, almost a sixth sense to imagine them profiting in a role other than the one they felt most suited to. Where a player would consider himself a midfielder, Wenger might see in him the makings of a defender. Where a player would consider himself a winger, Wenger might see in him the makings of a striker. Four members of the Invincibles main XI were crucially repositioned by Wenger: Henry, Lauren (who arrived as a midfielder), Touré (another midfielder) and Ljungberg (formerly a central playmaker).

In August 1999, shortly after signing, Henry expressed how he needed to rediscover the striker's mindset. He had played centrally in his youth, but having spent almost all his professional career since his debut out wide, he had become unaccustomed to thinking about scoring. In fact, most predatory strikers will admit that scoring needs to be something not far off an obsession. 'I need to rediscover the scoring instinct,' he said, 'That automatic reaction in front of goal.'

It was not the easiest task, and self-doubt, or self-consciousness, is a natural part of the process. Wenger was certain that Henry, a superb student of the game, would graduate with honours.

'You don't doubt your ability,' says Henry. 'I was going through a phase where the boss wanted me to play as a striker again. I was saying to myself, *Hang on a minute, I am in the national team, I won the World Cup as a winger. Am I wasting my time trying to relearn being a striker?* That was more the thing. It is frustrating. I felt like I wasn't helping anybody there. I did forget that I had it. I forgot about goals. When you play as a winger you have to assist the game, help the left back, it's not your job to score. You lose that killer instinct that I had when I was young. I had to learn – if you can say – how to kill.'

Vieira recalls how intensely Henry worked, and how strongly Wenger believed in his adaptation. 'It's all credit to Arsène because Thierry always loved playing on the left-hand side, the position he grew up, and I remember when he came to Arsenal in his first few games, and training sessions, he was missing so many chances,' he says. 'We were laughing about it. But all credit to him after because of the amount of time he spent on the training ground working in front of the goal. To adapt himself to the number nine position – how he will make this run? how he will play with his back to goal? – he worked really hard for it. That's why I'm not surprised he was scoring that number of goals afterwards.'

The captain, who had known Henry since they had played in

France's junior teams together before both progressing to represent Les Bleus at the 1998 World Cup, felt a responsibility to help his friend adapt. 'We were close. I knew how good he was. But I never knew he would reach that level though. The level he reached at Arsenal was unbelievable. He was there with the best.'

It helped that Arsenal gave Henry the atmosphere in which he felt encouraged to flourish. They supported him, but also, once he started to fly, they adored him. Vieira is certain that emotional nourishment was a big part of the picture. 'He is a really sensitive guy. Thierry needed love. He got the love at Arsenal and I think that is why he was that good. He knew how important he was for us, and that's why he performed. All the players showed him how important he was for the club, and for us. He liked that. He liked that kind of responsibility. He knew that we all loved him and that's why he just went and performed and played his game. Thierry was really happy.'

Bergkamp picks up the thread: 'I think he liked a compliment, yeah, definitely. For Thierry I think it's difficult to get criticism. Sometimes he would phone up a newspaper. I was thinking *I can't believe that he does that*. But he's so intense. When somebody would say something, where I would say just leave it – it's gone in a week – he would phone them up and say, "OK, this is what I think, this is my opinion." It's very strong. Of course he needed compliments as well. You forget that sometimes because he is so good.'

Did he feed off the fact he was perceived as the main man?

'Oh he loved that, of course,' says Bergkamp. 'In a way, at a certain point he deserved that role. In that group everyone was expecting him to take that role. Maybe I was the main man before, and when he came he became the main man. I thought it was fantastic. I loved it, to just feed off him and help him and make him look even better. For me it's brilliant because it helps make the team even better. Plus he would feed back, he would give it back to me and to other players as well. In every interview he mentioned the others. He would say the back four was fantastic today, or that pass from Dennis was fantastic. Take the spotlight, you can have it and you deserve it. He loved that. That's what helped the team.'

Having the best player in the league in their team was a constant source of reassurance and inspiration. 'It gives you strength,' explains Vieira. 'Because you know that he can change the game at any time. The year that we went invincible, that was our strength. We knew that Thierry is going to score the goals, or Dennis is going to create the pass for him to score the goals. So when you have Henry and Bergkamp, something is going to happen. So what is important is not to concede a goal. Because you know they are going to make you win games. And then you have the support of Robert, Freddie, Ray . . . So even if we went 1–0 down we knew that we were going to score.'

Henry himself took his role in the team as the peak point seriously. He felt motivated not only by the affection and esteem, but by the fact it was his responsibility to do his bit within the squad's Musketeer mentality. One for all, all for one. 'I felt it was my duty to do what I had to do,' he explains. 'I'm the striker. Most of the time, I'm going to be at the end of the move, or creating a move for someone else to score, because that's the position where you play and I knew what those guys were expecting from me. It wasn't only down to love. Obviously, we're all human beings, right? If you go to work and you feel that type of love around you, you're always going to work better. That's not a bad thing, but that doesn't mean that you're going to deliver. When you have those guys looking at you, expecting something from you, you've got to deliver. Whether it's Chelsea at home or Watford away – no disrespect to anyone – you have to deliver.

'But I was also looking at Dennis or Patrick or Lauren or Ashley Cole or Kolo Touré. The whole squad. When you're looking over your right shoulder, you're like: *OK, he's ready*. When you're looking over the left one, you're like: *OK, he's ready*. When you're looking behind you, you're like: *Those guys are ready.* That was in my mind when I was looking at the opposition goalkeeper in front of me and the net. I knew the guys behind me were ready. So it was just a continuity of what that team was giving me to be able to finish.'

Sol Campbell felt that Henry's temperament was part of what pushed him to strive to be the best. 'Sometimes he would be kind of touchy. He was very delicate sometimes, like an artist. I'm sure he would be like some kind of Picasso. Obviously there's different degrees in some players where they need a hug round the shoulder every day, or once in a while. Thierry is very sensitive. But he was strong at the same time and he's just a wonderful footballer as well. He really blossomed there. It was the right place for him to be nurtured.'

Keown watched him develop into the finished article with amazement. 'Thierry Henry was unplayable,' he says. 'You can't say that lightly. At the start he came with rapid, unbelievable talent. He was quite rough on the edges, he didn't have a style, he didn't have a rhythm. He created this style about his game which was ruthless, but then there was a rhythm to it, the way that he used to run. It became much prettier on the eye and it smoothed off the edges. He glided by the end of it. Like poetry in motion. The way that he'd go in and out of players, we always did that on the playground, but I'd never seen anyone do that at senior level. It was just dream-like.'

Henry was not the only player Wenger had plans for. But for Freddie Ljungberg, Wenger's idea for a positional shift prompted serious doubts. 'I had questions in my own head if I should stay or not,' he admits. 'Arsène knows that. I played centre midfield or number ten. I'd played there my whole life. I'd never been a winger, and never in a million years thought he saw me as a winger. He explained that if I went out there, I had more freedom.' That argument was based on the physical requirements expected of a central player. Ljungberg laughs as he describes himself as a midget, and the idea that he could thrive in the heartland that had been occupied by two powerhouses in Vieira and Petit was something Wenger was concerned about. He wanted Ljungberg to have the space and time to do damage. 'If I played centrally, other players would batter me, and we'd get nothing out of my game because it would be too physical. So that's how he spoke to me about it. I became a winger,' he explains.

But not a happy one. Not to start with, anyway. 'I felt lost,' he admits. 'I can say that honestly that first year, I had no idea what I was doing. If you ask most coaches, my strength in my game has always been my tactical awareness, knowing where people are, opening up games, my timing of runs and this and that. But I had that timing as a central midfielder, because that was my strength, and I'd done it my whole life. I knew when a defender came at me, small things like that, it was in my brain, and my quick feet. I felt so lost, I really didn't like it.

'I didn't play as well as I thought I should, and so after a year, in the summer we had a meeting with my agent. I said, "What the hell am I doing? I'm not a winger." We had some offers to go and play as a central midfielder somewhere else. But I'd never not made it. I made the decision to come because I like Arsenal, I like Arsène, I like my teammates. I thought, *Try and see if I can make it.* I changed my attitude that summer, from complaining to trying to learn. As a twenty-one-year-old I had to learn how to become a winger.' The way he knuckled down and adapted prompted Wenger to describe his evolution, at the time, as 'one of the satisfactions of the year'.

Ljungberg spent nine years at the club, and towards the end got the chance to return to his old posting. He was back in the middle as Arsenal journeyed all the way to the Champions League final in 2006. 'I never felt so comfortable playing at Arsenal as then,' he confesses. 'I absolutely adored to play there.' The sentiment reveals a lot about Ljungberg's determination and willingness to sacrifice something for the team. He recognized that he could be an integral part, and a successful part, of the team even if it meant being used in the way that was not his most comfortable. And Wenger recognized that Ljungberg had the personal qualities to make it work.

Lauren was another one identified for modification. He had been a midfielder during his career in Spain, but caught Wenger's eye as a right back for the future. The question of how he felt about changing position makes Lauren burst into laughter.

'Nobody knows what is in Wenger's head!' he says. 'When I first came I was playing as a right winger. He thought I was capable of playing as a right back, but at first I didn't know it. It was something progressive. He told me, "Lauren, I think you can play as a right back and replace Lee Dixon." At the beginning it was a bit difficult.' Not only did he have to learn about a new post, but also a new system, as 4–4–2 was the order of the day at Arsenal and Lauren had been playing in a 5–2–3. 'I began to understand the system, and my teammates, and the movement from a defensive point of view. It was not about convincing myself, more about readapting myself. Arsène gave you the confidence in yourself to realize that you could play in a new position. The most important thing about Wenger was that he believed you could perform there – as if he expected you to do it. If the manager doesn't believe in you, there is nothing to do.'

Lauren had his own experiences of trying new things in football before he joined Arsenal. He was born in Cameroon, but having moved to Spain at a young age, his first call-up for the national team of the country of his birth threw up a fundamental challenge. He could not speak French, so communication with his new Cameroon teammates and all the staff was a problem. They were all somewhat bewildered by this guy who showed up from Spain but could not really make himself understood. Lauren adapted, and became integrated enough to be a valued member of the side. In 2000, he was part of the Cameroon team that won the Olympics and the African Cup of Nations (when he was voted Player of the Tournament).

That turned out to be an eventful year, as he also began his Arsenal adventure. 'When I first came here I was shocked in the way that everything was organized,' he recalls. 'I had to get used to the experience of being away from Spain, and to come to a huge club like Arsenal was something amazing. Training, food, even food timing as you have to eat early, the language, the culture – everything was a shock. But at the same time I found a friendly environment, managed by professional, nice people. People who helped me to understand the environment, and how to play at a big club.'

He namechecks two of his new defensive partners as particularly influential in that regard. 'For me the most important was to play with someone like Sol Campbell. At the time when he was one hundred per cent he was unbelievable. He could cover the spaces when you were out of position, he was always there at the right time. And a guy that I like from that time was Martin Keown. People have their own preconceptions about him outside the club, but from inside he used to talk to youngsters, he used to advise you to do this or that, he was the kind of guy that took care of the youngsters and that was important for me.'

In turn, Lauren did the same for Kolo Touré. 'I remember the day he came to Arsenal along with his wife, I took him home for Christmas,' recalls Lauren. 'I talked to him. He needed that. As somebody did that for me, I had the obligation in some way to do that for somebody else. It doesn't cost anything.'

Touré was a wild card. Wenger had long been a supporter of African football, and was interested in tapping into this well of raw talent. For example, when a friend said he had seen a talented prospect playing in the Cameroonian league, he phoned every Monday for six months to find out how he was progressing before taking him on. That prospect happened to be George Weah.

Wenger also kept a close eye on developments at a football school
a friend of his had set up in the Ivory Coast. Jean-Marc Guillou, an
ex-footballer who represented France in the 1970s, was the driving
force at ASEC Mimosas in Abidjan, who were fast-tracking the
best players they could find by offering a quality of coaching and
facilities that were uncommonly strong by African standards.
Wenger had an eye on Kolo Touré from when he was seventeen.
'Technically he might have been less gifted than some of his young
teammates, but he had that charismatic attitude which makes a difference,' he recalls.

Kolo, the sixth of nine children, had the opportunity to join
ASEC at the age of fourteen, but his father wanted him to attend
a normal, academic school. Guillou's idea was to create a pathway
from the Ivory Coast to European football, but without many
examples it was difficult to persuade families there was much
chance of these dreams becoming a reality. Touré sensed a unique
opportunity.

'I was one of the luckiest boys in the Ivory Coast,' he says.
'When they made this academy they told us we had the chance to
go to Europe, especially to Arsenal or Monaco. For each player,
we knew that one or two of us would go through to one of the
teams where Mr Wenger trained. He knew about the quality of
this academy and for him it was very important to get players from
Africa who could deliver. I wasn't one of the best from my team. I
wasn't really thinking it would happen to me. They used to send
jerseys and we would have a draw to see who would win the
T-shirt. I won one, but it was from Monaco. One of my friends
won Patrick Vieira's from Arsenal. I really wanted that one.

'Wenger saw us at a tournament in Rotterdam. We went to the
final and played against Real Madrid. We knew he was coming to
watch us and everyone tried to do their best. But Mr Wenger is so
clever because he is not looking only for the talent of players. He
is looking for something else as well. He looks for players who
want to make a career. There is a difference between pure talent

and really wanting to succeed. It's a question of application, desire and hunger. You can find talent everywhere but those qualities are important. He wants a rough diamond he can polish.'

Touré was blown away when he first set foot in the dressing room. 'I swear I couldn't believe it. I was shocked. I was scared to go anywhere. I used to see the players on TV and to be able to be near . . . I was so surprised at the way they were. They were so nice, so humble. I was scared to say hi. In Ivory Coast I was used to being polite – *hello, hello, hello*. I could say hello to you three or four times in the same day. They gave me a fantastic welcome.'

For Wenger, the master of reinvention, finding a settled position for Touré, a player with an unbridled enthusiasm to try anything you asked of him, was a journey with some diversions. He represented Arsenal in every outfield position at some point or another, and was so useful as a utility player it was not obvious where, if anywhere, he would nail down a consistent role. Midway through the Invincible season, searching for the right word to describe him, Wenger couldn't help chuckling as he likened Touré to a 'mad dog'.

In pre-season of 2003–04, Wenger tried him out in the middle of the defence and it struck a chord. Even Touré didn't expect it. He had never envisaged a career at centre half. 'That's Mr Wenger. That's his touch. He sees something else,' notes Touré. 'Of course I was happy to try it. Honestly, it's a challenge. Sometimes it is difficult to change position, in your attitude you have to show you can cope with it. You have to help the team.'

Touré developed in that role, with Lauren to his right, Campbell to his left, Lehmann behind him and Vieira in front of him. It exemplified a side of Wenger's coaching that is fascinating. Organizing, and the minutiae of tactics are secondary to creating the best situation for a player to develop. He wants his players to learn in order to think for themselves, and think in order to learn for themselves.

Lee Dixon observed exactly how this worked as he watched

another member of the back four, Ashley Cole, come through. When he compared it to his own evolution, the way this home-grown kid absorbed his lessons was strikingly different. Dixon was personally grateful to be educated by the contrasting methods of George Graham and Arsène Wenger. One instilled the basics of defensive discipline. The other inspired freedom of expression on the field.

'George drilled us into very knowledgeable individuals, and a defence that could almost play with its eyes shut. I don't know whether Arsène could do that. Well, he couldn't!' exclaims Dixon. 'That's not his style, he is not that knowledgeable about the defensive side of the game. He doesn't push people around on the training pitch; he creates environments. A perfect example of that is Ashley Cole. Ash couldn't defend to save his life when he got into the Arsenal team – and he'd agree with me. But he had arguably one of the best coaches around for him in Tony Adams standing next to him. Tony had him on a piece of string. Arsène didn't coach him once. Arsène doesn't particularly know whether the left back is in the right position or not! But he knows that Tony knows. So he put Ash next to Tony and said, have a look at him. That blend of experience is the perfect platform for Arsène to do his stuff. Because that's what he is brilliant at – creating environments to prepare players to be the best they possibly can. And to have an environment where people can learn from the people around them.'

It wasn't only defenders who taught them. Attackers doled out plenty of lessons, too. Touré remembers how the back four gelled, and improved, because they had to give everything to deal with what they confronted in training. 'Every day we were working as a four,' says Touré. 'He used to put seven strikers against four defenders and we had to deal with that. We had to find a way to stop Henry and Bergkamp and Pirès! You are playing against the best players, so when you play in the league against other teams you find it easier because you have prepared against the best. That made us. We were challenging every day against the best attacking players in the world.'★

A new-look back four – or back five including Lehmann – was born for the 2003–04 season. The only link to the legendary George Graham defence was Martin Keown, who was getting used to his new role as a guide and helper as much as a presence on the pitch. He was thirty-seven years old by then. He was happy to pass advice on to Touré, in particular, to help him to wise up to what problems might need solving during games.

'I'd vowed that when the day came for someone to take my place, I would help them. I wouldn't stand in their way,' Keown says. 'The reason that happened was because the gaffer had created an environment and a pattern of behaviour, and I followed that. So he guided me, and I was guiding Kolo Touré really to take my place. He came over a young skinny kid with a big smile on his face. I remember him doing one-v-ones, with another kid from Greece, Stathis Tavlaridis, and they thought he was going to be some big player, but you could see this kid getting more and more frustrated because you just couldn't beat Kolo. The boss told him there are a lot of big centre halves here, so full back or a wide position looks your best bet. But he came back after that first summer and he was twice as big, he'd put muscle on. I felt a personal obligation to really help him and for it to work. We were talking all

---

★ The prospect of polishing another member of Touré's family never happened. Kolo's younger brother Yaya had a pre-season trial in the summer of 2003, just as Kolo was trying out his new position at centre half. But Yaya was not eligible for a work permit, and was so impatient to make progress he wouldn't hang around at one of Arsenal's partner clubs, KSK Beveren in Belgium, until the papers enabling him to move to London were secured. 'Yaya was a fantastic player and Mr Wenger saw that. They wanted him to wait,' recalls the elder Touré. 'He had a big decision and took the decision to go somewhere else. I wasn't very happy he chose to go to Ukraine. I wanted him to stay close to me. If he could have played for Arsenal in that time his career would have started even earlier.' For Wenger, this was one who got away.

the time about opponents, about his performance, about what he'd done well mostly. And trying to understand his role in the team.'

Touré, the skinny kid, the mad dog, the gamble who could play anywhere and cost next to nothing, became indispensable. Watching Kolo Touré's development had made Wenger come out with one of his typically thought-provoking proclamations. 'Every gifted player can play everywhere,' he said. That resonated with Bergkamp, who had grown up in the Ajax system where everyone spends some time playing everywhere to enhance their overall understanding of football. Wenger's penchant for shifting players into different positions echoed.

'It reminds me of Johan Cruyff,' he says. 'I think the philosophy mainly was who are your eleven best players? And then if you pick them it doesn't matter if you've got two right wingers, you put one right winger on the left wing, but you've got your eleven best players. The second right winger is so good and so intelligent that he can do his thing on the left wing. I think Arsène is always looking like that. I remember with myself, he put me as a right-half for a few games, European games as well. I can understand this idea. You want to put those players in there. You just work with them and try to get them to adapt to that position. Arsène was teaching the young players some stuff, if it wasn't taught by the experienced players. Because that was the character in the team as well: we teach each other.'

PART TWO

NOVEMBER 2003 – APRIL 2004

5
Trust

In Brazil, three footballers with Arsenal connections went out for dinner at the Confederations Cup in the summer of 2013. Discussion turned to the good old days, and Gilberto looked at his old teammates, Edu and Sylvinho, and recalled that feeling he had when he was standing in the tunnel as part of a team who felt on top of their world. As this chain of powerful athletes — most of them bearing the physique of a middleweight boxer — linked up they could almost sense the gulping fear in the opposition lining up next to them. Exchanging glances was enough to confirm what they were ready to do together. 'We looked into the eyes of each other,' says Gilberto. 'We knew that was the day for another victory, no matter who we faced. Of course we respected everybody but when we looked at each other we could feel that energy.' It was like an electrical surge.

Patrick Vieira became the social secretary for the group. He liked to organize dinners. Reflecting on the creation of the Invincibles years later, completely spontaneously, many of the players made a point of mentioning Vieira's dinners. It may well be that the cuisine was particularly memorable. But more pertinently, the atmosphere in these gatherings struck everybody as vital.

Bonding in the old days tended to revolve around the pub, perhaps the betting shop, maybe a nightclub. That wasn't Vieira's scene, so he arranged evening meals. Sometimes they would take place at restaurants, sometimes at players' houses. Often wives and girlfriends were included, to make for a more relaxed and sociable environment so it was not all about football.

'It was to bring us together,' explains Vieira. 'That's why I think the majority of us are still really good friends. I know sometimes it's difficult when you spend the day together and go out in the evening together again – it can be too much. But it is important to build a relationship. The objective of going to eat outside is to get to know each other better. You talk about something you don't normally talk about, and the guy who you are sitting next to who wears the same shirt as you, you realize how much you shared about your life when you were young. It brings you closer to him, and then when you are out there on the pitch you know that he will watch your back. This kind of team relationship is really important. And we had a really good laugh at those dinners.'

Even Bergkamp, who generally preferred to stay at home, could be persuaded to join in. He felt the group was unusually close. In a team environment it would be normal to click with some people but not be particularly fond of others. Bergkamp called this vintage 'a friends team'. He remembers going out to an Italian restaurant on New Year's Eve during the 2003–04 season, with the Edus, Gilbertos and Vieiras. At midnight they went upstairs to celebrate and it almost felt like fate that they should bump into a familiar face. 'Thierry was there as well!'

Was it luck that the characters just gelled together?

'I think that was the main thing,' he says. 'That team had a good connection on and off the pitch. The way it was off the pitch was new to me. We saw each other, we went out for a meal, we saw each other at home. Seven or eight players with their wives. And that was a connection I hadn't seen before. We knew that we were playing good football, and from that the relationship grew off the pitch as well. We all loved football and still do. We stayed after training to do some extra work. There was a lot of humour as well. We could really relate to each other, we could really make fun of each other and it was accepted. On and off the pitch it was friendship, but not like we couldn't tell each other the truth.'

It was a very productive atmosphere. On the whole they were

mates, they liked each other and they felt a strong sense of togetherness. Yet because they were competitive and highly driven, and all strove to be successful, there would sometimes be flare-ups and debates, which were actually welcomed as a means for developing and improving. Everybody accepted there were times for joking, times for concentrating, and times for straight-talking and challenging each other and themselves. It was all for the communal good.

But wasn't that honesty sometimes hard for people to take, when you are amongst such extreme competitors?

'Yeah, sometimes it's not easy,' says Bergkamp. 'You talk about experienced players who were names – big names, some of them. Some of them were arrogant. Without being negative, it was a good arrogance. They stood for something, they had an opinion about it, an authority. But somehow it was accepted, and maybe I played a role in that as well. Patrick played a role in that. Patrick can be arrogant. I can have my opinion as well. But we can all see the other side. We wouldn't accept it to become a fight, or become something that would be bigger than what it was about. I think you've got to have that in a group. We all had egos, but we knew when to stop. *OK. Leave it now, we do it your way.*'

Is the effect of players discussing football amongst themselves underestimated in the influence it can have on the team?

'A good manager would listen to that. A good manager would know what happens in the squad. Arsène was brilliant at that, he knew: *I've got players from twenty-five years old to thirty years old at the peak of their careers, of course I have to listen to them, of course I have to know what their opinion is, otherwise I am shutting it down.* Most of the time we were at the same wavelength, but sometimes we had different opinions.'

Was it like a creative tension?

'It is. It's more talking about players in confidence, talking about football in confidence. We knew if I talked to Patrick about Kolo

Touré or Sol Campbell it would stay there. But at the same time, we would talk with those players about the same thing, it's not like it would create something bad.'

Martin Keown recalls brainstorming gatherings in the dressing room that resembled a hothouse of football thinking; the self-styled University of London Colney. 'We would have our own meeting amongst ourselves,' he explains. 'We wouldn't have to wait for the manager; we had a couple of meetings where we felt we had to discuss what was going on amongst ourselves. Thrash it out. There were a lot of people in that dressing room who would speak up, who cared for the team. People say that does seem like we're doing the job for the boss. No, no, no. He's promoting that type of leadership. Self-learning. We're the ones out there, we're the ones in the middle of it. The group. There were a lot of leaders. If we needed to have a meeting amongst ourselves we'd do it.'

Sol Campbell felt the atmosphere was almost designed to bring the best out of such high-calibre players. He liked the moments of friction and the serious conversations. If something within the team needed saying, it would be expressed candidly. As soon as it was over, everybody understood that views needed sharing and metaphorically shook hands over some common ground. 'It would boil over, properly blow over on the training ground from time to time,' Campbell recalls. 'But that's normal. I think with tension – the right tension – and friction, that's when growth occurs. As a human being, as a club, you can't have it just all singing and dancing, tickety-boo. That's not going to work. You need to find out who's who around you. You need to find out if that person can actually go the whole hog when you're in a tough game. It just sorts people out – who's here for a jolly-up or who's here to actually win.

'We wanted to make history. You know, people weren't wasting their time there, just collecting the pay cheque. There was an

Stopwatch always in hand, Arsène Wenger controls training.

Practice makes perfect.

And they're off: Henry scores in the first game of the season. The new man, Lehmann, watches on.

High stakes, high intensity, high rivalry at Old Trafford.

On the precipice of losing . . . Van Nistelrooy's stoppage-time penalty cracks against the crossbar.

The volcano erupts.

Wenger: 'These guys have a special charisma.'

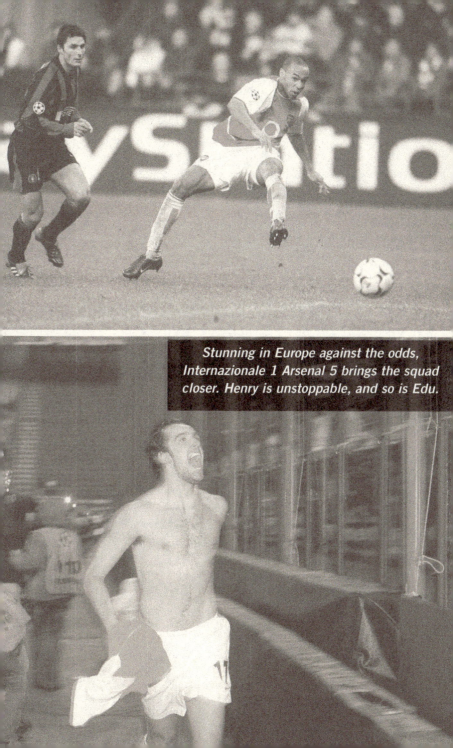

Stunning in Europe against the odds, Internazionale 1 Arsenal 5 brings the squad closer. Henry is unstoppable, and so is Edu.

Home sweet home.

underlying respect and friendship with everybody. And that's a beautiful thing. It's very difficult to get. It's very difficult to replicate. It's like everything was just all aligned. You can't buy it. It all happened over the course of, say, three, four, five years. Certain players came to the club, certain players left, it all slotted in and produced something amazing. It's so special.'

Touré loved the scene, and how the unity off the pitch was welded to synchronicity on the pitch to create what he describes as 'double power'. The gatherings were important to him as a young player, to help him feel he belonged and was trusted. 'One day it was a party at Patrick's house, another it was Lauren's house, then Dennis's house, and we joined each other with our wives – it was a big family. You have to trust your teammates on the pitch. We used to have meetings to discuss our vision, and which direction we were taking. We used to all sit together and talk. Everybody can make his point. The manager listens. We all ended up sharing the same vision. It was great.'

Touré becomes thoughtful, suddenly, when he remembers the situation that sums up, for him, how personally football and friendship could intertwine. His mother, Touré Hélène Bonontio, died young, when he had been in London for less than a year. He was twenty-one years old and far from home. Because religious traditions dictated she be buried quickly, he could not make it home for the funeral. Lauren offered what support he could. 'I was talking to him the whole time at the training ground all week. I wanted to do something special for him,' he recalls.

Arsenal played a match against Birmingham that weekend, and Touré was a substitute. 'Lauren told me, "I am going to score a goal for you, for your mum,"' he remembers. 'We played the game and Lauren scored, I swear, it was unbelievable. He pointed to the sky. He came to me. I felt it in my heart. He is my man. That's why I say this team is special.' Lauren also remembers it vividly. 'Suddenly it was a corner, Dennis Bergkamp's cross, and I went straight to him. He would do it if it was me. This is the emotional way, but the football way.'

★

Life on the road in football means spending many hours with your teammates. Journey after journey – by bus or sometimes train or plane to and from away games. Overnight stays in the hotel. The players must get used to each other's foibles.

Gilberto used to strap his mandolin onto his wheelie suitcase. For him, that was non-negotiable. If he went, his instrument went too. 'I am just a guy who insists on this,' he laughs. 'Music is something I love. For us Brazilians it is a really good combination – we combine football and samba. Sometimes I was playing in my room, if we were in the hotel after dinner I would play a bit. Not much because I didn't want to disturb anybody. Thierry was the other side of my room and the next day when I arrived for breakfast he would say, "Ah, I heard you playing, playing, playing. [He imitates Henry crooning] *Braaasil, Braaasil* . . . It was funny.

'Everybody brought their own flavour. It is chemistry. It's a combination of respect, culture, personalities and the profile of each other. Everyone at that time was a great player, who represented their countries, but also we represent Arsenal. We had one focus. To do the best we could for the team to win. That is what we always thought about. This kind of collective respect gave us power to fight for victory in every game. That's what we did every day.'

Lehmann paints an evocative picture of life on the bus when they travelled. He sat with Bergkamp, at a table of four, and others would join them. 'I sat next to him for years,' he says. 'The Germans and the Dutch they have a special relationship. They always take the piss out of each other. We had an international table. It was Dennis, it was Freddie, it was Gilberto. It was the two old guys, you know? He was just sitting there next to me, and I think he constantly thought, *What an idiot German.*' Lehmann gives the impression that he and Bergkamp were the team's Waldorf and

Statler from *The Muppet Show*, two disagreeable but amusing old guys chewing the fat in inimitable style.

In 1967, Celtic won the European Cup with a team of local boys. All but one of the squad of fifteen Lisbon Lions, as they became known, were born within ten miles of Celtic Park in Glasgow. Their life experiences would have been relatively similar. In terms of upbringing, environment, cultural references, even dialect, they were all more or less on the same wavelength.

The situation in twenty-first-century football, which had exploded into this fast-changing, horizon-shattering, globalized phenomenon, made for a dressing room the Lisbon Lions might have been fascinated by. Here was a united nations under a red-and-white-cannoned flag. There were ten different countries represented in the Invincibles (eleven if you include Vieira's birthplace of Senegal), from three continents.

On the surface, without the connector of football, if you introduced Ray Parlour, an Essex boy who likes pubs enough to own one and is a notorious joker, to Gilberto Silva, a placid guy from Lagoa da Prata with a strong sense of social justice who loves playing the mandolin, the bond of friendship would not necessarily be expected to spark. Or – again, take football out of the equation – try introducing Jens Lehmann, a strong-willed German who educated himself to degree standard, to Kolo Touré, a devout man from the Ivory Coast who gave up school to chase the football dream. Or – no football, here, remember – introduce Sol Campbell, a thoughtful, intense guy raised in East London as the youngest of twelve children born to Jamaican parents, to Sylvain Wiltord, a rebellious livewire from the Parisian suburbs with a taste for zany humour. Or introduce Freddie Ljungberg, an easy-going Swede who was into fashion, to Lauren, a keen boxer born in Cameroon and raised in Spain.

Different roots, diverse personalities, disparate interests. Through football, the incongruous became congruous. Through being part of the same team, they found so much common ground and a genuine warmth being in each other's company. The fact they extended their interaction to dinners outside their workplace gave them the time and space to find out more about each other's lives. The differences became something they cherished.

'For me it was like a book to learn,' says Ljungberg. 'It was amazing. Most players thought it was very interesting to learn how different cultures worked and how we can make it work together – because that can be a problem. I must say, I like travelling, I like people, and I felt every day was like an education of how other people are. I think that's why I fell in love so much with London as well, because people are accepted for who they are, for me it feels like I can breathe. Maybe it sounds philosophical, but we learned so much from each other. Because of the values of the club, you have to adapt your culture to what Arsenal believes in. I always thought that was quite special.

'I remember the English boys were saying that they wanted us to speak English in the dressing room, and for me that was quite special too. There was understanding, of course a group from France or whatever can speak their native tongue, but it just became a togetherness because everyone tried. I didn't understand a word Ray Parlour in his cockney accent was trying to say when I first got there, but I learned, because everybody tried to interact with each other in their language. I thought that was quite useful, and I thank the club for that.'

For the foreign legion who joined Arsenal, having somebody like Parlour, an indefatigably hard-working player, around the place gave them an insight into the club, and the culture that had been around for aeons before they showed up. Parlour was integrated into the ways of Arsenal from a young age. He was spotted as a twelve-year-old, although Arsenal needed to be persuasive as he came from pure West Ham territory. Parlour's father was reticent when Ray told him he wanted to give Arsenal a go, and needed to drop the fantasy that his son might play in claret and blue before giving his blessing.

At first Parlour used to take the 'old push and pull train' from Barking to Seven Sisters with a handful of kids from his area. Training took place in a local school, with gymnastics apparatus up the walls, and the boys played five-a-side. At fourteen he signed schoolboy forms, and represented Arsenal on Sunday mornings. He steadily progressed until he was taken on as an apprentice come his sixteenth birthday, and began to make a serious impression on the then youth team coach, Pat Rice. 'You've got thirty apprentices – all wannabe footballers – and that's when you've really got to apply yourself and do the best you can,' recalls Parlour. 'But Pat Rice was a great manager. I mean, he loved you getting stuck in, loved the work rate and I was right up his alley, really.'

The day job then contrasts strikingly with the life for today's young footballers. Cleaning dressing rooms, lugging training kit around, polishing the boots of the first-team players you were detailed to do jobs for, was all part of the process. 'You've got to make sure they're spotless, those boots. You always wanted a bigger player, because you get bigger Christmas tips at the end,' Parlour remembers. 'We had to go to the ground, bundle all the kits up, put them on the back of the coach, off we go from Highbury to St Albans – probably about an hour journey – and then, when we got there, we got all the kits out, set them all out for the first team, then we'd get all their boots ready. We used to clean the dressing rooms on a Friday. The apprenticeship gave you a little bit of character. It made you more desperate to make it. It gave you that bit more drive. I mean, a little bit of hard work? You think, *This is what it's all about.* So when you do make it into the first team, it's been well worth it.'

Parlour's break came when he was seventeen. 'I always remember the game – Norwich away. I didn't get on. I was sub. I went down on the train, because someone got ill. I got picked up from the station, taken to the hotel, and I always remember you had to do a speech in those days. The new player into the squad had to stand up at dinner. I was so nervous. I knew Tony Adams, because he came from Essex as well, and I said, "Tony, what do I have to do?" And he said, "Oh, just say thanks and whatever. Say something about the manager's tank top, all right?" But he was stitching me up, with George Graham. So, I stood up and said, "Oh, it's really great to be here and I'm very, very honoured to be with these great players." I went round the table – the likes of the late Dave Rocastle, Michael Thomas, David O'Leary. So, it was all going really well and then I went, "Oh, by the way, Boss, we all love your tank top." And his face! All of a sudden, I'm having a go at his clothes. And all the players went "Aaagh!" So, Tony stitched me right up.'

When it came to new players, it was up to the club's old guard to pass the baton about the club's fundamental belief systems. Ljungberg had been there only a week when Pat Rice pulled him aside for a pep talk. 'He said, "You know, Freddie, at Arsenal we have certain principles of the respect that you're supposed to show everyone else around the club. Everyone is equal, we show everyone respect, and that's special, that Arsenal spirit. If we don't win a trophy every year that's a massive failure, so you know that's what you have to achieve within Arsenal Football Club." It was very inspiring. I was extremely proud to be part of a club that had those standards. I felt proud every time to have the badge because of what it stood for. To me that's what Arsenal still stands for, why I still support it. It maybe sounds silly, but when I changed club afterwards I would still go and shake hands with the cleaners every morning, or the receptionist, whatever. A lot of players don't at other clubs. And that was something I was taught at Arsenal: you show respect to everybody, everybody has the same value and brings something so this club can go forward. And I felt that was special.'

Rice found himself wanting to pass on messages that had been passed to him by former players when he was a youngster desperate to make his mark. 'I used to go round the dressing room saying what was said to me when I was a kid of fifteen,' he says. The messages were simple. 'Be good to those on the way up, son, because you'll need them on the way down,' he intones.

'Remember who you are, what you are and who you represent.' The maxims were at the core of what was drilled into Arsenal players for years. 'All of us, as football players, when you go out onto a pitch, the only thing that you can guarantee is that you can give a hundred per cent. You can't guarantee that you're going to win the game, and the management can't guarantee that you will play well. But the only thing that you can guarantee is that you'll give your all. That's what the Arsenal supporters will love you for. They'll forgive you for everything. But if they don't see you competing for them, then they will just go off you.'

Thierry Henry is a good example of how a player can come from abroad and become so absorbed by the club and what it represents he wants to lap up its history. Henry – naturally a voracious watcher of football and someone with an exceptionally astute knowledge of the game – wanted to learn all about Arsenal. He studied stories from the past. When he arrived David Dein gave him a video of Ian Wright's goals with the message that he, too, could earn such a place in the club's pantheon. 'This is what you've got to do,' Dein said prophetically. Henry watched it intently, soaking up the nuances of what it took to become Arsenal's record-breaking goalscorer. He was quite struck, and explained later, 'I said to myself, *He's no bigger than me, no faster, no more muscular, but he scores more goals*. I watched him closely. He put a hundred per cent into everything. When he called for a pass, he shouted at the top of his voice, and when he got it, he'd smack it into the back of the net. I just kept thinking, *This is a goalscoring move*.' When Henry was still waiting for his first goal in Arsenal colours, Wright was the man, the name on top of the charts. Six years after joining, Henry would be presented with a golden cannon in recognition of breaking that record, and Wright proudly did the honours.

'I remember a quote from Thierry, him saying he fell in love with Arsenal because of me,' says Wright. 'That really made me feel good, because I know what Arsenal means to him, and he knows how much Arsenal meant to me. To have anything to do with Thierry, what he went on to do with our club and what he went on to do in world football, whether it was his appetite for goals or the runs he made, that's humbling for me. I would have given anything to have played, or been around, when he was there. If I could have stayed, and seen Thierry in, I would have loved that. It's one of my biggest regrets.'*

Gilberto was another who arrived with a huge desire to embed himself in his new club. He was thirsty for knowledge. 'When I arrived I wanted to learn,' he says. 'Because before I went to Arsenal I didn't know much about English football. We saw a lot of Italian and Spanish football in Brazil, but not much from England. We had a bad image of English football because of the hooligans. It wasn't the only thing people talked about but we were aware of the violence. When I arrived I thought, *I don't want to generalize. I want to learn about what things are like here.* It's easy if you just listen to what people say on TV and radio but you have to find out for yourself the real story. I want to hear from the people who were there.'

With this perspective in mind, it isn't just fellow players who have the dominant role. Behind the scenes, the staff at the training ground became part of the welcoming committee. Vic Akers, the kit man, was somebody Gilberto naturally gravitated towards. 'Vic is the kind of guy who has a lot of stories to tell,' he recalls. 'From his experience at the club. He has been there a long time, met so many players, so many people with different characters. He has a lot to teach you. He keeps his way of doing things, very calm, relaxed, positive. I always liked to be close to him because I knew I could learn a lot by hearing what he had to say. He experienced

---

* Wright elaborated on why he thought Wenger felt he wouldn't be the influence he wanted for this new breed of striker. 'I think I stopped playing football in my heart in 1998. Arsène is so surgical and clinical, perhaps with my exuberant nature he didn't want that. He might have thought that affected the way they prepared. It all worked out brilliantly though.'

different eras of the club. You learn a lot from everybody. Vic was one of them. David Dein was one of them. Arsène is another one. Also the English guys who work for the club. I want to speak to them, learn from them, about their lifestyle and their culture and the way they see football.

'For me it was the best experience of my life, those six years as a professional at Arsenal. It was the longest time I spent playing for one club. I learned a lot with them. English guys, French guys, Jens from Germany – everyone sees Jens as a tough guy with a big personality but he is a fantastic man. There was one fact I have to mention: everyone was a winner themselves. Inside of everybody is the winner's mentality, the winner's personality. It was hard to accept losing any game. We would go back, look at each other's faces, and move on to the next game to prove that we were ready to win again. This winning personality combined with the way everyone learned from mixing up our cultures made a great environment.'

Wenger's backroom staff was handpicked to embody that all-important sense of trust. Pat Rice, his number two from day one, was kept on as Wenger was adamant that having a club man, someone who had been ingrained in Arsenal and English football, was a necessity. Wenger also brought his own coach with him, Boro Primorac, whom he had known in France and taken with him to Japan. He speaks nine languages, has a great eye for football and, above all, could be trusted with absolutely anything.

'Boro was quite a nice foil for the manager,' says Keown. 'He is very close to him. They both have a great love of football. He always used to sit at the back of the bus, chat to the players, get a feeling of the mood. It was never a bad move. It was about joining in the togetherness. The boss would sit at the front with Pat, planning for the next game.' Primorac's relaxed nature and dry humour made him a well-liked middleman who could float comfortably between Wenger and the players, a role that is vital in any club. Keown particularly remembers Primorac's favourite jokes, which by the sounds of it, would get him more or less every time. 'He always seemed to have a toothpick after a meal, but he would shake hands with you and the toothpick was protruding through his hands. You would end up being stabbed by the toothpick. The other one was the boot, where he would hold the laces and throw the boot at you, but just as you thought you would get hit the taut laces stopped it.

'Boro was quite technical as a coach. His technique was good so he would often do the demonstrations. The boss would never really join in. Boro would start things off. The tempo of the first pass often sets the tone for the rest. That was Boro's forte. He is an encyclopedia of international players. If you were playing an international match he would be brilliant. His knowledge is great. He might say, "You've done well to miss that match because the Montenegro striker is world class," and you'd never have heard of him or seen him. That striker would rip the England team to ribbons and you would think, where did Boro get that from? Him and the boss would sit and eat their dinner off their laps all night watching football on TV.'

Rice felt the staff, rather like the players, brought diverse qualities to the group. A brainbox Frenchman, an astute Yugoslav, a hot-headed Ulsterman, and a mild-mannered Englishman. 'I'm volatile, I can fly off the handle,' says Rice. 'Arsène's not like that. Boro will tell you exactly how he feels, he won't mess about. We were different in that Arsène was quiet, Boro was fairly quiet, I was the big mouth. And of course you had Gary Lewin, the physio, as well, who is so placid. As far as Arsène, Boro, Gary and I were concerned, we used to have a thing whereby up until maybe Thursday or Friday when the manager picks the team we would disagree. We would argue our points. But at the end of it all as soon as the manager makes his mind up, that's it finished, there's no more disagreements, we go with what he wants. So he will go into the game, his decision will be final and we will back that up. We didn't want to put indecision in the manager's head.'

It's like there was a huge Venn diagram of trust, all overlapping –

Wenger and his staff trusted each other. Wenger trusted his players, who trusted him, and one another. It's paramount. Through all the talking and all the practising they did, all those strands of trust deepened.

Martin Keown bumped into Luís Boa Morte on a coaching course not so long ago and their conversation evokes exactly how that sense of trusting your teammates works. Boa Morte was only at Arsenal for a couple of the early Wenger years, and although he never managed to hurdle the dividing line from squad player to part of the establishment, he was needed in some cameo appearances. Keown asked Boa Morte about how it felt to be a young player coming through, and he replied that Wenger made him feel as important as everybody else. Keown picks up the story: 'I said, "Well, because he did that to you, you took a really important penalty in the quarter-final of the FA Cup against West Ham away." He said, "Yeah I did." I asked him if he was surprised I remember that, and he was. I said, "Well, my life was in your hands but I trusted you to do it, because the manager trusted you and he trusted me so it was this feeling, that if he's going to believe in you, we're going to believe in you too, and it paid off."

'You care for each other. There's a love for one another. People don't want to use that word, but I thought that Wenger set that influence. Because you get some managers who would trust you, they've all got good knowledge, but not all of them care for you. But he cared in such a way that you gave more for him. He spread that. He certainly spread that to me. I felt that I was being more caring, or more helpful towards other people because of what he did. I felt that habit and behaviour came from the boss.'

The way Wenger trusts his players is unusual in some ways – certainly in terms of strategy on the pitch. In the modern era, where the cult of the manager has become so imposing, Wenger can be quite relaxed in terms of trusting his players to know what to do. Coaches generally want to instruct as much as possible, and quite often players actually want to be told exactly how to play.

Wenger's approach is more subtle. He encourages his players to work things out for themselves. He does not want to work with robots. He dislikes the idea that so much in football is premeditated, with routines worked until they can be done blind-fold. At times, that has looked like a flaw, when his sides have been exposed by more diligently organized opponents. But when it works, there is nothing Wenger appreciates more than a team that interprets the game according to a philosophy he simply defines as 'the game we love'. Ideally, everyone can express themselves within the team framework, connected, together, yet able to play with freedom and use their imagination. It is more free-form than many managers would even dare to try, because it leaves so much more to chance.

Come the turn of the year, with 2003 segueing into 2004, there was so much to admire in that game they love, but there was still work to be done. Although they had not yet been beaten in the league, and a familiar foe had lost three times already, it was Manchester United who were top of the table on New Year's Day. Just after the halfway mark of the season, after nineteen games played, the men from Old Trafford had a point more. Come January, something odd happened. Arsenal lost a match for the first time in almost three months. It was only the Carling Cup, a 1–0 defeat against Middlesbrough, and the majority of the team that played in the Premier League match three days before were rested, so it wasn't the end of the world.

But as it turned out, Arsenal lost the second leg too. Martin Keown was sent off, and José Antonio Reyes confirmed the defeat with a late own-goal, so it was an uncomfortable one to absorb. And even though it was the Carling Cup, the poor relation of English football trophies, it was still a semi-final.

That rotation, to juggle resources sufficiently to power on in the league and in the cup competitions, could give you a tactical headache sometimes. Wenger was about to enter a period where he would have serious food for thought.

6

Turbulence

Arsène Wenger attended the 2010 World Cup in South Africa, combining television punditry with his general desire to study players and trends in football. Something that impressed him throughout the tournament was the number of people from distant lands who approached him to talk with vast knowledge and passion about English football. One morning, as he was taking breakfast at the Radisson Blu hotel in Johannesburg, he was approached by a Kenyan man who asked for a photograph. They started some small talk. 'You know,' said the man, 'in our country it is all Man United and Arsenal.' Wenger offered an amiable reply. The Kenyan went on: 'You know that when you lost against Man United, my cousin committed suicide after the game.' Wenger was flabbergasted. After decades in the job not many things had the capacity to leave him reeling in such a way. 'At first I thought he was joking,' Wenger recalls. 'The two guys who were with him said, "No, it's true, we were at the funeral." You could never imagine that. You could never think when you drive home from Islington that somebody, somewhere in the world, has committed suicide because you lost a game. How many are you responsible for . . . ?'

The daily life of a high-profile football team tends to exist in a bubble. For managers, particularly, stepping outside that bubble to dip into non-football pastimes can bring a nagging sense that you ought to get back as quickly as possible. That certainly seems the case with Wenger, a man who gives the impression that a second not devoted to thinking about football, and how to eke the best out of his resources, is a second wasted.

Pat Rice remembers thinking he had never seen anything like it in terms of someone immersing themselves so completely in football when he began to get to know Wenger. 'First of all, I'd never ever heard of him, to be perfectly truthful with you. I doubt whether he'd heard of me either, so it was mutual. I remember he stayed in the West Lodge Park hotel, and I used to go and pick him up and take him either into Highbury or the training ground, because he obviously was just finding his feet. But the thing that struck you whenever you went into his room – he would maybe be getting changed, he'd say, "Come on, come up and have a sit down while you're waiting for me" – you would think that someone had been in there and papered his room with DVDs. Because whichever wall you looked on there was either tapes or DVDs plastering the wall. He never used to go out, he just stayed in the hotel room and watched videos.'

David Dein tells a story about Wenger's car, which exemplifies how devoted he is to his calling. It is, according to Dein, the ultimate second-hand vehicle. 'It doesn't have any miles,' he quips. 'Most nights of the week he's watching football from around the world. So he goes every day to the training ground which is only a few miles away and then he comes back.' The commute from the Wenger home in Totteridge to the training ground at Shenley is roughly a quarter of an hour on a slow day. The only other routine journey is down to Highbury for match days, possibly with a diversion via Whetstone on the way back, for dinner on the local high street. 'He's not great company if we lose, I can tell you,' adds Dein. 'It's a one-way conversation, because he's upset about it. It's a game of emotion, of tension, of feeling, of passion. He's a bad loser! And you wouldn't want it any other way.'

The time these two men spent talking about football was not far off non-stop. Compared to the normal rapport between the two major drivers of policy at any football club, their relationship was unusual in that their chemistry made them a doubly strong partnership – as friends as well as colleagues. Dein wanted Wenger to know he was with him every step of the way. On match days, it was important for him to seek out Wenger both before and after the game, regardless of result. 'I had my own routine,' says Dein. 'I would go to the dressing room to talk to the boys, just to shake their hands and wish them luck. But not within an hour of the game because that's private time for the manager. I would never go into the dressing room within twenty minutes of the end of the game. You've got to let emotions cool down a bit. But the manager needs to know that someone upstairs cares. He had to feel he was part of the family, we were in it together, good times and bad times. I wanted him to know that if he was wounded, so was I.'

In the second half of Wenger's Arsenal career, the part where trophies were elusive and problems more complex, there was a tendency for seasons to hit a perfect storm. The period where a number of competitions collided, injuries began to bite and fatigue began to tell, threw Arsenal off course. Each year, Wenger would be faced with a pile-up of dilemmas. For which games can you afford to rest certain players? How best to prioritize to get the maximum out of the most trusted match winners? Which balls needed juggling, and how often, to survive the onslaught of challenges, and keep the best players fit and fresh enough to thrive?

Wenger sat next to Pat Rice on the team coach for sixteen years. If his loyal assistant told him the story of how few players Arsenal used when they won the Double in 1971, the contrast would have felt sharp. Just sixteen players in total, and two of them – the prodigious maverick Peter Marinello and the genial, home-grown left back Sammy Nelson – didn't even get to a handful of games each, so the core squad was just fourteen players. To win the league and FA Cup.

There was no Champions League as we know it back then. The European Cup was not such an overpowering affair. It didn't have quite the same capacity to wrest attention so heavily, and so often, away from the domestic scene over the course of a season. Still, Arsenal were involved in another continental competition that year, defending the Inter-Cities Fairs Cup that they had so thrillingly won in 1970, inspiring the crowd to pour onto the pitch in wonderment. Come spring, they were chasing a treble.

As the prizes came into sight in 1971, Arsenal's schedule was intense, with seven matches packed into twenty-two days:

9 March	FC Köln (h)	Fairs Cup 4th round
13 March	Crystal Palace (a)	Division 1
15 March	Leicester (h)	FA Cup 6th round replay
20 March	Blackpool (h)	Division 1
23 March	FC Köln (a)	Fairs Cup 4th round
27 March	Stoke (Hillsborough)	FA Cup semi-final
31 March	Stoke (Villa Park)	FA Cup semi-final replay

Hazard a guess at how many changes the manager of the time, Bertie Mee, made to his starting XI over that period. Perhaps Rice asked the same question of Wenger one day on one of their motorway chats. And the answer?

None. Not a single change. Team sheet after team sheet. Bob Wilson, Pat Rice, Bob McNab, Peter Storey, Frank McLintock, Peter Simpson, George Armstrong, George Graham, John Radford, Ray Kennedy, Charlie George.

★

In the spring of 2004, Wenger mulled over his options. Three trophies were on the agenda and they faced three matches against major opposition in less than a week. After thirty matches Arsenal were top of the league – still undefeated – and had seven points' breathing space. They were in the FA Cup semi-final, against Manchester United. Just over the horizon they were awaiting the home leg of a Champions League quarter-final against Chelsea, a club they were in the habit of routinely beating, followed by a league game against Liverpool. Arsenal had reason to feel optimistic. Deep down, most of the team looked around Europe and felt at least as good as anybody around – arguably better.

On their arrival at Villa Park for the FA Cup semi-final, a sudden buzz went round when the team sheet dropped. No Henry. Wenger had decided to rest his most powerful weapon. It wasn't an easy call – never is – but this manager who has always trusted science and logic to help him to make his choices felt that Henry physically could not be at his best for a run of three heavyweight bouts in six days. Henry hadn't played in 2002 when Arsenal went to Old Trafford and won the title at their place.

How many are you responsible for? . . .

It is impossible to think that way. It would send you mad. Wenger's immediate responsibility is to his team, his squad, his club. Life in the bubble. The task in hand involves carefully managing this three-game series, this triple challenge, to build on their momentum, gather speed, and set up the sprint finish. Wenger took Henry out of the starting team and chose Jérémie Aliadière in his place. Henry's young compatriot had just turned twenty-one. He had done well in the League Cup run that season, and was suddenly thrust into the limelight with a rare big start in a big game. It backfired.

MANCHESTER UNITED 1–0 ARSENAL, 3 APRIL 2004

With a hop, skip and a jump, Sir Alex Ferguson did his own version of Porto coach José Mourinho at the final whistle, his face resembling a cat that had won a lifetime's supply of the finest French cream. To the soundtrack of 'Where's your treble gone?' cascading from the Trinity Road stand, he relished a tactical and emotional triumph.

This was a double for United in terms of satisfaction. Not only can they provide a season of underachievement with consolation in the form of the FA Cup, they have also kept their 1999 achievement sacred. A first-half goal by Paul Scholes was enough to win a contest that was competed with noticeably more spirit and determination by the men from Old Trafford. This was their season – they knew it and showed it.

And so Arsenal were defeated for the first time in a domestic competition they have taken seriously this campaign. With all due respect to Middlesbrough, who took the honours in the Carling Cup semi-finals, this was one Arsenal will not take with a pinch of salt.

But how seriously were they taking this? A clear signal that Arsène Wenger was making a priority of the Champions League arrived with the team sheet, which confirmed rumours that Thierry Henry would be rested. His place was surprisingly given to Jérémie Aliadière, a rookie playing his first match after three months sidelined with knee trouble. He was nowhere near a match of this intensity and had as many kicks in 58 minutes on the pitch as the top man did on the bench.

As for United, having this season endured a defensive crisis and had question marks hanging over the creativity of a midfield shorn of David Beckham and Juan Sebastián Verón, this was the day their attack was at its weakest. Ferguson was deprived of his top three strikers – Ruud van Nistelrooy through injury, while Louis Saha was cup-tied and Diego Forlán deemed too tired after returning from international duty in South America.

That they were able to compensate owed everything to a well-devised game plan that was followed to the letter by every United player. Much depended on Ole Gunnar Solskjaer, the lone ranger, who was full of endeavour and intelligence. Support was particularly effective from wide positions, where the riveting Cristiano Ronaldo, often assisted by Ryan Giggs's roaming runs, posed a constant danger. Ferguson had identified eighteen-year-old Gaël Clichy as a weak link and instructed his men to direct traffic along his side.

It paid off after 32 minutes. Gary Neville exposed Clichy with a disguised pass to Giggs, who cantered into the box and cut the ball back for Scholes to stroke past Jens Lehmann. Quick, decisive passing pinballed round a statue-like Arsenal defence and United were in raptures.

It must be said that they had ridden their luck. Arsenal's blistering start saw Dennis Bergkamp denied by Roy Carroll's block and then Wes Brown on the line, before Edu chipped against the crossbar and Kolo Touré's header was clawed away by the Northern Ireland goalkeeper.

Breathless stuff, but it was downhill fast for Arsenal. The next chance fell to Robert Pirès, whose free header was back to the old routine after that comprehensive nod at Chelsea in the Champions League. When Patrick Vieira's header caressed a post in first-half stoppage time, Arsenal were cursing their luck again.

After the interval, United set out to hold what they had and before long there were two clear signs of Arsenal's increasing desperation: Bergkamp fell over John O'Shea's ankle and crumpled theatrically in the box, then Lehmann saw fit to shove Ronaldo off the ball.

Time for Wenger to acknowledge that his gamble was failing and just before the hour he sent on the attacking cavalry – Henry and José Antonio Reyes. Bet he wishes he had not. Henry was in one of his hands-on-hips, thousand-yard stare moods. Reyes, on the other hand, was dynamic and looked the one player capable of rescuing the game for Arsenal, until Scholes's malevolent tackle from behind ended his efficacy. 'It is a big blow to us not only to lose, but to lose players,' lamented a grim-faced Wenger. 'With such a short squad, that is a massive disappointment.'

Observer

Arsenal drove south from Villa Park frustrated. But the two major goals remained in their hands. Henry returned, the team dusted themselves down, and the air grew heavy with expectancy as Chelsea arrived at Highbury in the Champions League. The quarter-final first leg at Stamford Bridge had gone well enough, with an away goal in a 1–1 draw to build upon at home. And yet, something nagged. Arsenal had been so dominant, cocky even, in the closing stages of the first act, there was a hint of opportunity missed. Chelsea's defender Marcel Desailly had been sent off with ten minutes to go, and with a little more ruthlessness that 1–1 scoreline might have turned into a 1–2 victory, with an extra precious away goal to feather the cap.

Patrick Vieira remembers a feeling of mild discomfort at the end of that game at Stamford Bridge. 'We should have won that game easy – we battered them at Chelsea!' he exclaims. 'You could smell that we may have let our chance go. We knew we missed the chance to kill them. On the other hand Chelsea got lucky. The mental approach completely changed with that draw against ten men. The doubt came in our mind, and the confidence went to them.'

Wenger gauged the mood carefully. 'You never know what the psychological consequences of a defeat will be on your team,' he observes. Come kick-off of this all-London duel, Arsenal started brightly, and Reyes struck to give his team a confidence-boosting lead. Yet Chelsea struck back. Twice. The second blow, from Wayne Bridge, was deadly, coming so late that Arsenal were left crushed, dazed, and in no position even to attempt an unlikely recovery that would require them to score twice to overcome the away goals advantage that Chelsea now enjoyed. The seventeen-match hex that Arsenal held over Chelsea had ended at the worst possible moment.

Two competitions extinguished in four days. From treble to terrible. The mood was sober, and even years later, lasting regret about the ones that got away is manifested in hard stares and rueful shakes of the head. 'We underachieved in the Champions League,' says Vieira. Ray Parlour agrees. 'The lads really thought, *Champions League football this year, this is gonna be our year . . .*' Bergkamp still strains for a proper explanation. 'Maybe we needed more confidence to go in those sort of games,' he suggests. 'It was more like, *Can we live up to it? Can we reach that level? Is it not too high for us?*

Maybe a little bit of confidence was missing. But if you look at the quality of the team, we could, we should, have done better. Especially with those games against Chelsea. It was a shame.'

Jens Lehmann articulates how he is so bitterly frustrated, he even has a conspiracy theory, as the league fixtures on either side of this series pitted Arsenal against high-calibre opponents, too. 'I think it was the stupidity from the FA, and probably intended, to put us in two weeks against Man United in the league and cup, twice Chelsea, Liverpool and Newcastle,' he tuts. 'So the best four teams in England we had to play them every three days. Mentally, normally we should have beaten Chelsea easily, because we were better. But we were so tired at the end of this Champions League game, and this was the biggest disappointment, because this year we deserved to win the Champions League. But due to this idiot schedule we were just too tired, we couldn't come back. It is still one of my major disappointments. We were probably the best team in the world, but because we had to play the biggest teams every three days, we've been knocked out of the Champions League.'

*

There is no time for navel gazing. Chelsea, chasing hardest in the Premier League, pick up another three points while Arsenal are tripping up in that FA Cup semi-final. The gap at the top is trimmed to four points. Arsenal may still be undefeated in the league, but on the back of two brutal blows, confidence is shaken.

Liverpool travel to Highbury and attack swiftly. The high-pitched screech of the Highbury screamer, a fan whose piercing cry can often be heard just as the opposition are about to score, signals a crisis as Michael Owen steers his team into a 2–1 lead at half-time. Arsenal are shell-shocked. It is as if everyone – the players, the management, the supporters – had been cruising serenely and feel stricken to be suddenly carried towards a crashing, unavoidable, waterfall.

Henry evokes the sense of desperation and impending doom brilliantly: 'I felt that the stadium stopped breathing,' he says. 'We were having such a great season, people were talking about the treble, and in a week, we lost everything . . .'

Vieira had seldom felt anything like it. 'I don't know how to describe it. It was really strange,' he says, grappling for words. 'You are going through different emotions. You go through the season and get so much pressure. You get so much stick from outside if you don't come through. Emotionally that was one of the hardest ones.'

Gilberto felt the same. 'That circumstance against Liverpool shook everybody,' he recalls. 'We had been winning the games in the league but everyone thought to lose this game was possible. We didn't want that.'

Sol Campbell remembers trying to weigh up what was going on. 'What's happening now? Where's it going to go from now? Are we going to just capitulate, and the season just' – he makes the sound of air hissing out of a balloon – 'flatline?'

So what the hell are they going to do?

It is not unusual for the dressing room at half-time to be quiet, thoughtful, concentrated. This time all the levels have dipped to below normal as they try to recharge and refocus on what they need to do. Martin Keown, a substitute for these three pivotal games, is worried. He has been with the team every step of the way during this key period, watching from the sidelines, from the team coach, from the dressing room, as the season began to unravel and unspool in a way they didn't seem able to control. At half-time, he looks around and feels alarmed by this sense that everyone is almost traumatized by the situation.

'There were World Cup winners in there, European winners, and I think it was a massive loss for all of that to happen in one week, psychologically,' he recalls. 'At the beginning of the week we were going on all three fronts and suddenly at the end of the week we only had the league to go . . .

'Only the league? Hold on!'

Keown thinks he needs to speak out. To do something to shatter this strange, shocked, inertia.

'I could feel for everyone, the manager and Pat. And I just felt at that point at half-time we came in, and it was a case of how are we going to lift this group? There was a sense of us feeling sorry for ourselves and everything's going down the pan.'

The oldest player in the squad asks Wenger if he can impart a few words.

'I always spoke before the game, but I never spoke at half-time. I asked permission to speak because I could see that they were down. I spoke from the heart,' he recalls. 'Look, fellas. We're feeling sorry for ourselves. This is the best group of players I've ever played with. If we get that first goal then this ground, this crowd, are just waiting for us, and it will turn on its head.'

This notion of Keown geeing up his teammates – or challenging them if he felt that was necessary – was fairly commonplace, especially before matches. 'I used to say in the dressing room, "Look around you. No disrespect to anyone, but it's taken me a lifetime to get to a group of players like this. There are no players I'd rather play with." Then I'd quickly remind each player of the talent they had and how the opposition player was quaking in their boots about what they were up against. "Because I've trained against you all week so I know what you have. And I'd sooner be playing against that lot than playing against you." They just needed reminding. And they used to giggle at what I was saying, because they were almost embarrassed by the praise. But then they'd go out and do the business.'

Bergkamp remembers how Keown's homespun motivational speaking could provoke a mixed response, but he admired it. 'It doesn't matter who you are, he will say what he feels. He's got respect for you, but if you're Dennis Bergkamp or Thierry Henry, or Ray Parlour, or whoever, he will tell you to your face what he thinks of you,' Bergkamp says. 'That's sometimes very annoying.

But it can be very helpful as well. For me it was really strange coming to England and other players complimenting you. That's not done in Holland, you don't give compliments to a fellow player. *Oh, you were fucking brilliant today.* You don't! So when players do that to me – and Martin was one of them – I would look at him . . . [He mimics a mildly appalled expression] *Are you taking the piss?* That's not done! But he would tell you as well if you should have worked harder in the game. *I wanted you to make the difference today, come on now.* So he's genuine, he's honest.'

Keown soaked up the metaphorical punishment if some players occasionally rolled their eyes when he started up. If he felt he could make even the tiniest percentage of difference, he would far rather speak up than keep thoughts to himself. 'They probably got fed up with me,' he confesses. '*Talks too much, he's always in our ear.* I'd always be on the pitch with something. "I think we need to change our studs, lads," and they'd be like, *Fucking hell, our studs are fine!* But you were adding whatever you could to the party. Even when I was injured, the boss would allow me to come in the dressing room and say a few words. I only ever tried to encourage people.'

Arsenal retake the field against Liverpool knowing precisely what is on the line. The season is at a crossroads. It will be defined by which avenue they take.

'If you have a disappointment, you must shake yourself,' explains Gilberto. 'You must move on and target something. This is what we did. We had a disappointment but it did not have to be a destruction. To lose our full focus, on what we wanted to achieve? We came back in a very positive way. We changed totally our behaviour. We had to move on and push ourselves back up to do something totally different. We stuck together to avoid a bigger problem for everyone. We found a way.'

That way, beautifully, takes the form of Arsenal doing what they do best. A slick passing move just after half-time brings them level. Henry drifts in from the left touchline and jabs the ball to

Freddie Ljungberg, who volleys the ball into the path of Robert Pirès. The man who has a knack for arriving at exactly the right place at exactly the right time delivers. It is perfect one-touch football. Three touches – one from Henry, one from Ljungberg, one from Pirès, and they make it look as easy as kids playing pass the parcel – revive the entire team. The colour returns to Arsenal cheeks, the blood pumps round every player, the spark electrifies their game.

Some years later, a discourse with Pirès about his knack for scoring goals is interesting.

'Knack? What do you mean, knack?' he asks.

It's a difficult word to translate. Three people round the table with a grasp of both English and French are scrambling to find the right term. It is like smelling goals, arriving suddenly and bang!

'It's the feeling,' says Pirès. 'That's how I scored lots of goals, in fact. I anticipated a lot of things. What I wanted every time is that the defender misses his control, or his pass, so I could come in. I anticipated his error.'

So it was a question of thinking ahead all the time?

'I've found the word,' Pirès exclaims. 'It was more instinctive. It was instinct.'

Back in the game against Liverpool, Arsenal's quest to turn a point into three, to breathe fire back into their season, goes on. When Henry seizes the moment, something extraordinary happens. Henry calls it 'more than a goal'.

Liverpool are camped around their box, defending in numbers, as Arsenal probe. When Gilberto flicks the ball to Henry, level with the centre circle, there is an obstacle course of players in front of him. Ten Liverpool players are lined up between him and the goal. Ten opponents waiting, ready to disrupt. Henry revs up. Didi Hamann chases, stretches, tackles thin air and falls over. Henry surges on, into the box. He dummies, this way and that. Jamie Carragher is bamboozled, off balance. Henry sprints on. By now the cavalry have arrived and he has Pirès to his left, Ljungberg to his right. His two teammates become decoys as Henry finishes his virtuoso salsa with a flourish, bending his shot past Jerzy Dudek. He wheels away, screaming. His teammates run after him but he is in his own world and appears not to see them. Inside Highbury a cork is popped, and all around are fizzing, exploding individuals simultaneously letting out so much pent-up tension.

'It was one goal that was more than a goal and whenever I see that goal I can still feel what happened that day in the stadium,' remembers Henry. 'It is the only time in my life that I felt a stadium breathing again. I never had that feeling ever again. We didn't know where we were at that particular moment. We were kind of losing our way, and then we went [with his hands he forms blinkers around his eyes] and finished the season like this.'

Looking back, he suggests there is something almost mystical that, in this essential moment of this essential game of this essential season, he was hanging back, uncharacteristically deep. 'If you look at that play, I don't even know what I was doing there by Gilberto,' he says. 'Because we were attacking. There was a cross that was cleared. I remember saying to Gilberto, "Give me the ball." It's just the desire that the team had and the confidence that that team had in me – I felt like I had to deliver every game. That's what I felt like and that's how I used to play.'

In the crowd, Nick Hornby was struck by how the season's work became distilled into one moment. 'The goal where Thierry dribbled through everyone was the single most important moment of the season for me,' he recalls. 'We'd lost to Chelsea on the Wednesday and lost to United, gone out of two competitions, losing at half-time in the league. Is this all going to fall apart? That game I was worried at half-time. Completely racked with uncertainty. Then to see him do that, just take the ball and score a George Best goal.'

Alan Davies is still in awe. 'I've watched it, I don't know, a hundred times,' he says. 'I always say to people about that goal: watch Jamie Carragher. The poor bloke! He gets destroyed because

Henry sells him two dummies in the blink of an eye, and he buys both of them. You have got to be a good defender to even be quick enough to buy the first dummy. He looked like an Action Man where the upper part of the body had been turned to face the wrong way. When Henry stuck it past Dudek it was just joyous.'

An insight into Henry's remarkable drive comes as he describes how he had developed a deeply personal sense of determination against Liverpool. It was rooted back in the 2001 FA Cup final, a game that even today makes the players involved curse and wonder how defeat was snatched from the jaws of triumph. Arsenal were comfortably on top, and Liverpool struck lucky when they avoided the double punishment of conceding a penalty and having a player sent off as Stéphane Henchoz handballed on the line to prevent a certain goal (it would have been Henry's goal). Two late sucker punches from Owen bulldozed Arsenal. 'That game was a joke,' he says. 'I was devastated. I came back home – how can you lose a game like this? It was so hard to take. I said to myself, especially when I used to play after against Liverpool, I had something special . . . Every time I used to play against Liverpool I used to think about that FA Cup final and make sure that they were going to suffer, not us, again.'

Henry secures the result with his third goal of the day. Bergkamp's assist lofts perfectly into his path, and his shot ricochets off the goalkeeper, bounces back off his shin, and pings in. The showman peels off his shirt, holds his hands aloft, and soaks up salvation. The completion of that hat-trick is like the climax to a symphony when the tone shifts beautifully, thankfully, from discord to harmony. The mood is transformed from churning tension to visceral relief. Hearts are soaring.

Henry feels that while it is natural to become fixated on certain goals as critical, like a stick of dynamite to smash down walls and clear the path ahead, everything behind that goal matters. 'People remember that goal, but if Robert didn't score before, then it's not 3–2,' he explains. 'We put ourselves in that situation and it just so happened to be me that turned the game around. People will always remember that game, but you still have to score against so-called lesser teams. You still have to put yourself in the situation where you can stay at the top of the league. I just felt that every time I was on that field I had to deliver. But the thing is, I'm sure Robert was thinking the same thing. Patrick was thinking the same thing.'

The captain, Vieira, remembers the feeling of waiting for the inspiration from within to pull the team up as they hung over a cliff face by their fingertips. On this occasion it was Henry. 'We were expecting someone to do something magical and it happened,' he says. 'We wanted for him to do it. He was there for us. When you are struggling you expected him, or Dennis, to do something. When you have Thierry and Dennis up front it is easy.' The beauty of this team is that while Vieira felt that way about Henry and Bergkamp, for example, they felt the same way about him. 'We knew the strength of each other,' he adds.

Ljungberg expands on that feeling of faith in the team to find its path. 'It's weird,' he recalls. 'But I always felt the trust in my team-mates, I knew how good they were and what character they had. I never thought once that we wouldn't come back in the second half and do it. And when the goals started to go in, it just felt amazing. I felt power come back into my body. I can actually picture certain elements of that game still to this day – there's not many games you can do that with. It's just because there was so much pressure on that game and it was so important for us players to show ourselves. But it's hard to explain. You just felt, *It's turning. Here we go again.*'

ARSENAL 4–2 LIVERPOOL, 9 APRIL 2004

What are you made of, Arsenal? It was the question Haunted of Highbury was asking at half-time as Liverpool were on course to continue the path of destruction begun by Manchester United and Chelsea.

What was at stake did not need spelling out. Here was the crossroads: one way pointed towards cataclysm, the other catharsis.

When Michael Owen slipped Liverpool into a 2–1 lead on Friday, watching Arsenal was like looking at a boxer being pummelled on the ropes and wondering how much more punishment he could take, whether there was any defiance left somewhere in the pit of the stomach to summon a recovery. With morale on the floor, to recover from going behind twice demanded what one Arsenal coach described as (pardon the expression, but nothing else suffices) 'big balls'.

Losing two ferociously contested and finely balanced cup games is one thing, but to throw away nine months of excellent work in the league would be madness. Arsenal knew it and responded superbly. And, let's face it, it would have been understandable had they wanted to sneak out of Avenell Road and run away from the volcanic pressure of this very public implosion.

Thierry Henry said that the cup exits 'felt like the end of the world'. He may not always be the man for the big occasion – critics cite a series of key fixtures in which the alter ego of this magnificent forward plays as if he has a big, dark cartoon cloud hovering an inch above his head – but on this most crucial of Premiership days he delivered so comprehensively that he went home with the match ball and Gérard Houllier's nomination for goal of the month.

'When you are a winner, you are never in doubt,' Henry said. 'If we had doubts, we wouldn't have come back from 2–1 down at half-time. We came out with such hunger and I have never seen the team feel such vibrations. We responded with our heart. It was extraordinaire.'

Observer

Pirès doesn't really like to overanalyse these things. Asked about what was going on during that half-time against Liverpool, his reaction is effortlessly laid back.

'And at the end?' he asks pointedly.

Yes, but what happens when the pressure is bearing down and the team go in at half-time?

'But at the end?!' he begins to laugh.

Seriously, how can he react like that when it looks so tough?

'At half-time it was 2–1 for Liverpool. For us it wasn't over. That's how we won 4–2.'

Simple as that.

The crashing waterfall evaporates. The anxiety fades. The title is absolutely, incontrovertibly, back on. Oh, and after that week of weeks, Arsenal remain unbeaten in the Premier League.

7
Leadership

Day one of any new adventure is bound to come with swirling emotions — anticipation, eagerness, excitement, a frisson of fear. In the autumn of 1996 Patrick Vieira arrived at Arsenal's training ground with Rémi Garde — an experienced pro who spoke some English and signed for the club on the same day as him partly to act as a sort of chaperon — unsure of what lay in store. 'I really didn't know what to expect,' he recalls. 'My first training session was when Tony Adams announced he was an alcoholic. I didn't really understand what was going on. My English wasn't that good so I had Rémi to translate for me. I was just asking myself where the hell I am. [His voice drops to sound notably underwhelmed] OK . . . What's going to happen now?'

Only very occasionally do the curtains open on a player's career and the audience is instantly, completely, bowled over. The overture, for Vieira in Arsenal colours, was memorably arresting. With a mood of instability off the pitch — between managers, and with news of Tony Adams's admission of alcoholism only a couple of days before all over the papers — and some humdrum performances on it, Arsenal were straining for focus when they hosted Sheffield Wednesday in September 1996. They lay tenth in the table. The teams immediately above them were Derby County and Wimbledon. The circumstances were not particularly auspicious for Vieira as he made his way through the Marble Halls and into the home dressing room to get changed and readied to take his place on the substitutes' bench for the first time.

For the opening twenty minutes or so, Vieira was so intrigued

as he was assailed by the flavour of a tight English ground and the
sights and sounds of the crowd packed close around the side of the
pitch, he found it difficult to focus on the match itself. 'To be honest, I wasn't really concentrating on the game,' he confesses. 'I was
really looking at the fans, and the atmosphere in the stadium.'

Sheffield Wednesday took an early lead. Rumblings of frustration coursed down from the stands. A couple of minutes later,
Ray Parlour was injured, and all of a sudden Vieira was ushered
out of his seat, told to do a quick stretch, and he was on. It was the
first impression most Arsenal fans had of this new kid, and by
extension, the first glimpse of Wenger's intentions. He trotted
onto the grass, this tall, lanky yet powerful boy with an elegant,
confident air and these limbs that seemed unfeasibly long. Purely
from a physical perspective, the way he looked suggested a contrast to the usual midfielder of the day – shorter and stockier,
hardworking runners in the manner of David Hillier and Steve
Morrow, who would soon be ushered out. 'When I came on I
didn't have time to really think. I didn't have time to feel pressure.
I just played. It turned out the way I was hoping,' Vieira smiles.

Immediately, like a flicked switch, Arsenal's game was transformed. Stylistically, it was as if the backdrop of the George
Graham era was lifted, and the Arsène Wenger palette rolled down
in its place. It was mood altering. With Vieira in the middle of the
pitch, the team began to purr, the passing began to click, the pace
of the game accelerated. Arsenal recovered from 1–0 down to
thump Wednesday 4–1, and although Ian Wright made the headlines with a hat-trick and his 150th goal for the club, it was the kid
whose arms he leapt into to celebrate one of those goals whose
name was on everybody's lips as they left the ground. The Arsenal
supporters were awestruck.

'I'll never forget the sight of him,' says Alan Davies. 'From that
moment on, the ball came from our back four into Vieira's feet. It
went to Vieira's feet for the next five or six seasons. Prior to that it
would go to the number nine, Alan Smith or John Hartson. He was

like one and a half players, Vieira. He was that good. Put the ball into his feet he would elude people, shrug them off, if someone put in a challenge he liked it. He was a monster. As soon as he got possession he was on the move and looking to pass.' There was a ripple effect of Vieira coming into the side. His presence and style of play seemed to impact on those around him. Defenders didn't need to bypass midfield any more with a view to pumping the ball quickly to a big man – in fact the old-fashioned robust English striker role would soon become redundant. Hartson was sold within four months, as Nicolas Anelka, gifted and whippet fast, arrived to replace him. The heart of midfield now had two roles – to simultaneously protect the defence and become a creative hub.

Wright, an early beneficiary of the new style, was staggered by Vieira. 'I had never seen a midfield player like that, he was almost feline in his movements, so tall and elegant. He has this beautiful walk on him and he played football the same way. When I saw him, the first thing I thought was some of the midfielders in England are going to eat him up because he was quite slim and skinny. Then when we started training we couldn't get near him. He got the ball, held you off, just amazing. He is really strange looking, but how he took to the Premier League, we knew we had someone world class on our hands. Look at the time he had around himself, pure top quality. We were looking at a midfield player we hadn't seen the like of.'

Dennis Bergkamp wasn't playing on the night of Vieira's debut. He was injured, watching on, and a player as attuned to precision football as he was sensed this wave of incredulity as everyone watched something so new, so unexpected, so eye-catching. 'When he came on he changed the game. He completely changed the game! And I think in the stadium everyone was thinking, *What happened here? Did I really see it right?* I remember people talking to me about it. He was there and then he controlled the ball, and when you think he was going to lose the ball he would pass and put someone in. He was a different sort of player. He was one of the first modern midfield players. He was so, so dominating. We had two midfielders, but it seemed sometimes he was the one really dominating the area in front of the two central defenders, which is so important in our system. And no one would go past. Then he could accelerate to the front and assist the strikers.'

Martin Keown was playing, and felt the magic spreading through the team. 'That's because his first pass was a thirty-to-forty-yard diagonal pass, done in a nonchalant way,' he explains. It certainly wasn't what Highbury was used to. 'When he turned up at the club with Rémi, and this sounds wrong, he was like a stray puppy that turned up with an international player.' Keown remembers the conversations around the training ground: '*Who's Rémi Garde? Oh he's got a couple of international caps for France. OK, who's the kid with him? The skinny kid? Don't know, someone said he's a player . . .* And it turns out the stray pup is a world-class player, a truly world-class player. And actually a world-class human being as well, which is also even more enjoyable.'

Nick Hornby remembers how Vieira's debut reflected on Wenger before the manager had officially arrived. 'Every Arsenal fan remembers Vieira's debut,' he says. 'Him coming on and saying, *Bloody hell, what is this?* And the game changed, they went from losing to winning, and he was a kid. You thought, *Can Arsène do this, every time we have a need of a player in a certain position, will he produce someone who we've never heard of who will turn out to be a genius?* And of course he did for two or three years, although there were some funny ones as well.'

Vieira laughs heartily at the notion that it felt like he was blasted down from the moon that night, twenty-eight minutes into a game that started bleakly against Sheffield Wednesday, appearing suddenly on the centre circle to show Arsenal a new way of being. 'That game is still in my mind, of course,' he grins, years later.

*

Spooling back to the beginning, those first few weeks before he got on the pitch made an impression on Vieira. Quietly observing

what was going on around him, some typically Arsenal characteristics sunk in. Looking back to that first training session, and the
moment Adams called his teammates over for a chat, most of the
guys who thought they knew him so well reckoned their captain
was going to announce that he was their new manager. It was during that limbo period in between Bruce Rioch departing and
Arsène Wenger arriving, and many of the players had taken to
calling Adams 'boss' anyway, as he was organizing and leading in a
typically dominant way.

Although at the time Vieira was extra bewildered as even
Garde's translation of Adams's speech to his teammates was shaky
(he had missed the all-important word – alcoholic – so they were
both bemused until a fuller explanation clarified matters a little
later), in hindsight he was struck by the atmosphere he was coming
into. 'What surprised me is the fact that when he announced it,
everybody was clapping their hands,' he remembers. That supportive round of applause told him something about the closeness
of this team and their mutual respect for one another. 'They didn't
leave him by himself. The relationship they had between them –
Tony, Ray Parlour, Paul Merson, Steve Bould, David Seaman,
Nigel Winterburn, Lee Dixon, Martin Keown – it was really
strong. The English really stuck together to try to support Tony.
After the first few months that's when I realized how much they
love the club, and that's when I understood what Arsenal was all
about. Day after day, week after week, month after month, I saw a
team who was really sticking together. With time I understood
how unified they were. It was really powerful.'

When he arrived, Vieira's priority was to try to play football so
that he could push his case to be included in the squad for the
1998 World Cup which was scheduled to take place in France. It
had been a struggle to make inroads as a young player at AC Milan,
where his promise had been noted but where opportunities at the
expense of his established compatriot, Marcel Desailly, were
limited. Vieira was mainly kicking about in Milan's reserves. He

was impatient to play. For the manager-in-waiting, that was a great sign and Wenger sent Dein to prise him away from Italy.

'I was really scared the first few training sessions because I thought I was going to play straight away and I didn't,' Vieira recalls. 'Training wasn't going the way I was expecting as everything was new. It was difficult. I knew that what you do in training will make the difference in how you adapt yourself. To be one of the boys I had to show them what I was capable of.'

Wright remembers how they began to connect by teasing one another. 'We were always quite derogatory to each other in our playfulness,' he laughs. 'He used to get his swear words all mixed up and I used to get him every morning. You have to say good morning in France, and there's a newspaper there called *Le Matin*, and I used to say *Bon matin*, knowing it was wrong. He would get so annoyed. "It's not even a word!" I used to say it to him every morning. *Bon matin*!'

Vieira underestimated how much he would learn to love Arsenal himself, feel such an integral part of it. Soon, it was not just about playing football, and settling in, but about representing something.

There were complications along the way. That sense of him being targeted that made Martin Keown feel he needed to act as his personal minder was genuinely demoralizing. A distasteful incident in 1999 saw him sent off at West Ham and involved in an altercation with Neil Ruddock, an old-fashioned bruiser, who provoked him into a spit of retaliation. Two red cards within seventy-two hours at the start of the following season left him at a very low ebb, and questioning whether English football was for him. It wasn't really Vieira's style to be driven away from something he believed in. He cooled down, and played on. In 2001 he was made vice-captain of Arsenal, with a view to taking over the full captaincy when Adams retired at the end of the season.

The honour was tinged with some internal wrangling. Although Vieira had been made captain of his boyhood club, Cannes, as a teenager, he was not totally convinced it was the right thing for Arsenal. He had observed Adams's super-determined and vocally inspiring style of leadership. He was not in that mould, preferring to lead by example rather than exhortation. There were also a bunch of vastly experienced professionals around him, a fair bit older than him, which sat strangely at first.

'When Arsène told me I was captain I wasn't sure,' admits Vieira. 'When I looked at the players around, players like Lee Dixon, I needed to speak to them. I spoke to David Seaman about it. I needed them to give me their blessing a little bit. I knew that I would be a completely different captain to Tony Adams. Tony is more vocal. I am more reserved as a person. But if Arsène gave me the captaincy it was because I was a leader in a different way on the pitch – to bring the team together from the way I played rather than the way I was talking.'

Henry watched his friend, whom he had played alongside for France's under-21s and then senior team, evolve into a natural – albeit different – skipper. 'When you watch the game, you wouldn't see Patrick shouting at everyone. But Patrick was so good and so dominant that he didn't have to shout,' he says. 'Just the way he was playing was enough for us . . . *We better wake up. He means business. Let's follow him.* I remember games when that guy was playing alone in midfield. No disrespect to anyone, but you knew he was going to get the ball. Arsenal fans knew that, the opposite team knew that, the press knew that, everybody. He was just a lovely guy, nice to be around, but when he was on the field – different story. You better be awake and make sure that you're going to be able to fight.

'Sometimes, when you play away from home against a lesser team – no disrespect to anyone – it's raining, the first ten minutes, you're not in the game. And then suddenly you see Patrick going and slide-tackling someone and smashing the guy and getting the ball and just driving like he used to drive, doing a box-to-box run with the ball. And you're like: *Oh, OK, let's go.*'

The subject of the captaincy is where one of Wenger's idiosyncrasies became important. In a country like England, which historically values the armband as something revered in team sport, Wenger spoke often of his preference for what he calls 'shared leadership'. He believes the captaincy in itself is little more than symbolic, and that, ideally, a team has a multitude of leaders who relish inspiring one another. Think about some of the characters who formed the spine of the Invincible squad and would naturally contribute in terms of leadership. They didn't need to be told, it was an innate part of their character: Lehmann, Campbell, Keown, Vieira, Bergkamp, Henry. Between them, they had diverse leadership timbres. Some were serious talkers, others gently encouraging, some just oozed an air of confidence that made you feel good to have them by your side, while others were more fiery and gritty.

As for the rest – perhaps not blessed with what is perceived as authentic leadership characteristics – they were all fighters. Lauren, Cole, Touré, Ljungberg, and even Mr Nice Guy Pirès. You think he's not a fighter? You think he isn't driven to succeed whatever the circumstances? His was just a different kind of fighting – without the desire to win the technical fight he would not have adapted sufficiently to be voted Footballer of the Year in his second season in England.

It takes toughness to make yourself successful when the challenge looks overwhelming, as it did initially for Pirès. On his debut he memorably sat on the bench watching and wincing – Wenger told him it was best he took a look at the demands in store before throwing him in. A more brutal football was a culture shock, and it took guts to learn how to master an environment that felt quite alien. 'People think it's only the matches which are hard, but it's every day,' he says. 'Every day training is complicated, it's difficult. When you train with Tony Adams, Martin Keown, David Seaman, Ray Parlour and others, you are forced to learn. You grow. It was important for me, physically and also mentally.'

He admits he was not fond of tackling, but the team clubbed together to cover all the bases. 'For example, when you had to go into a duel, I didn't go. It was Tony Adams, it was Martin Keown, it was Ray Parlour, it was Patrick Vieira. They did it for me,' he explains. 'I didn't have that quality – because it is a skill. I had other skills. We had a very strong mix. Players who were less strong than me technically were much stronger physically.'

Having said that, Campbell thinks fondly of Pirès's contribution when tempers were up. 'He was very quiet but then he likes causing a stir on the pitch,' he reckons. 'If there's any pushing and shoving, he always seems to be there and then he scuttles off at the back, it makes me laugh!'

That give and take within the team extended to leadership. Even though he was the captain, Vieira actually asked certain players to shout at him, give him a blast, when it was required. As Jens Lehmann puts it, 'Patrick was somebody who you needed to kick up the bum sometimes. Because he was very laid back, and he knew, *Oh, I'm the greatest.* Being great doesn't always help.'

Vieira had a particular rapport with Campbell, who specialized in directing traffic from behind him, and could be relied upon to poke him with a verbal stick. 'Patrick wanted me to shout at him all the time to wake him up,' remembers Campbell. 'He'd say, "Sol, I like it when you shout at me because it gets me going!" Patrick was just a gentleman, but his strength was within his play, his mannerisms, his determination to win the ball, to break up attacks, to get the ball forward, make the right pass, score goals. He did it more through his stature on the pitch. He was a Mr Arsenal. It takes different types of captains to run a team. Some of the lads did his shouting for him. But he was just the calm guy doing the right things on the pitch at the right moments.'

Vieira has no qualms about the fact he benefited from Campbell giving him these alarm calls during matches when he started to drift off. He liked it. 'Yeah, that's why that generation was so good, because we were so honest,' he says. 'I was telling him, when the game was easy and I can get a bit lazy, I can be switched off quickly. I notice it when I start to make a silly mistake. It's a lack of concentration, really. Sol was really good because when I started to make one mistake he would shout at me. He would shout, "*Patrick, come on!*" He'd tell me I was better than that. He switched me on straight away.'

It certainly seemed to work, and was an example of how well these players knew each other, and each other's game, and how willing everyone was to do whatever it took to help one another. With the powerful personalities around him, Vieira was an outstanding captain, and some forceful performances during the season's winter slog in 2003–04 made Wenger stop and reflect about how well his midfield gladiator had grown into the role. He was so pleased that Vieira had resisted the temptation to quit in previous seasons when he felt English football had it in for him.

'I was worried he would go,' Wenger said at the time. 'There were critical phases he was on the edge and felt victimized. But always after a few days he came back and said, "No it's down to me. I have to improve my behaviour and attitude." His self-critical view got him through. Now it looks to me as if he has gone over the top of the hill incident-wise. If you look at the reasons for our consistency since the start of the season, of course it is down to the attitude of the team but also to the work Patrick has done with the players. He transmits a mental understanding, and he has seen that before from Tony Adams.'

★

Edu, one of Vieira's sidekicks in midfield, gives an insight into how shared leadership can work. For him, one of the strongest leaders of the group was Henry. If Vieira was one step removed from Adams in the context of the English stereotype of captaincy, then Henry was another step removed from Vieira. For Edu, what he saw in Arsenal's supreme goalscorer made a lasting impression. Nowadays, Edu is director of football at his boyhood club,

Corinthians, and he constantly looks for someone with Henry's presence inside a squad. 'I always say, I would like to have the mentality that I saw Thierry had in that time. He *always* wanted to win. Every game. Every training. Everything. If he was playing cards, he had the mentality to win. In the squad to have someone who is always pushing the guys, pushing himself, to win every game, was special. Sometimes it can be a little bit heavy. This is Thierry. But having someone to push us on to win meant a lot for the squad. His mentality was unbelievable. If every squad has a Thierry, the squad works better. I like for Corinthians to always have a guy like him but they are very difficult to find. And to be so gifted and be able to score so many goals, Thierry was the complete footballer.'

These strong characters strengthened one another. Lehmann drove them to give only their best in training. Keown was in everybody's ear constantly. Campbell kept Vieira on his toes. Bergkamp worked with such intensity at his craft he was an example for everyone. Parlour pushed himself to physical limits. Gilberto strove to be super-professional. Ljungberg, Cole, Lauren and Touré were teak-tough competitors. Henry hated losing, full stop. Vieira stood tall with that armband on and any opponent knew there was no easy ride. Good luck taking that lot on.

Tony Adams had a maxim which sums up how he feels about the strength of a team: 'You need seven.' He believed it was imperative to look around your team and know there were at least seven who would back you up with everything they've got, no matter what. You could probably carry the rest along with you. The Invincibles had no problem reaching that magic number and beyond.

Everywhere they looked was a collaborator they could depend upon. Keown, for example, sings the praises of a couple of the supposedly quieter members of the group, who were not necessarily the first to attract attention. Gentle by nature, but men with giant spirit. 'Gilberto was a fantastic man, a great leader, a very humble person. He arrived into the dressing room as a World Cup winner, and almost apologizing for that, but never played with any apology. I thought it was an outstanding addition and he raised the bar. The French players looked across and saw a quality individual. Very driven, and always playing for the team, not for himself.

'Lauren was a very together person, very determined, knew what he wanted, you weren't going to have to carry him at all. But he was a winger playing full back, and at first he got the feeling, *Do we rate him or don't we?* That maybe came from the fact there were all these English guys at the back and suddenly he wasn't English. But he was a really tough cookie who came in and an exceptional player. Another winner. You knew you could rely on him very quickly. He stood up for himself at the start. You know that you can win things with those sorts of players.

'There was a real sense of lots of leaders in the group, lots of winners in their own right. There was an aura around a lot of those players, Henry, Vieira, you see them today, they still carry themselves in a certain manner. A big charisma.'

*

In terms of the fundamental quality of a basic hunger for winning, there was not one member of the squad who fell short. This addiction to winning accompanied the team from training ground to match. It permeated the atmosphere more or less wherever they were. Parlour remembers that training matches were regularly tougher than what they faced come the main event against another club. 'In training on a Friday, you could have an eight v eight, and for Arsène Wenger it must have been his worst nightmare with injuries because he's watching sixteen guys kicking lumps out of each other,' he says. 'Because that team wanted to win so badly and it was competitive. I mean, there were proper tackles going in. You could have gone through the motions and Wenger wouldn't have said a word, but that's the competitive nature you need in any team. It's great that you can take that winning spirit on a Friday afternoon on to the field on the Saturday. Now you've got sixteen born winners all together in the team.'

When Vieira led the squad out of the Highbury dressing room, into the compressed space of the tunnel, with its chink of light and grass and atmosphere at the end, Arsenal sensed their opponents shrinking. Arsenal had a big team of winners, and a winning team of big men. It was highly intimidating. Martin Keown remembers how the visitors would look up, whispering.

Parlour takes up the theme. 'Highbury was so tight, in the tunnel, that you could sense the nerves in the other team. You look at them and they're going: *Look at Henry, Bergkamp* . . . all these great players lined up alongside them. You could just sense that they were going to try to park the bus, as they say, try to defend as long as they can, and if they lost 1–0 or 2–0 that would be a good result for them. We always used to say to each other, "They think they're going to lose already; let's not disappoint them." We got a buzz out of that.'

For the likes of Ljungberg and Cole, who were not the tallest, being part of that collective gave them metaphorical extra inches. As Ljungberg recalls, 'It is not so much about we were so big, I just felt everybody wins, everybody was dying in training, there were bust-ups, this and that to win, so when we stood in that tunnel, I knew that the team would do anything to win.

'And if there was a fight – and people can say it was wrong at Man United, but they tried always to bully us when we played – all of a sudden we stood up for each other. Every other team knew that you can pick on us and we will stand up for each other. Inside the team, I personally felt it was good. We showed everyone else how much we will protect each other. And that's what I felt every time we stood in the tunnel.'

Vieira searches for the perfect word to describe how he felt at that time, lining up with his teammates, next to absolutely anyone. 'We were . . .' he ponders, then smiles as it comes to him, '. . . Monsters.'

8
Wengerball

You didn't need to be a comedian to poke fun at what had become of Arsenal's style come the dog end of the George Graham era. The team had evolved a strategy based on super-resilience and mostly hoicking the ball up to Ian Wright, their explosive, maverick striker, as quickly as possible. It was perfect for cup runs, and Arsenal won three different cups between 1993 and 1994, but it wasn't always pretty. Alan Davies and his friends used to dream up silly diversions to deal with some of the tedium at Highbury. 'There was a real lull,' he says, chuckling to himself. 'We used to have a little wall in front of us in the West Lower — we were in the front row — and we'd put a coin on top of the wall and move it along until there was a corner or a throw in, just to amuse ourselves because the football was so unbearable. That period when George signed John Jensen and Stefan Schwarz and Eddie McGoldrick. We used to sit there and shout "Hayes . . . Groves . . . Papin!" The idea that someone like Papin would turn up and be in that team was laughable. In the seventies or eighties Rudi Krol was supposed to be coming and he never came.'

There's a broad canal just round the corner from Dennis Bergkamp's boyhood home. The scene is typical, suburban Amsterdam. The clean lines of the canal split the streets, bicycles are propped up against the apartment blocks, it's pretty quiet. Here, against the wall of his building, he spent so much of his time as a young boy repeatedly kicking a ball. Touch, touch, touch. Instep, outside of the foot, toe, laces, harder, softer, left, right, with a bounce, without a bounce. Touch, touch, touch. While most boys would have been satisfied just to keep the ball-to-wall game going, Bergkamp got an extra kick out of analysing the science of the way the ball would respond according to how he made contact. It fascinated him.

The rebirth of Arsenal, from a stylistic point of view, began with Bergkamp. He played the orchestra's first note. He was the oboist, whose clear, pitch-perfect A tunes every other musician around him. He starts, the rest respond. In terms of creating a new identity, he arrived, he elevated the standard, he embodied a nod to the Dutch ideal of total football – technical, inventive, collective – and he was a joy to watch. Within a year of his arrival, everything began to flourish as strong personalities came who could take this idea, and effectively turn the solo into a symphony.

Wright credits Bergkamp as the most important signing in Arsenal's history. 'Dennis changed the DNA of what our game was about,' he reckons. 'The player he was, our game had to change because you couldn't bypass him. Then Arsène Wenger coming in with his total football, it was brilliant. I could only wish I was four years younger. I knew the great times were coming.' That's quite a statement from a man who had won medals, would break goal-scoring records, and had fallen in love with the club even before the great sea change.

'It all started with Dennis, to be honest,' assesses Vieira. 'If you have Dennis Bergkamp in your team you cannot play kick and rush any more. We had everything at Arsenal. We had technique, you can say we had brain with Dennis Bergkamp, we had pace, and that's why it worked. We really enjoyed playing together, and that is the freedom that Arsène gave us. We were really lucky to be in that team that was winning and enjoying it so much with the style and the football we were playing. That is the vision. The manager has his philosophy, and then he brings the right players for his philosophy and the way he wants to play football.'

As a supporter, Nick Hornby watched it evolve, quite unexpectedly, right in front of his eyes. He was intrigued to observe how Wenger completely redefined what Arsenal meant to people. 'I can't think of many football clubs that have a brand, actually,' he says. 'An actual brand as opposed to they're famous. Probably the only two are Barcelona and Arsenal, and Arsenal have done it through one man. At Barça they have to play football a certain way, but they also have the resources to achieve that. So it's quite remarkable that one man has taken something that meant one thing and turned it into something that meant the opposite. Within six or seven years everyone had forgotten the old Arsenal. And now when foreign people talk about Arsenal, or they play Arsenal football, everybody knows what that means and that's a relatively recent invention.'

Bergkamp's arrival was serendipitous in that he was such a natural fit to instigate the change in advance of Wenger. The philosophy he absorbed at Ajax, the way he inherently thought about football, blended well with the incoming coach. The Ajax Academy, a football school renowned for the way it educates its youngsters, teaches according to what they now call the TIPS model. It stands for technique, insight, personality and speed. All these things resonate totally with Wenger's footballing dogma.

Reflecting on the evolution of Arsenal's style, Bergkamp sees these components, which were so prevalent in the squad, as keys to the way they formed *their* game. The interplay that became a hallmark with, say, a burst of seemingly instinctive exchanges between Bergkamp, Henry and Pirès, was based as much on insight as pure technique. 'I always try to copy the words that Arsène once told me: the ball always goes through the intelligent players in the team,' Bergkamp explains. 'When you name those names, they're all very intelligent players, they saw the game, they saw the openings.

'The understanding was right. Why? Because we played to each other's strengths. So I knew exactly what the strength of Thierry was, or Patrick or Robert. That was the power in that team, we knew exactly where you could connect on the pitch. You also knew what the weaknesses were of the players. So you're always looking, as Arsène says, to make the right pass and put a player *in his strength*. With Thierry, I knew exactly what he wanted to do, he knew exactly from me what I could do for him. On the pitch we had all those connections happening. Maybe there were two or three players who weren't on the same level as we were, but they gave something else, they gave power to the team, or defending. They had the intelligence as well – when we get the ball we give it to Patrick or Thierry or Dennis. They don't want to do silly things. That's what Arsène wanted.'

When a new player arrives, can you see that intelligence in them immediately?

'Yeah. You know that they always try to overachieve in the beginning, try to show themselves. But within those moves on the pitch or the way they control the ball, you would always know, OK, *this is a good player, this is a player I can play with*. Robert was a player who wanted to play one or two touches. Patrick the same. Thierry is different. You have to play him in, or you have to put him in a position where he can play one against one. It could be behind the defenders, or it could be in between them. It didn't take long, but after a few training sessions you knew exactly what a player's strength was, what his weakness was, and how you as a team could grow.'

How unusual is it to be in a team where you can develop that high level of intuition about each other's game?

'It's really rare. I had the same sort of feeling at Ajax, but those were all upcoming players, young players. Of course, we could play football, but young players are always up and down, and people say "That's fantastic" and the next week they say "Oh, that's rubbish". But I was lucky in the Arsenal teams that they were all a certain age, where they were at their best. The connection at Arsenal stood out for me, it was really special. Because we played with each other for a few years we knew each other through and through, on and off the pitch we could really tell each other the truth, and be honest to each other. We knew that we could grow, because of that.'

Many of the players confess that the player they looked for first when they had the ball was Bergkamp. That habit went all the way back to the goalkeeper. 'Always,' says Lehmann. 'It wasn't Thierry, it was him. Because he was the converter. Or the conductor. I knew I couldn't give the final pass, but he could. Technically he was so good that I knew I could always give him the ball. Even when he was thirty-six or something like that.'

The influence he brought to bear on the team manifested itself in so many different ways. The way that he trained, with such intensive concentration even when he was well into his thirties and a totally established club icon, chimed. He never took it easy. The perfectionist in him ensured that every day offered the chance for refinement, if even by the tiniest increment. The way he thought about the game set a high bar. On the pitch in particular, he was always thinking ahead, trying to see moves taking shape, where the runs were coming from, clicking it all together. The oldest of the regulars in the Invincibles team may not have moved the quickest, but the others were hard pressed to think more quickly.

The speed of the team – speed of thinking as well as movement – seemed sharper than anyone else in that era. 'We were on a different level, I felt,' says Bergkamp. 'As an athlete, or as a football player, going out somewhere doing your thing but knowing already that you will be successful on that day, is amazing. You're so confident and so full of quality and talent that you know you can make a difference. We had the same feeling as a team. I remember some goals, the timing, how quick it was from one side to the other side. It was not like we were a counter-attack team. In those moments, for the front four or five players, we knew exactly what was going to happen in the next ten to twelve seconds, and that's a fantastic feeling. And then it's all at the highest pace, with the highest quality. Let's go.'

Ljungberg felt that collective speed of thought evolved from the fact the group spent a lot of time analysing the game. 'We all liked to think football,' he says. 'That I agree with. When people ask me about how we played, stepovers take a lot of technique, for example, but the speed of the pass, how it got smashed around to each other, that was the hard thing. Top teams do it, when the field is really wet and it gets smashed around, one touch. Before you get the ball, you need to think, *Where's the ball going after this?* Because the ball is coming at real speed. With the speed of the ball we could still control it. It's not that we ran faster than everyone else, but the ball moved faster. Everybody thought how to get it faster to catch the opponents out.'

Lehmann agrees that the speed was critical. 'What is the fastest thing on a football pitch?' he asks. It feels like a trick question. 'It's not the ball,' he says, grinning knowingly. 'Nobody is faster on the pitch than a thought. And then the ball comes. And then the players come. So quick thinking was vital. I'm still convinced that we played a much faster football than the team today. We were playing one touch, two touch. When you look at the team today, it's three or four touches. Normally you say football is progressing so fast now. But I can honestly say between 2003 and 2006 we played such a fast football. Everything was faster. The opening, the finishing.'

There were times during the Invincible season when the goalkeeper was in a very privileged position, as Arsenal were zooming forward at full throttle, slicing through opponents, in his direct eyeline. 'Plenty of games I was standing at the back just watching, because we had so much possession, we were playing so fast, we were playing tic-tak-tic-tak-tic. One touch. It was amazing to see. I said to myself, *What an amazing group*.'

A remarkable illustration of how Arsenal's new style made an impression outside their own family occurred towards the end of the Invincible season. In March 2004, they travelled to Portsmouth for an FA Cup quarter-final and put on such an irresistible show, the opposition supporters felt compelled to raucously applaud the away team while in their own home.

PORTSMOUTH 1–5 ARSENAL, 6 MARCH 2004

'Can we play you every week?' inquired the Portsmouth fans cheerfully at 5–0 down. Now either that is inspired irony, or the fantastically loyal Pompey fans had it in them to appreciate that with Arsenal in town they were able to watch football from another planet.

Something extraordinary happened here in the 71st minute. Arsène Wenger made a triple substitution: off came the imperious Patrick Vieira, the irrepressible Thierry Henry, the impish Freddie Ljungberg and they were given a standing ovation by the Fratton Park faithful.

'Their fans were fantastic, even at 5–0 down, and with fans like that Portsmouth don't deserve to go down,' said Henry, warming to this unexpected love-in. Wenger said he had never seen anything like it.

Seventeen places and light years separated these two teams. 'They're the best team in Europe, possibly the world,' wheezed Harry Redknapp. 'I think they have moved on to another level. At five I thought, "This could be anything." '

Come the final reckoning it was easy to forget, though, that Pompey really made a fist of it for the opening 20 minutes. But Arsenal are both beauty and the beast. They swept the road before beginning the procession . . .

Intimidating, poky little Fratton was something Portsmouth were depending on. Cracking noise, swirling rain, skiddy surface, thudding commitment – all the ingredients were there to try to unnerve the Gunners.

But Arsenal's noses are not so easily put out of joint. Perceived wisdom was that Pompey would have to make it a bruising game to win through, but Arsenal supplied more than their fair share of bone-crunching moments (both Kolo Touré and Henry were lucky to escape bookings for reckless challenges). If they have to play hard to play beautiful they have the armoury to do exactly that. With Vieira leading by awesome example, Arsenal made sure they won the physical battle before the ballet began.

As if the searing pace of Henry was not enough to contend with, his partner José Antonio Reyes drove at Portsmouth with lightning runs. 'The amount of runs he makes is absolutely unbelievable,' said Wenger. 'His and Thierry's pace caused big problems for their defence.' Reyes crashed a half-volley against the crossbar with his first chance. Henry went one better with his. Capitalising on Petri Pasanen's loose clearance, Arsenal's top scorer shimmied, cut back and lashed past Shaka Hislop.

Some of Arsenal's interplay afterwards was irresistible. The cushion their dominance merited arrived just before the interval and in exquisite style. Edu picked up a loose ball and exchanged a delicate one-two with Vieira. The Brazilian then arced an artistic pass for the energetic Ljungberg to strike the second. Then, in stoppage time Portsmouth couldn't deal with an Arsenal corner and Touré rifled a third from the edge of the box. By the time Jeff Winter whistled, the Pompey players looked like they'd been caught in a tornado.

What to do? Redknapp sent on Steve Stone for Eyal Berkovic but frankly by now the personnel was irrelevant. Arsenal were so commanding Portsmouth were struggling to see the ball, let alone touch it. After stringing together a move of what seemed like 100 passes, Reyes found Ljungberg, who rolled the ball onto Henry, whose precision finish nestled into the far corner . . .

'Come on Pompey, get a goal!' someone shouted. And after two attempts rebounded off the woodwork, it finally came in the last minute from Arsenal's old enemy Teddy Sheringham. Oh well, seems they are not perfect after all.

Observer

It was universally understood that work at London Colney translated directly into performances come match day. The message comes across loud and clear. 'You play how you train. If you train well, generally you're good in a match,' says Pirès. 'If you think training is training and game is game, you lose the game,' adds Gilberto. 'We had to be careful not to injure each other but we had to train seriously. This for Arsène was really important. He showed everyone the importance of being serious in training sessions. If sometimes someone did something which was not in accordance with what he thinks, he stopped training and spoke to the players. Everyone understood his mentality and the way he approached everyone.'

Even years down the line, most of the players can remember key moments when Wenger stopped the play to deliver a particular message, or catch them for a tête-à-tête, which would become a touchstone for how they should mould themselves to become an Arsenal player, and a better fit for the Arsenal system.

Gilberto remembers this well. 'Arsène was very important to show the way he wants me to play, the way he likes the team to play,' he says. 'I remember well my first few games. It is quite common in Brazil in the position I played that the ball gets passed to the side, then turns to another side. That is what I was used to. Suddenly one day he came to me at the training ground and talked about what he wants from me. He said, "Oh, what you are doing is good, it's great, but I want you to play *forwards*. That's the way we play in England. That is what English football is about." I understood. It was really important the way he approached me to say that. I had to listen. Everyone understands the importance to play forwards. I had to get into the team and adapt to the system. Not them to me. I got the message.'

Ljungberg absorbed the impact of an early lesson, too. 'There was a moment in training, not long after I got there, I did my man inside and had an angle, outside of my foot placed shot into the corner. Nice goal, thanks very much. And he stopped the game. And I got a proper bollocking. What's going on? I've just scored. And I haven't been there very long, and he says, "Freddie, the striker's standing there, pass it to him, he can roll it into an open net, why are you shooting? You've done great to go past this defender, but you need to pass it to the striker." And in my past coaches had not told me that, they were like, *Oh great he scored*, and they don't say a word. And I remember so vividly he stopped the game, gave me a bollocking. "The next time you always pass. You pass, you pass, you pass . . ." I learned that very quickly.'

That was a trademark of Wengerball. It might be Ljungberg making the run and then cutting the ball back for Henry, or Henry searing into the box and squaring for Pirès, or Pirès darting into space and tucking the pass to the onrushing Vieira. It worked, Ljungberg says, because selfishness was not tolerated.

Henry describes it as 'the joy' in the team. 'Look at how we used to set each other up. We had situations where one guy could score, but no, he was going to cross it for a guy that was in a better position. And that was the way it was all over the field. We were just passing the ball. In two, three, sometimes four passes, we were already in your box finishing the movement. No one was keeping all of the ball. Everybody was passing to the guy that was in a better position. Nobody was trying to showboat. Most of our goals were just like that. People thought it was easy, but it's not an easy thing to create – being unselfish and trying to help each other. Not only from a defensive point of view, but an offensive point of view. It's difficult to fight against glory. We are all human beings, so sometimes, if you're in a good position, you're like, *Oh, I can score*. But the point is not you scoring. Arsenal has to score.'

Isn't that going against a goalscorer's instincts, though? 'I'm not an Alan Shearer or a Michael Owen. They are natural-born scor-ers. I will never be. I wasn't that type of striker. I was scoring goals, yes, but at that time anybody in our team, even if they were in a great situation to score, was passing it if someone else was in a better position. That was like second nature for us.'

For Ljungberg, it was essential they all shared the same philosophy. 'We all saw football the same way, that the main thing was to win, not who scored,' he stresses. 'Sometimes I heard a commentator say, "They should shoot from there!" But that was not the philosophy we had in the team. Without meaning to be cocky, our team had made it as players. Some were in the top three in their position in the world. They didn't have anything to prove, they didn't have to score this goal to play tomorrow. That gave us that feeling we could be so generous. There was no ego whatsoever. That's how I felt within the team. That's Arsène behind all that. But then as well I think it developed within ourselves, because we showed each other respect and we were friends. People say, "Did you score today?" I don't really care, we won, who cares. That was an amazing feeling to have. I remember I could say, "We won 3–0 and Sol was amazing." Sol didn't score a goal but you understand what I'm saying.'

Parlour remembers being uncertain about what to expect when he first started training under Wenger. 'But I remember David Dein said, "This man will take us forward." From day one, the training regime was great,' he says. 'The lads started to put the ball down. I loved George Graham, I thought he was great, but there was a lot of focus on defending, win 1–0, not great football. Suddenly we had freedom.'

Was training fun?

'Oh yeah. I loved it. You had to concentrate, but it was always very enjoyable. No disrespect to other managers, but it was a little bit same old thing, forty-five minutes of that. And you think, *Oh, I've had enough now*. Your concentration goes after probably about fifteen, twenty minutes working on one thing. Wenger knew that, so then he goes on to something else, totally different. Then your mind is still working. That's why everything was always on the clock. He always knew the time span of people's top concentration.

'I'll tell you why I was so impressed with Arsène Wenger. He was on the training field every single day. He never had a day off. He never once came into training and said, "The first team are in the gym, warming down from the game, I won't bother going out today." He was out there with the other players, teaching youngsters, whoever it was, on that training field. And that is a big thing to do. As a manager, it's so easy to leave it if the first team were elsewhere. But he was on that training field trying to make the other players ready if they were needed.'

For Pat Rice, the most striking aspect was how precise everything was. 'The actual training system and the way that we trained was completely different to how we'd done it before,' he says. 'Whenever I used to referee the games – and we would play a game for fifteen minutes at the end of the session – I can remember Arsène shouting out to me, "Pat, look at your watch, seven and a half minutes." He would come up to me and say, "When I say it's fifteen minutes, that means seven and a half minutes each way, that doesn't mean seven minutes or eight minutes, it means seven and a half minutes." And everything was done to the clock.' At first Rice was slightly bemused. He felt it wasn't necessarily enough to allow players to get into the flow. But he was soon convinced it had great merit, encouraging players to focus on something specific to work on during the mini-game. Sometimes Wenger would stop the game and send the players on sprints, then straight back into the second half. 'It was just to see if you could switch on and off,' explains Rice.

Sometimes Wenger would move the goals into the corner of the pitch, to create a situation where angled, crossfield passes were the focus. Other times, if you completed ten passes in the opposition half you would be awarded a goal to drum home the beauty of possession and attacking the ball. There were drills where the ball could not leave the floor. Lots of tricks, lots of detail, lots of precision. It all came together to produce this swifter, slicker, approach. 'You would have sessions like that, then all of a sudden you would bring that into the games that you actually play on a Saturday,' says Rice. 'They would be dragging the opponents all over the place.'

For the team's defenders, adapting to this new style, this new freedom, was both exhilarating and frightening, as all the default mechanisms, the defensive methods that were so well honed, would be challenged. Full backs were all of a sudden liberated to become auxiliary wingers. Lee Dixon remembers it as 'tremendously exciting' being able to look up and see options in front of him and be challenged in terms of making the right choice to build an attack. Martin Keown was more dubious to start with. 'Full backs bombing off meant cover you expected to be next to you was sometimes absent.' But as he discovered, practice meant more or less perfect.

'I was watching Hungary play with Puskás on the TV recently. They had this system where the full back just flew forward and every time I stopped the screen, they had six players in the opposition box,' he exclaims. 'If you did that with Arsenal it was the same. When Wenger first came I was constantly saying to my full back, "Are you sure?"' The reply would come back that the boss was telling him to go forward, but Keown was not immediately reassured. 'I'd say, "Just occasionally can you stay in?" We were not throwing caution to the wind, but by playing people in full-back positions who were happier going forward, the full back almost played like a winger.' What emerged was a series of players shifting positions to fill in for one another.

It was no coincidence that the two full backs, Lauren and Ashley Cole, were athletic, pacy and had experience of playing as wingers earlier in their careers. It was also not a coincidence that the players in front of them (Pirès and Ljungberg) were smart enough to adjust themselves. Nor was it a coincidence that the anchor midfielders, Vieira, Gilberto and Edu, read the game comfortably enough to move around the pitch to fill any gaps.

Lauren describes how he and Cole would take turns to go on

the offensive by gesturing with a pulley motion. 'Who goes, who stays?' he says. 'You know that when Ashley Cole goes up, you cannot go up at the same time. So one goes, the other one stays. It's like balancing.' Sol Campbell's role in the defensive chain was vital, as he welcomed the job of organizing those around him. 'I was very quiet off the pitch, but when I got onto the pitch, I was a different animal,' he says. 'I'm very vocal, I'm a very good organizer. I move people into position before it becomes a problem.'

All over the pitch, patterns emerged: the core defensive triangle between Lehmann and his two centre halves. The link between the full back and winger. The fluid movement of the attacking players. The central midfielders had the flexibility to overlap with any of those areas. These patterns became instinctive because of the practice sessions in the Hertfordshire countryside.

'We went through a lot of team shape with mannequins,' explains Keown. 'When you play on Saturday it's off the cuff, but if you've practised it through the week, without an opposition, with mannequins, when it comes to Saturday it's familiar. I'll just make that diagonal pass into midfield as we have been making that same pass during the week. You're just stepping with the team. Years later I spoke to Patrick and said, "When I got the ball I literally had three passes. I'd give it to you, or if not you then Dennis, and if not him then Henry." And he said, "When I got it I used to give it Dennis." And when I went over to speak to Dennis, he said, "When I got it I just used to give it to Henry or put it in the back of the net." And really it was very simple. You're climbing a ladder through your team to the opposition goal as quickly as possible, and you're only giving it to the player that's better than you in front of you.'

For Bergkamp, the essence of training was in the enhancement of patterns. 'Keep practising the patterns,' he says. 'Keep practising the passing. We did the sprints, we did tactical games, positional games. But when you've got a team who already know all the patterns, who already know the strength of each other, and you are doing that at the highest pace, then you make other teams look silly, to be fair. It's like you're on a different level.'

In 2004, after their wobbly week was realigned, momentum was rebuilt and Arsenal cruised down the home straight towards the league title. 'It was a machine, like a train,' says Pirès. 'In fact the train advanced on its own.' He begins to laugh. 'There was no driver on the train!'

★

Good Friday, 2004. The title is in sight. Leeds United arrive at Highbury, where the expectancy is tangible. The team feels powerful. The crowd is excitable. The songs are lusty. It only takes six minutes for Arsenal to slice through their opponents. Vieira jabs the ball forward, Wiltord dinks it to Bergkamp, who caresses a pass, so beautifully weighted, for Pirès to sweep confidently in. The pattern is made to look ridiculously easy. 'We shall not be moved,' chorus the Arsenal fans.

Then Henry takes over. His masterclass is such he goes one better than a hat-trick. He scores four. The fourth has a touch of the absurd about it, as he is running at such velocity he actually trips himself up, but has such astonishing balance he is still able to strike ruthlessly at goal mid-fall. There are two assists from Gilberto, one from Pirès, and Bergkamp earns a penalty. On the day, there is some rotation, as Wiltord and Clichy seamlessly slot in instead of Ljungberg and Cole. Every member of the squad is simply loving this football. 'You don't want the ref to blow the whistle,' says Henry. 'You want to play that game your whole life.'

Nick Hornby felt something similar as a supporter. 'There are loads of games that everyone remembers about Thierry, but my two top memories of that season, one was the Liverpool game, and the other was the Leeds game. It was a friend's fortieth birthday on the day of the Leeds game and I felt a little bit bad about it at the time, but I said I'm just not going to your party. Sometimes maybe I'd miss a home game for a friend's fortieth birthday, but not that season, not the way they were. Thierry was sensational. I remember sitting there thinking, *I wouldn't be anywhere else but here. I wouldn't be at a friend's birthday party.'*

David Dein, who back in 1996 had tried to reassure the big group of British players when Wenger was appointed that 'this man will take us forward', watches on from his perch in the Directors' Box. After the many conversations he has had with Wenger over the years, as his friend, confidant and trusted deal maker, seeing Wenger's vision being played out is extraordinary. This is the fruit of the daily work.

'One has to understand Arsène's philosophy,' says Dein. 'Firstly, he is a teacher. People used to call him a professor. He gets his job satisfaction by nurturing talent – from an average player to a good player, from a good player to a very good player, from a very good player to a world-class player. That's what he does. He is always the first one at the training ground and the last one to leave. The first bit of kit he puts on is his stopwatch. Everything is precision. He really does enjoy taking talent and watching it develop. In terms of style, Arsène uses two expressions. "Progression with possession" and "explosive pace". Together, they scare a defence. Watching it was like poetry in motion. We were seeing football from another planet.'

By the time the floodlights were turned off at the end of that Good Friday, Arsenal were ten points clear in the Premier League, with five games remaining. Before they played again, their closest challengers, Chelsea, effectively raised the white flag. They could only draw at home to Everton and were beaten at Newcastle.

Now Arsenal had the chance to seal the title tantalizingly close to home. Just four miles away. In the home of their nearest and not so dearest neighbours, Tottenham Hotspur.

9

Sanctuary

The shrill ringtone of a mobile phone disturbs the focus that Arsène Wenger appreciates as a foundation stone for concentrated work. 'He was trying to tell us off, but it wasn't his way, really,' remembers Ray Parlour. With perfect comic timing the chiming suddenly turned into a chorus. 'About four mobile phones went off, just like that, all at the same time, and he said: "Right, that's it! No more phones! Next phone that goes off, £10,000 fine." And he was serious,' adds Parlour. A couple of days later, at the team hotel, the players went through their normal routine. Go for a walk, back for a twenty-minute stretching drill, then lunch. The stretching was always quiet, no chatting, a time for easing mind and body. All of a sudden a phone goes off. It keeps ringing and ringing. The players, transfixed by this soundtrack, looked nervously at each other. 'Whose phone is this?' queried a stern-faced Wenger. But it didn't belong to any of them. 'OK,' he said, walking back towards his bag, 'it must be mine.' His face creased into a giant smile, as he confessed, 'That's £10,000 for me!' Parlour retells the story with classic mischievous schoolboy spirit. 'He broke the ice with that. He was a very humorous man. People don't see that, but he was great fun. I loved him to death.'

Noise is an essential part of the atmosphere of football. Traditionally, it is a game which is played out with sound effects. On match days, the accompaniment of the crowd is an elemental part of the experience, whether it is a hubbub of grumbling and cursing or the massed tidal-wave roar for a goal. At the training ground, at the very least there is the thump of leather boot on ball, shouts between teammates, instructions, whistles, teasing, chit-chat and laughter.

When Wenger first arrived at Arsenal, he was a little taken aback by the ambience in the dressing room. The music, with Ian Wright emphatically singing and dancing to crank up his own exuberant tone, took him by surprise. He pulled over Patrick Vieira to ask, 'Is it always like this?' Wright remembers getting a lot of quizzical looks from Wenger. 'I'm not sure he really knew how to take me because I was like a child with a disorder,' he confesses.

While Wenger did not wish to curb too much enthusiasm, he did want to instil more calmness and consideration into the general atmosphere. The ambience at the new training ground is noticeably tranquil, and clearly influenced by some of the concepts Wenger became accustomed to in Japan. When he spent some time living in a hotel there, and noticed the attention paid by those performing tasks which would be perceived as menial in the West, such as tidying up or arranging flowers to decorate the lobby, it made quite an impact. 'You learn to respect the dedication of everybody to what they do,' he says. 'You think you are doing your job well and then when you see them work you think you are a small man. They treat a leaf from a tree like a human being. With respect. It's an amazing experience.'

At London Colney, everybody must take off outdoor shoes in a sort of buffer zone before arriving at the interior, so as to ensure all muck is left outside and inside is spotlessly clean. So much of the design was created to maximize the feeling of light and space with a nod to feng shui principles. Some of the little touches, such as a waterfall in the gardens positioned in the eyeline of those working out in the gym, clearly have an effect. 'The whole flow of the place was great,' says Campbell. 'Football is all so mad. It's nice actually to get to a place where you can just calm down, zone out and concentrate on your game and then go back to the madness. You know, if you have madness on the pitch, around football, and then you come back into the training ground and there's more madness, when does it stop? When do you have time to think and create an amazing team and try and win championships year after year?'

Although the players never saw him as a disciplinarian, he encouraged habits that would convey positive vibes towards each other and their environment. 'There were simple rules, like I have to say hello to you when I am coming in,' says Lauren. 'Some people may say that is stupid. But you have to do that to your teammates, to everyone from the guy who is cleaning to the directors. It is no different. It made you show respect to everyone. That's the connection. If you unite, you are stronger. From the human and professional point of view it was important.'

Lehmann sensed an immediate contrast to his life in German football. 'Here you had to perform on the pitch – no excuses, no apologies, nothing. You also had to concentrate in training, and focus in the gym. But apart from that, on a daily basis, it was so relaxing,' he says. 'In Germany, you're constantly stressed.' He had a panic before his first game in England when he misjudged the London traffic and was late for the team meeting, but it summed up the difference for him that he was given latitude when he expected punishment.

Wenger set the scene for a more serene, settled atmosphere. The change was felt more emphatically on match days, considering the English game was used to the stereotype of managers leaning on the fact they could engineer an effect, a reaction, by screaming out rollockings and proverbial tea-cup throwing. Wenger was different. He seldom raised his voice. Pre-match team talks were brief and based on logic, not emotion, and were all about Arsenal and not the opposition. He advocated a period of silence at half-time for everyone to cool down and refocus before any specific instructions were handed out, by which time players would be in the right state to listen and take a message on board. He preferred not to give any big speeches immediately after a game.

'He's really calm and cool,' says Bergkamp. 'Maybe once or twice he would shout. But I think a manager should be able to make a difference tactically. So if something goes wrong in the first half then he should be able to change that at half-time. You move ten yards to the left . . . we have to find the striker more . . . you have to be closer to that player . . . those sort of things. If you've got a coach who only shouts, "We have to do more! We have to give more. We have to go for it one hundred per cent!" it doesn't work with players from twenty-five to thirty because they're like *Yeah, yeah, yeah*. We have to talk at a reasonable level. "I see this from the outside, guys, this is what's happening . . ." Tactically make one or two changes and that's it, you can deal with that. Arsène is like that. The one or two times when he really got upset is when you don't give enough as a team, if you just play at sixty per cent then he would really tell you. That's normal.'

Keown at first found it surprising for the manager to keep his counsel after the heat of a game, but he learned to appreciate it. 'After the game there's nothing said at all,' he recalls. 'Because Arsène probably learned you can only do damage after a game, and it never looks as bad on the tape so he wants time to reflect. And again, people take that information in much better when they've had a period to calm down. So that's the reason for that. Did I agree with it? I think I did in the end. I think it is a much better environment. I don't think he needed to bollock us.'

Most of the players welcomed that Wenger wasn't constantly talking to them. There was one notable exception. Lehmann interpreted his quietness as an extra pressure.

'Arsène put me under a lot of pressure psychologically, without saying a lot,' he says. 'I remember when I first came I always had a habit to do some shots after training, so players gathered around the penalty box, and I would alternate with the other keeper. After a while I realized he was always standing behind the goal. I looked at him and at every goal the keeper conceded [Lehmann imitates a dismissive gesture] he didn't say anything, but just the way he looked – *Oh, rubbish* – was just a simple example of how he psyched people. You knew you couldn't afford to make a mistake.'

That pressure, in Lehmann's case, was epitomized later in his Arsenal career, when Wenger dropped him – something the player took as a fundamental challenge he felt duty bound to respond to. It built towards a climax at the 2005 FA Cup final, when there was much speculation that Arsenal would be searching for a new

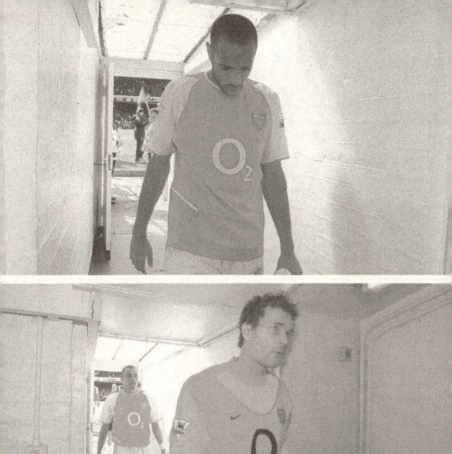

A season's work in peril: out of the FA Cup, out of the Champions League, and trailing 2–1 to Liverpool at half-time . . .

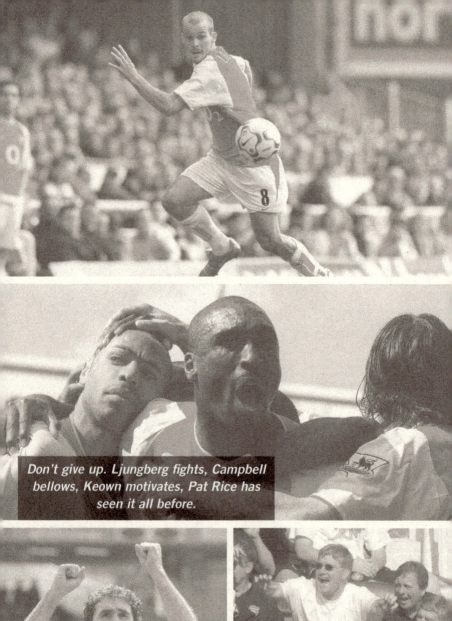

Don't give up. Ljungberg fights, Campbell bellows, Keown motivates, Pat Rice has seen it all before.

Salvation. Pirès has the knack to make it 2–2 against Liverpool, and passes the baton to Henry for 4–2.

Arsenal champions in the white heat at White Hart Lane. Vieira's lightning break stuns the home crowd.

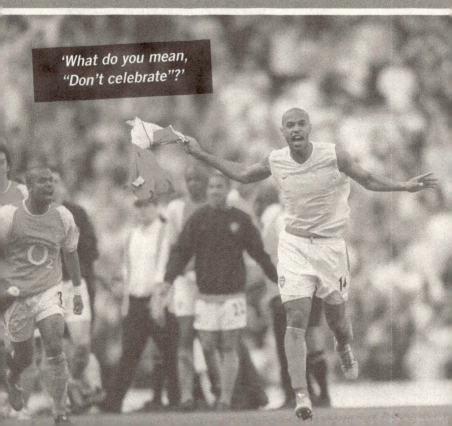

'What do you mean, "Don't celebrate"?'

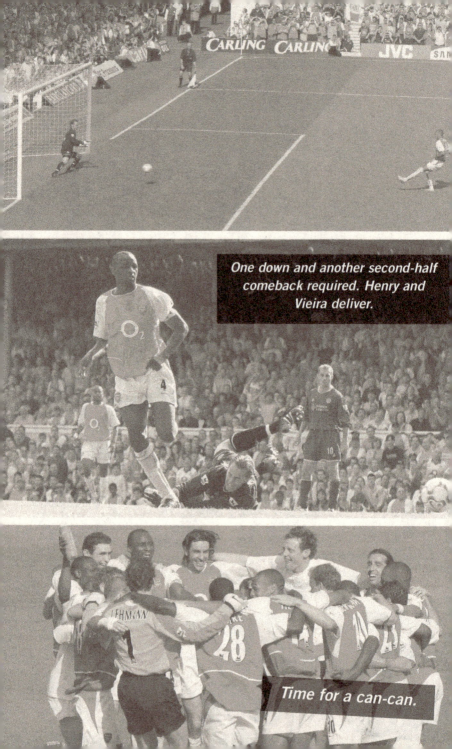

One down and another second-half comeback required. Henry and Vieira deliver.

Time for a can-can.

'It's beyond belief.'

goalkeeper. 'At Arsenal I learned to explore my limits,' he explains. 'I knew if we get a new goalkeeper, I must make sure he's not better than me. The pressure in that game was intense. I knew that I wanted to win this FA Cup. In the extra time there was a long ball and I had a one-on-one with Giggs and I hit the ball and he hit me. I went back and carried on for another half an hour including penalty kicks, and then after the celebrations on the pitch, which took another half an hour, I came into the dressing room, took everything off and went into the shower. And all of a sudden, I think it was Ray, screamed at me: "What happened?" I had such a knock, such a big thing, the size of a football. "What is that, is it broken?" And I didn't feel a single pain because I was so full of adrenaline. The tension was so much. The pressure was so high, because I knew Arsenal would take somebody else if I made a mistake in that game, and I didn't want to have that. I liked it. It pushed me to my limit.'

All managers must retain an element of mystique as far as their players are concerned. It is important to locate the right point between on the one hand being the boss, remaining detached and somehow untouchable, and on the other being a friend who is a supportive presence to the players and undeniably on their side.

For a man like Lee Dixon, who witnessed how Wenger handled the manager–player relationship from day one at Arsenal, and now observes him as a pundit, it is interesting how mutual admiration and affection were integral, but only up to a point which Wenger did not like to cross. 'I don't know him, although I have been around him for years,' says Dixon. 'I like Arsène a lot. He's got a really cool sense of humour, he can be really funny, he laughs at himself. He can be difficult at times – he is not very good at confrontation, which you would expect him to be. He finds it very difficult to front you up and tell you why he's dropped you because he cares about you, so it is very difficult for him to look you in the eye. He can be quite awkward at times in that very powerful position he's in.

'He made me a more rounded player and person. I've had lots of sit-down chats with him about any subject you want. He can talk about anything, in a knowledgeable way, not a know-it-all way. He is just so educated. So if you need to know what double glazing to have or what thermal tog to have on your duvet, he's your man!'

Although Wenger was mindful of not becoming too close to his players, he always wanted the best for them, and was very thoughtful about how they were in their general life. Despite the relentless demands on modern managers, Wenger made an effort to think person first, player second. Perhaps nobody felt that as strongly as Edu, who was grieving for his sister in his early days at the club and found every aspect of his life – personal and professional – immensely challenging.

'I would call Arsène Wenger my father in London,' he says. 'I didn't start very well but he wasn't worried about whether I was playing well or not on the pitch. He was worried about my life. He was worried about my father, my mum, my brother, if they were OK. He would say, "Don't worry about the technical way, I want to see you fine with your family, settled in London with the club, and after that I am sure you will be OK." He understood how hard it was for me and my family at that moment. He understood everything, all my needs, all my sadness. He was the guy who was fantastic for me.

'Arsenal was the club which helped me in the most difficult moment I ever had in my life. Arsène Wenger and the club had the patience to let me try to be good again. They let me have time to try to be myself. I think of that a lot. Sometimes you can arrive at a club, have problems, and the club can say, "Listen, go back to Brazil, stay there for a year, and then we will see how good you are." That wasn't the way they treated me. They kept me there, they gave me time, and I know how important they were for my life to help me recover. Every word I am saying is completely true. You can imagine for my mum, my father, without knowing anyone in London and not speaking English, Arsène Wenger and the club were fantastic. My parents still remember that. The club were always, always, thinking about my family. That is in my heart. It is not only a football club. That's why I always have Arsenal with me.'

PART THREE

APRIL 2004 – MAY 2014

Dennis Bergkamp stares intently across the table. 'What did Jens say about the game?' he asks. There was no way of sugar-coating this. Jens said he was very upset. 'Because he thought we didn't win it,' Bergkamp says, still amazed by the surreality of a storm cloud in the middle of the happy haze of league-winning euphoria. Bergkamp vividly recalls how Lehmann was in a blur of fury at White Hart Lane due to a sudden brain freeze which made him think Tottenham's late goal had tripped up Arsenal's quest. 'It happened twice in my career,' says Bergkamp, as if that makes this phenomenon even more remarkable. The first occurred when he was a seventeen-year-old with Ajax, playing one of his first European matches ever – a European Cup Winners' Cup quarter-final against Malmö. The Ajax goalkeeper Stanley Menzo got himself so befuddled about the away goals rule, thinking Malmö's solitary away goal counted for double, he was the only person in Amsterdam who thought Ajax were out when they were unquestionably through. 'He was so annoyed. "God damn, they are through,"' Bergkamp recalls, laughing. 'We said, "No, no, no, you can't keep adding, Stan!" but it was the heat of the moment. I thought of that when Jens did it too. He was so annoyed. Everyone was celebrating and he was so frustrated. "But Jens, we won it!" He turned around. "Really?" It was such a strange moment.'

When Pat Rice boarded the bus for White Hart Lane on 25 April 2004, taking up position next to Arsène Wenger, he did so with a unique perspective. Rice was the only man who had taken that particular journey in such extraordinary circumstances before. On

3 May 1971 he was the home-grown right back in the Arsenal party that crawled up the Seven Sisters Road knowing the size of the prize at stake: they could win the league in the most emotive of locations.

Crowds had thronged all day (there were at least as many loitering outside as managed to get in – an estimate of more than 100,000 in the area) which made for a crackling sense of occasion. The Tottenham perspective was summed up neatly by their captain, Alan Mullery. 'Arsenal have got as much chance of being handed the title by Spurs as I have of being given the crown jewels,' he said.

Rice doesn't even like to say the word Tottenham. When he made a poignant appearance at the Emirates in the spring of 2014, back on the touchline that had been his vantage point for so long after a grave illness, he couldn't help himself when he was asked and referred to that place in N17 as 'the dark side'. The habit was ingrained. For him it was the name that should not be spoken.

'As far as I was concerned, it was *the* game,' says Rice. 'It wasn't about winning the league, it was about beating Tottenham. And Sol was the same. People say to me, "What is it that you hate about Tottenham?" And I say it's not the players, and it's not the people that work at Tottenham, but it's Tottenham. When I was a kid, Arsenal weren't the greatest thing, but they had the great Tottenham side of 1960–61, Bobby Smith, Johnny White and all of them. So the Tottenham supporters gave the Arsenal supporters unmerciful stick and rightly so. It's come from that. There's something you take from having been a child. You never forget it.

'Going there in 2004, the players knew what they had to do. We knew that Chelsea were at Newcastle, and that they were playing early, but we knew we had to do our job. We had to get the players focused – not that they needed it – because news of what was happening at Newcastle was coming over all the time. You could feel it in the crowd as well. As far as getting the players to concentrate on the game, I don't think there was any trouble there.'

The mood on the bus was a little different compared to the expedition thirty-three years previously, because the atmosphere in this particular fixture had grown increasingly virulent over time. Compared to the 1971 occasion, where it is estimated the crowd was a fairly even split, with no record of any particular problems, this time there is one, heavily policed, segregated corner reserved for Arsenal. An all-seater stadium, the highest category security operation, and a greater sensitivity to the fact this rivalry can boil over underpinned a tacit understanding that if Arsenal achieved the result they required, sentiments could be complex and potentially alarming.

The players themselves were conscious of how volatile it was. 'I must admit we were a bit worried about Sol, of course,' Bergkamp says. He was not alone in retaining vivid recollections of the first trip to White Hart Lane after Sol Campbell had crossed the North London divide. November 17th 2001. Bergkamp shakes his head at what he saw that day. 'As a warm-up we used to run on the pitch. From side to side. He was running next to me and I could hear the whistles and everything. I was a little bit scared. I've never experienced that and when he came on the pitch the hate – there really was hate in people's eyes. They could do something to him, they could really hurt him.'

Keown describes how that situation was, in his eyes, the making of Campbell as an Arsenal player. It came a few months after his shock arrival. Arsène Wenger had called Tony Adams and Keown over to explain that Campbell was the future, he would play, and the two veterans would share duties alongside him. Those kinds of conversations are not the easiest to have, but Wenger went for honesty, and Adams and Keown were experienced enough to accept the situation. Keown learned to appreciate his new teammate's qualities. 'Once he got going he was unstoppable,' says Keown. 'And I felt like that train started to really fire when we went to Tottenham and he walked out. The windows had come in on the bus, I've never seen such anger towards us, and when you walked out onto the pitch you saw people snarling. They felt that they'd been sinned against, you know? And Sol really responded that day and he took off from that. We shared it with him, and we didn't like the Tottenham fans either, so when one of yours is the figure of hate you rally round.'

Campbell's own words for that day? 'Barbaric. I think they knew what I had to go through just to get through the game.'

★

During the week leading up to White Hart Lane in 2004, Bergkamp decides that the best way to deal with what is bound to be a significant moment for Campbell is by lightening the mood. Every time the centre half receives the ball in training, Bergkamp boos loudly. 'It's for you to get used to it in time for the weekend,' he tells Campbell, who ends up laughing along with everyone else.

Come match day, of course it's edgy, but there is welling excitement too, which builds as the news filters through that Chelsea, who kicked off a couple of hours before Arsenal, have faltered at Newcastle. The mathematics become simple: one more point is required. Arsenal need only to draw at Tottenham to clinch the title.

It's warm. Under the glow of spring sunshine, the players look controlled, purposeful, driven. Needless to say, in the tunnel they catch each other's eyes and share that contagious winning feeling that has been brewing for months. As they emerge into the arena, out of the protected interior and into the white light, white heat, white noise, Henry glances towards the red corner. He checks to see where his people are. He can't seem to take his eyes off that section of the stadium. They are applauding madly. He puts his hands above his head and claps back, staring at the Arsenal fans as if he wants to absorb all that support and turn it into power in his limbs.

Henry kicks off. Within the first fifteen seconds of one- and two-touch football, the ball zigzags between nine of Arsenal's players. Pass, pass, pass. Henry to Bergkamp to Vieira to Cole to

Campbell to Gilberto to Touré to Lauren to Parlour. Tottenham players are straining to get close enough to interrupt the flow. Once they do, they earn a corner. Pressure for Arsenal? Hardly. They break like forked lightning – sudden, explosive, blinding, a handful of connected bursts all at once. Tottenham are scorched.

When Johnnie Jackson takes the Spurs corner, Gilberto meets it and nods straight into Henry's path. In a heartbeat he is sprinting, full pelt. He is so fast, so elegant, he almost appears to be skating across the turf. He is not alone. Bergkamp accelerates just ahead of him to the left, Vieira motors through the middle, Pirès races along the right.

Four prongs of lightning detonate simultaneously from the same source. Henry clips a pass into Bergkamp, whose piercing cross zips across the grass for Vieira. One of those famously long legs extends. His right foot prods the ball home. The goal – in collective speed and execution – is breathtaking.

It's symbolic of everything Arsenal work on at the training ground. For a start, it shows how speed is of the essence – three of the four players involved take only one touch (Gilberto, Bergkamp and Vieira). The other, Henry, does his damage by his afterburner dribbling. The whole move is electric fast. Another element which resonates is how, watching it unfold, it's obvious how each player intuitively puts the teammate he passes to 'in his strength', as Bergkamp describes it. Nobody needs to break stride to be in absolute control of their body, the ball and the move. The synchronicity is beautiful.

Vieira remembers it so fondly, being a part of this shock of speed and power at such an important moment. 'You had the technique and quality of Dennis, the pace of Thierry and my power. This is one of my favourite goals. I really loved that,' he says.

Ahead after a mere three minutes, Arsenal are effortlessly comfortable, and craft another goal before half-time. The build-up again is a masterclass of the style they had perfected. When Lauren picks up the ball just inside the Arsenal half, he begins a spell of

Invincible

possession with a passing rhythm that is almost hypnotic. Seven passes, six different players involved. They cruise around and wear out the opposition, waiting for the moment to suddenly shift gear and zoom away. One of Wenger's catchphrases springs to mind: 'Progression with possession'. Suddenly they whir faster. Pirès canters forward and guides the ball to Bergkamp. With razor-sharp thinking, he pirouettes and slides the ball to Vieira, who has appeared galloping up the left. He tucks it back for Pirès to drill into the bottom corner. By the time the move gathers speed it is all one touch again. It is devastatingly effective.

Pirès defines that first half as 'perfect football'. He had a particular gift for scoring in North London derbies, and proudly announces the figures years later. 'Eleven matches, eight goals. Thank you, Spurs!' He laughs delightedly. 'I didn't do it on purpose. When you play and you are lucky enough to score in certain games, you are happy. It turned out to be against Tottenham.' He may give the impression it is slightly coincidental, but also he stresses that the most intense games inspired him. 'That day there was lots of pressure. To be champion, we needed at least a point, and you are going to your enemy. And that's war! Already when you arrive in the bus, *oy oy oy*. It was hot. You feel the pressure. I prefer it that way. It stimulates you. It gives you strength, energy, it's incredible. And those two goals . . .'

For Pirès to have an essential say in the finale is meaningful. A damaged cruciate had sidelined him for most of the run-in to the 2002 title, and he had experienced the bizarre insider-on-the-outside feeling of any player who misses the coronation for one reason or another, but his injury actually inspired a moment that will live with him for the rest of his life. He had been recuperating in France as his teammates finished off the job, and travelled back to Highbury for the celebrations still hardly able to walk. As he limped to collect his medal, all his teammates fell to their knees and bowed to him. He was blown away. It is one of his favourite images. His mother has the photograph. 'I have it in my mind,' he says, tapping his head.

Bergkamp felt they crystallized something important with that two-goal salvo at White Hart Lane, as if triumphing in this manner was the ultimate confirmation of their chosen style. 'Most of the time the games over there are difficult, really difficult,' he says. 'We never seemed to play our best game there, because of the rivalry and the emotion and everything that happens. But I remember at that time we could really play our game and that's something we were very proud of, because we created an Arsenal style of playing, and we could produce it at a championship-winning game, at your main rivals. Those goals were absolutely Arsenal.'

At half-time it feels weirdly relaxed. Arsenal are so obviously on top. Perhaps it is complacency, perhaps Tottenham deserve credit for doing everything they could to provide two moments to answer Arsenal back, but the second half changes course. Jamie Redknapp thumps in a goal from long distance with around half an hour to go. But it is a bizarre penalty incident three minutes into stoppage time that salts the Arsenal mood, just as they are mentally getting so close to the sweetest finale. When Tottenham have a corner, Robbie Keane tangles with Lehmann and both players end up in the net. When they get back up Lehmann tries to push Keane out of the way; Keane responds by shoving the goalkeeper over. The referee consults his assistants for what seems like an age, books both of them and awards a penalty. Keane scores, runs off into a celebratory cartwheel-come-somersault, and Lehmann is plunged into turmoil.

In 1971, the endgame had come with a pressure that was even more ferocious as Arsenal had to withstand a barrage from Tottenham which could have had devastating repercussions. An unyielding battle swung their way when Ray Kennedy arced a header in off the bar. But a 1–0 advantage had seldom been so precarious. Such were the mathematical complexities of the goal average system used at the time (a precursor to goal difference) that a goalless draw would have given Arsenal the title yet a score draw would have handed it to Leeds United. Tottenham duly threw themselves into the closing minutes. It was pure attrition as they endeavoured to sting the tale by turning their neighbours' joy into their own schadenfreude. Arsenal held their nerve.

A spontaneous surge, as half the crowd cascaded down from the stands and onto the pitch, turned Tottenham's home into the scene for their foe's unbridled celebration. There was such a multitude of red and white souls converging on the playing surface, eager to slap the backs of the players and hoist them on high, that the Arsenal captain Frank McLintock described it as a frenzy. 'So many thousands on the pitch and everybody wants a bit of you,' he said. 'I was up on somebody's shoulders and they all threw scarves round my neck . . . I was dying to get back to the dressing room to see my teammates because we were all separated for about half an hour. We just wanted to grab each other. All that training, all that hard work, all that running through ploughed fields. And then the reward. I loved that night. It was everything I wanted. Winning the championship at last and then bursting with love for your fellow players.'

All those years later, come the final whistle seconds after the restart following Keane's penalty, the echoes of the past became an essential part of the celebrations. The Arsenal contingent began to chant '71–2004'. All that is needed is a sequence of numbers, embracing two season finales, to distil decades of local rivalry.

While most of Arsenal's Invincibles are lost in the fever McClintock described, it is all a blur for Lehmann, distraught by his confused notion that the penalty had denied his team the title. It's strange how an unbeaten sequence to win a title is marked by these two emotionally loaded stoppage-time penalties confronted by Lehmann. One early on at Old Trafford. One towards the end at White Hart Lane. The first is missed, which brings the goalkeeper a sensation of wonderment. The second he is beaten, and left bewildered. With a fuzzy head he makes a beeline for the dressing room. The other player who exits immediately is Campbell. Removing himself from the microscope was a smart move. He doesn't want this moment to be about him. 'He went in to let everything settle down. If he is out there all the focus would be on him. With all the hassle he got before he has done well there,' observes Bergkamp.

Lehmann was not the only one who felt a draw was not the ticket – albeit for different reasons. 'I was a bit pissed off that we lost,' says Sol Campbell, looking back over this eventful afternoon, before breaking into slightly uncomfortable laughter.

Lost? But it was a draw, not a defeat.

'Well, for me it was a loss. It felt like a loss. Jens should have just kept it calm. I knew what Robbie was up to. He was trying to be niggly and back in and stamp on his toes and then Robbie did overreact and just went over like a gymnast. But he did well for his team at the time. He played for it and got the pen. Jens didn't have to push him, did he? I lost it in the changing room afterwards as well because I was so desperate to win. I wanted to win for other reasons that day. I wanted to just be complete. I wanted to almost finish people off. Not in a malicious way. I just wanted to win.'

Lehmann is wrestling with what has happened. He had become a target at set pieces throughout the season, once the league cottoned on to this combustible element in his game. 'It was funny because they were man marking me at corners, I'd never had that before,' he recalls. 'I remember a game at Manchester City where three people were standing around me, to prevent me from getting the ball, because they knew that was my strength, to get the ball, to catch it and to throw it forward, and then we were so fast and so dangerous. The referees in Germany are more restrictive to players who attack goalkeepers.' On this occasion, he gets wound up and becomes embroiled in one of those moments that supports the 'Mad Jens' nickname. It is a silly penalty award. He has to take the punishment.

'That was a very sad moment, actually,' he confesses. 'Robbie Keane came to me and all of a sudden he hit the floor, and the referee gave a penalty. People blamed me for that. Even the boss. I didn't know that we were champions when we went to the dressing room. So I sat there and I was really upset. And Sol came in and he was upset. He was upset with me. And the boss stood there mumbling something, and he wasn't really happy. "Jens, I've told you so many times to stop shovelling around with the opponents, and now we get a penalty for that." I said to him, "Boss, my fault." Somebody came in after a while and said, "Hey! Come on! We are champions, we are champions! Get out!" OK, I went out, cheered a little bit. But I was really upset.'

Meanwhile, out in the sunshine, the rest of the team are flying. It is Henry who leads the way. His intention, before the emotion of the situation overrules everything, was to try to keep cool at the end. 'Before the game the police came and said, "Do not celebrate if you win the title, we don't want to create chaos. If you score, don't run to the stand, we don't want any trouble. Be nice,"' Henry recalls. 'We argued a bit at the beginning: "What do you mean? If we win, we win. It doesn't matter if it's at Spurs or wherever." They insisted: "No, please. We don't want to have any problems." So we said OK.'

But the behaviour of one of his opponents on the day, Mauricio Taricco, riles him. The Tottenham full back reacts to Tottenham's late face-saving goal with a level of frenzied excitement that sits uneasily compared to the way Arsenal were instructed to tone everything down.

'I remember Taricco jumping around – and he got a cramp out of it by the way – jumping around and celebrating. Celebrating a draw. I looked at him. Are you kidding me? And he went "Yeeeahh!" I said, "You realize we needed a point to be champions. At your place." He was talking, talking. And I said, "Watch me after the game." If you act strong, be strong at the end. It's the rivalry, and we all understood what was at stake. But it was too hard for me to see them celebrating a draw when we're champions at their place. *OK. I guess we can celebrate, too. Now I am going to celebrate with my fans.*'

Henry is the unabashed band leader for the bellowing noise Arsenal's players wish to make at White Hart Lane. He looks like a man possessed. The stewards attempt to stop them from approaching their corner. Lauren is in furious argument with one of them. But the corner is calling the players with magnetic force, and there is no stopping Henry. He breaks through, bounces towards the away supporters, peels off his shirt to twirl around and around his head, and with the dam broken his teammates flood after him.

'Don't celebrate? That's a silly thing to ask,' says Ray Parlour. Touré couldn't wait to pop the champagne cork. 'When we see Thierry, a strong character, we thought, *OK, let's go*. We realized we needed to be happy,' he recalls. Edu still sounds astonished by what he experienced: 'I remember celebrating at the end of the game and the stadium was empty, except for only our section of fans. That moment stays in my mind, so enjoyable. That's what you strive for, moments like that.' Lauren reaches for the right words: 'It was intense. The happiness, when you win the league against your biggest rivals, we were just over the moon. We did at the time things that will stay there for ever.' Bergkamp simply relished it: 'The main thing on our mind was winning it over there. I thought it was a good game as well. The fans didn't care if we won or drew.'

Arm in arm, the team performs the cancan. They jump on each other. They cannot stop bouncing. They scream 'Champions'. Touré does acrobatics. Soon the tall, suited figure of Wenger comes back out from the dressing room, surveys the scene, and walks serenely across the pitch. His face doesn't crack until he gets to that corner. His players do not notice he is there at first. He watches them bounce, with the backdrop of the jubilant Arsenal supporters. Finally, he allows himself to break into an enormous smile before embracing his players one by one.

Once the bulk of the Tottenham fans have departed, and the team has gone to fetch Lehmann and Campbell, the party begins in earnest. The 2004 champions go back onto the pitch to relish their achievement in front of their own. An inflatable Premier League trophy appears and Cole, bare chested with Henry's arm around his shoulder, bounds upfield to plant it ceremoniously in the centre circle at White Hart Lane.

'One by one, roared on by the fans, each player held it up in the air with both hands as if it was the real thing,' recalled Cole. 'Then came my turn. I was the last one to do it. That's when the thought came to me: go and plonk this trophy slap bang at the heart of White Hart Lane. I ran, pelting across the pitch. Thierry and Ray Parlour followed. I got to the centre spot. I raised the trophy high above my head and brought it down like I was sinking a flag into enemy territory. It was like someone scored a goal. The Arsenal fans went crazy. It was the best moment.'

It's a poignant moment. Cole's connections to the club root back to boyhood. He grew up an Arsenal supporter. There is a famous photograph of him, beaming, as a ten-year-old on the pitch at Highbury, wearing an oversized red Arsenal soccer school T-shirt, cannon across his midriff, tucked into shiny replica shorts, with the league trophy (won by the team he idolized) in his hands. Cole was a gifted boy, and shone in the club's youth system. He developed into a tenacious and athletic full back, and he was so mobile when it came to joining Pirès and Henry to create the patterns to scare the daylights out of opposition defenders attempting to deal with that flank.

In the same way that Charlie George embodied something extra in 1971, as he was a local boy who used to watch Arsenal from the North Bank, Cole in 2004 represented that rare ideal of a genuine fan of the club transforming into a successful player. His brand of delirium on the pitch at White Hart Lane struck a particular chord. As a boy he held the silver trophy, pretending he was winning it for real. As a man he hoisted a plastic imitation trophy on the day he became a champion.

Vieira is full of fondness when he thinks of that. 'I always remember in the programme at Arsenal he was pictured when he was young in his Arsenal shirt with the trophy. Then he was doing it with the first team. That's fantastic. I love Ash. He's a good boy, a sweet boy. Ash was a guy everybody loved in the dressing room. He came through the ranks. Everybody wanted him to do well. For me he was going to be the next Tony Adams.'*

Bergkamp admired the way he pulled together the old-fashioned English heart and new style of continental football into one package. Even though he was young, he gave the older ones something to think about. 'It was great he was an Arsenal fan,' Bergkamp recalls. 'In a team like Arsenal, with all those foreign players, those sort of players can make the difference for you. I strongly believed through my time there that you have to have the English backbone – the spine, the philosophy, the strength, the power, you have to have that in your team. It was fundamental. Ashley was part of that. He knew what he had to bring to the game in spirit, yet funnily enough he was one of those players who could adapt to the European style of football. He would pass it to the midfield. He would have a one-two, even at the back, he would go down the line, sometimes be in the box. He adapted to the style of football which helped us, but it helped him as well, because he became a European-style player. He was fantastic.'

When Pirès reflects upon the trophies that graced that period, he believes the presence of the English players, who injected a

* Vieira later expressed his frustration that Cole left for Chelsea, and the future he envisaged for his friend at Arsenal never happened. 'I thought he was the best left back in the country. I tried to fight a little bit because I wanted him to stay,' he says. 'Ashley was supposed to be the next Arsenal captain. He was there from the youth, he grew up at the club, and to see him go, I was disappointed.'

gritty and gutsy undercurrent into the squad, was as fundamental to Arsenal's style as the imported flamboyance. 'I think our strength at the time was that we had English players,' he says. 'You come to England, because it's the best championship in Europe, everyone wants to come. But you *have to* keep the English guys. They are the core of the team, because they know the impact of these matches. If you don't have that any more, it's very difficult to win the championship.'

Like everybody else, Gilberto is lost in the moment. But a few days later the thought occurs that it could – and perhaps should – have been even more definitive. 'I thought we could have won that game and it would have been much, much better,' he confesses. 'Imagine to win the game at White Hart Lane and at that particular moment win the league? At the end of the day when you achieve what you planned for the season, it was fantastic. Even though we didn't win that game we won the league on that day, in that stadium. It meant a lot for us. Their fans got very upset, very angry, when we started to celebrate with our fans. They wanted to jump onto the field. At the end the security guys told us to go inside and we had such a big party in the dressing room, singing, dancing, jumping, celebrating. It was superb. What a fantastic atmosphere inside the dressing room.' That is their private moment. Nobody else but those players, and the staff, have an inkling really of the depth of feeling they share to have been roped together, trusting each other, as they climbed to the summit of their Everest.

For one Arsenal supporter, the chance to get a close-up view of this emotion was too good an opportunity to pass up. With tickets for the match like gold dust, Alan Davies had wangled his way into the press box as he had been writing celebrity football columns for *The Times*, and it turned out to be the only means of access on the day. As the press box in that stadium is just above pitchside, adjacent to the players' tunnel, he sensed an opportunity. Amidst the general hullaballoo Davies hopped over the wall and stood by the mouth of the tunnel.

'I was waiting there and the Arsenal fans aren't going home. Then the players came out. I am the first person there. I got an embrace off Keown. Henry came out and I got him to sign my programme. Didn't know what to say to him. Said, "You're a legend." Graham Stack came out, the reserve goalie for a long time. He had a nice character, seemed like one of life's enthusiasts. He was absolutely pumped. They couldn't contain themselves. I don't know how they stayed on the ground. Jumping, screaming. A real jobsworth steward decided to stop me going any further.

'And then I had to get out! I am recognizable as an Arsenal supporter and I'd been pretty rude about Tottenham several times that season in *The Times* so I knew I couldn't get onto Tottenham High Road; there were thousands of Tottenham supporters. I was standing there wondering how I was going to get home. My car was parked about half a mile away. Then I saw David Dein at the wheel of his Range Rover. I'd met him a couple of times. I tapped on his window. He wound it down. I said, "You couldn't give me a lift, could you?" He said, "Where?" I said, "Anywhere . . ." '

Out, out, into the night. Arsenal's players ride their bus out of there and back to the training ground. Almost everyone is euphoric. Lehmann still feels a little strange. It is only when they get back and Wenger has a word with him that he begins to make some peace with what has happened. 'It took two hours before we came to Colney, and then the boss said to me, "Jens I have to apologize, I saw it on telly, it wasn't your fault." Two hours.'

Did that equalizer really matter after all? He was a champion. They were all champions. And they had reached that point without losing a single league game. It was an extraordinary feat, unprecedented in modern football. Surely it was deserving of revelry to savour. 'I went out for about two days after that,' blurts Parlour. 'Don't tell Arsène Wenger!'

11

The Invisible Prize

Two little blonde girls are running around on the pitch at Highbury, laughing, as if they were playing chase in the back garden. One is seven-year-old Lea Wenger, the other eight-year-old Estelle Berg-kamp. There had been some discussion about whether the kids would be allowed onto the grass, when it was their dads who were meant to be the centre of attention, but they just pushed their way through and bounded on. The picture of innocence. They seem oblivious to what is going on around them, as an elated crowd of 38,000 onlookers bask in the glory and sing, in some kind of enchanted astonishment that it is really true: 'We are unbeatable.'

Step back a moment. It is the autumn of 2002. Arsenal Football Club, the defending champions of England, have good reason to feel cocksure. They carried the bulldozing form that had won them the Double the previous season into their new campaign. They are cruising along undefeated, playing with a bewitching blend of heavyweight power and delicate dexterity. A cluster of journalists make their way to London Colney, just off the M25, down a country lane, then an unassuming left turn into an unnamed driveway flanked by mature bushes to mask the private headquarters. The Arsenal training complex comes into view, a modern structure with a flowing shape, large expanses of glass overlooking the manicured pitches.

In through reception, up the stairs we go – not allowed straight ahead through double doors which lead into the inner sanctum – and through into the press conference room which is adjacent to the players' restaurant. There is the weekly version of *Waiting for*

Godot, before Wenger enters, sits down, and faces an interrogation which is usually respectful enough. Besides, at this point of his Arsenal career, he is buoyant, and gives the impression he is absolutely in control of the messages he wants to put out. He is very familiar with all the ploys as journalists try to coax what the trade calls 'a line' out of him, and far too clever to catch out unless he specifically wants to divulge one.

Arsenal are in rampaging form. They have just beaten Borussia Dortmund 2–0 in the Champions League (goals from Bergkamp and Ljungberg) and Wenger is looking ahead to a week that will bring these results: Arsenal 2, Bolton 1; PSV Eindhoven 0, Arsenal 4; Leeds United 1, Arsenal 4. They are hugely dominant and ooze authority. The questions are more or less routine, until the *Star*'s Dave Woods throws in one of those teasers that the press keep trying even though they are used to being knocked back.

Can you go a season unbeaten?

There is a pause. Woods recalls it quite vividly, as he noticed he could almost see Wenger's mind ticking over as he pondered whether to keep his real thoughts locked away, or open something of a Pandora's box.

'I remember he had been asked it quite regularly and he had said no, it was impossible,' says Woods. 'That day, as you often do, we tried the question one more time. I can almost see his face now. He had that 50/50 feeling. Should I say yes? Should I say no? I am not a mind reader but it seemed like he wasn't sure what he was going to say. He said yes, not in a hugely expansive way, but obviously it made headlines the next day.

'There was a buzz in the little huddle afterwards. In hindsight you can recognize how it was a major moment in that season. It was a moment that felt significant and unusual. You are aware someone has come out of their comfort zone. Most managers have boundaries about what they will and won't say. What goes on in the dressing room is out of bounds, and usually making what would seem an outlandish statement is out of bounds. I don't think he had made his mind up to say it in that moment. I think he felt, *Sod it, I may as well say it.* Managers of his level are always aware of how what they say can have a positive or negative effect on players.'

TREBLE-TALKING WENG TAUNTS RIVAL BOSSES: YOU LOT ARE TOO SCARED

by DAVID WOODS

ARSÈNE WENGER insists he isn't frightened to boast that Arsenal can finish the season unbeaten and win the Treble.

The Highbury boss also claimed other managers like Sir Alex Ferguson, Gerard Houllier and Claudio Ranieri also fantasised of pulling off such a remarkable achievement – but were too scared to say it.

He said: 'Do you think Man United, Liverpool or Chelsea don't dream such things?

'They don't say they can because they're scared of being made to look ridiculous. But it's not ridiculous because anything can happen in this job and I've a great belief in the squad and the team.

'I don't see why it's shocking for me to say we can win the Treble and go through the season unbeaten.

'Of course, if we lose people will say I've got a big mouth, but sometimes you have to take a risk.

'It's not impossible to stay unbeaten because it has been done by Milan.

'I've confidence in this team because we've not lost in 27 league matches and scored in 45 straight Premiership games.

'If I was to say I didn't have confidence, people would call me a liar.

'We know it's going to be difficult, but if you've the right attitude you can improve. And I think this team can improve.'

David Beckham famously predicted last season Manchester United could remain unbeaten – but they lost nine Premiership matches and won nothing.

Even Sam Allardyce, manager of Arsenal's opponents today, Bolton, admitted: 'The way they're playing, it's going to be extremely tough for anybody to catch up with them.'

Daily Star

A cluster of other managers, players and pundits were quick to join the naysayers. John Giles had a more thoughtful perspective than most as he had experienced his own manager saying something similar of a famously unyielding Leeds United side in the 1970s. 'The words conjured the memory of my old Leeds boss Don Revie, with tears in his eyes, saying: "We can do it – we can be the first team not to be beaten. We can shock the game." There are differences, however, in the statements of the two. Revie made his in the pain of a dramatic loss to Sunderland in the 1973 FA Cup final and he made it privately. Wenger did it in the open and after a glorious Double triumph. There is no doubt Wenger has piled pressure on his brilliant team. A season without a slip, without a game when things go wrong, would be a freak of nature. It's the toughest call in the game.'

Even Pat Rice, Wenger's right-hand man, felt a little uncertain. 'Arsène came out and said that this team can go undefeated, and I thought inwardly, *Well that's a big statement to actually say, because no one's done that, no one at all.*'

Inside the Arsenal dressing room, Keown was mildly alarmed by these headlines. 'The manager had gone public and said we could go unbeaten all season. I remember thinking, *Has he lost the plot?* We don't want that discussed publicly. But sometimes, and I always believe this very strongly, you have to talk about things, it has to be discussed first before it can become a reality. And actually when the manager said that, subconsciously it was, like, *Is this achievable?* But we don't want to wave a flag at ourselves, because everyone was trying double hard to stop us. And that's when it blew up against Everton with Rooney's goal.'

And so it all came crashing down, down, down.

Scorn was poured all over Wenger for daring to propose something so radical, so apparently arrogant. Rooney's goal was like some sort of medieval punishment for having such outrageous notions. There was an air of burn-the-witch glee from those who felt the very idea of an unbeaten season was worthy of contempt.

★

How curious that one season later, with the title secured and four games remaining, that prospect of an unbeaten season presented itself as eminently possible. Looking at the remaining fixtures – Birmingham, Portsmouth, Fulham and Leicester – it wasn't even just possible. It was probable. Had Wenger's mad prophesy been right all along, but just a year premature?

The morning after the night before (or perhaps a couple of mornings after a couple of nights in Parlour's case) Arsenal's players turned their attention to a new ambition. Up until that point it had all been about the title. With that vital mission completed, addressing a new challenge was not easy. They had crossed the line of the marathon, all the pumping adrenaline and momentum and concentration naturally wound down, and it was as if the next day the starting gun for a 10,000 metres fired.

The games should not have been ultra-complicated for undefeated champions. Birmingham (home), Portsmouth (away), Fulham (away), Leicester (home). As it happened, none of those opponents had anything riding on their results against Arsenal. They finished tenth, thirteenth, ninth and eighteenth, respectively. Three confirmed mid-table teams, and one already relegated. It was more or less holiday time.

The trouble for Arsenal, though, was that they felt like their bodies were already halfway to the beach, even though their minds knew they had to be absolutely committed to the job in hand.

Bergkamp explains how hard it was to re-spark their motivation. 'It was a big challenge, because you've got what you wanted, but then suddenly you can write history,' he says. 'To be on a high, then drop, you've got players who feel a few pains, thinking already of the national team games or whatever, that's hard. I remember for myself it only became a target when we got closer to the end. The ambition is to win the trophy, you win the trophy, and then you want to go on. Let's do this now. But for your body that's different.'

Ljungberg articulates how strange it is when the body and mind are not on the same wavelength. 'The important thing is always to win the trophy. It's about winning, not an unbeaten season. But we all decided we wanted to try and achieve it and be invincible. But that is hard, because whatever people say, when it's not life or death to win that game, to win the trophy or not, you go down a few per cent. If I was a betting man, I would bet for an upset. It's not as easy as it looks.'

Pirès puffs out his cheeks as he recalls that quartet of matches which would make or break the fresh aspiration to complete the season without defeat. 'You tell yourselves there are four games left, we *have* to make an effort,' he says. Touré adds he felt it was 'stressful'. Vieira found the matches strangely complex. 'At the back of our minds we wanted to do it, once it was all over the TV and that kind of thing. But we didn't want to put any more pressure on our shoulders.'

It was Henry who spoke about it most intently. His role as a leader was enhanced as the season reached its climax. He kept talking about what they needed to do, as if that would help to ignite muscles to work harder and faster. As Campbell recalls, 'He was the only one who was really thinking about it all the time. Thierry is always talking. He just wants to know everything and tell you about everything.' Henry agrees with that, as striving for more is some kind of fuel for him. 'I'm always the guy that is not too happy with what's happening,' he says. 'I am always trying to go further and trying to reach the maximum of what we can reach.'

But even he found motivation a complication as they basked in the glow of that title triumph in that most special setting. 'You know how it is. How many times have you seen the team who is champion, and the next game they are drawing 5–5 or losing 4–0? Because it's like a boxer. A boxer doesn't go in the ring to have fun. A boxer goes in the ring to kill. But what is there to kill? We are champions. We got caught into thinking, *You know what, it's Birmingham, we are champions, do we need to beat Birmingham today? Is it going to change anything?*

'The first game after Tottenham, everybody was like that. Remember, we had won the title *at the Lane*. If you are an Arsenal fan, what is going to top that? Then you go through the motions against Birmingham. It was one of the most boring games I have ever played. I don't even know if I touched the ball.'

The game was mind-numbingly dull, and finished goalless. But ultimately, those four games just needed crossing off, one by one. If they were not memorable, that was fine, as long as the run was sustained. As Henry recalls, 'I remember the boss coming every morning and saying, "Guys you are maybe going to be able to do something amazing. Are you realizing?" And we are like, *We are champions*. I remember Patrick looking at me and saying, "There is no fight. I need to have a fight. I need to know that we need to get some points." We were not realizing what was happening.'

Rebuilding momentum was a peculiar task precisely because the circumstances were not normal, not something a footballer would expect to face. Henry sums it up poetically by describing the Invincible season as an 'invisible prize'.

The goal was abstract, he says: 'There was no prize. At the end, what are you getting? You are fighting for something you will never see. We didn't know they were going to make a golden trophy. It hadn't been done before. We were fighting for a place in history. Something that has never been done before and may never be done again but there was no silverware or medal for it. It was kind of weird. I guess it was something we would look back on and think *Wow,* but at the time I don't think we realized how big a deal it actually was.'

With Birmingham chalked off, next up came Portsmouth. The scene of that FA Cup masterclass a couple of months before, where they had inspired that memorable ovation from the Pompey fans, was now a daunting hurdle. Arsenal trailed at half-time. Wenger reckoned the team were 'a bit nervous'. Henry remembers this one because the pressure began to boil over. 'I remember we all had an argument with each other in the dressing room because we were getting hammered in the first half. I was pretty vocal. Jens was vocal. Yakubu scored, we were 1–0 down, and we looked at each other: *WHAT ARE WE DOING?*'

Lehmann recalls the scene. 'It was one of these typical English games, 1–0 down, terrible pitch, opponents really fighting. Thierry said to me at half-time, "Jens, why didn't you save it?" I was upset. Then in the second half I made some good saves, and we scored, so we got a draw there.'

José Antonio Reyes was the saviour as he found the perfect moment to volley his first Premier League goal in a game that ended 1–1. He stepped up again to ease anxiety in the penultimate game of the campaign, a narrow 1–0 win at Craven Cottage.

Reyes was an enigma. In hindsight, his arrival was significant in that it demonstrated how powerful Arsenal felt at that time. They bolstered their squad from a position of strength, and at the same time sent out a message in successfully prising away from La Liga one of the most coveted young players in Spain. A move to Real Madrid or Barcelona was expected, but Arsenal in the peak of that era felt able to attract the best around. David Dein recalls how the Sevilla fans blocked the road so the car carrying their boy away couldn't leave. It was a big deal in every sense.

Although his Arsenal career would falter, and be filed away as a disappointment, his role in the Invincible season was significant. At a time when others were physically and psychologically fatigued, he popped up with critical goals to keep the unbeaten sequence intact.

Lauren, having grown up in Seville just like Reyes, tried to be some kind of mentor. But this homespun Andalusian found adjustment almost impossible. 'I remember speaking to Steve Rowley, the scout, before we signed him and I was telling him: "You have to sign him by himself. Don't bring his family." The big point about José, if I am talking in an honest way, was the family was against his progression. He's the kind of guy you have to leave alone, and take him out of the protection of his family. You can extrapolate that onto the football pitch – he is a fantastic player but is not consistent, because he has been overprotected. If you see the guy, he was unbelievable. You can see the movement. He comes, he goes, he finds space. He had the movement of a top player. The problem for José was mentally he was too weak to be consistent.'

Vieira admired his 'pure talent', but accepted that it was just one of those cases where player and club couldn't quite bond. 'What a fantastic player he was. But he found it really difficult to adapt, coming from Sevilla, where at four o'clock you go for lunch. In London at four o'clock you are at home because it's dark already.' Vieira laughs heartily. 'The Premier League was not for him. He needs to live in the sun, shorts and T-shirt all day.'

Reyes and Arsenal might have been an imperfect match, but his goals, and his presence when the regulars were so tired, made him an important member of the supporting cast of the Invincible story.

Those unremarkable games at the end, curiously, capture the spirit of the season for Henry more evocatively than the famous ones that felt so pivotal. It was the unexceptional moments that glue together the exceptional whole. The ground-out results when it was so tough, so close, so imperative, to plough on, mean so much to him.

'I know people always remember the massive ones, the famous goals. Old Trafford, the Liverpool game, whatever. But I remember Portsmouth at home,' he says pointedly. 'We were getting outplayed and Robert somehow got a penalty. I don't even remember how, but never mind. No disrespect to any other game we had, but that's why I always say: "You've got to make sure you don't lose against Portsmouth." That year, we didn't beat Portsmouth home or away. I remember Leicester away, Gilberto Silva scored and we drew. I remember Birmingham after we clinched the title at the Lane, at home. Because we could have blown it.'

★

One game to go. Ninety minutes from an achievement nobody except Wenger ever gave much credence to. Funnily enough, the only person in English football who even came close in the modern age was his predecessor at Arsenal. In the 1990–91 season, George Graham's team lost only once, and that in itself was regarded as some kind of miracle.

Outside Highbury the vibrations are celebratory and expectant. Leicester, Arsenal's opponents on the day, have been relegated. Nothing to play for? Not quite. Depending on results they could finish bottom, or third from bottom, which could be worth in excess of £1 million to them. That detail had been impressed upon the players by the club's financiers. Their team coach arrives, they head through the Marble Halls to the away dressing room, and the players wait for coach Micky Adams to give them the usual pep talk. Only on this occasion, he does something different.

'We sat down expecting the team written down on A1 flipchart paper, with all the strengths and weaknesses of the other team and what we would try to exploit,' recalls the Leicester striker James Scowcroft. 'On the day the manager just wrote the Arsenal team down and said, "All the best with this lot," and walked out. There was no point going through it, saying you'd better watch Thierry Henry and his pace in behind, watch out for Robert Pirès dropping off or Dennis Bergkamp getting the ball to feet or Patrick Vieira's runs from deep. We knew the team inside out because so much had been said about them. They did not have a weakness.'

To Leicester's pleasant surprise, the game does not pan out as predicted. 'Arsenal didn't seem that bothered,' remembers

Scowcroft. 'It was like a typical end-of-season game. We were able to start really well and were 1–0 up at half-time.'

Back in the home dressing room, the players are feeling tense. 'Sheesh,' exhales Bergkamp. 'One–nil down and we're all like, *Oh come on. Let's put the effort in.*' Gilberto, usually the epitome of calm, was annoyed. 'It was quite a strange game. It was like everyone in the team had lost their power. We had no energy,' he remembers. 'It was quite hard for us to come back into the game. I was frustrated. *Why are we going to lose this game? I don't want to lose this game! This is the last game of the season, after being unbeaten until then – why?! Let's change. Let's do something.* This was when the winning mentality came back on.'

Two passes from Bergkamp make the difference. The first, scooped deliciously to meet Cole's burst into the box, earns Arsenal a penalty. Henry steps up. Normally, he shows a level of composure and coolness that looks effortless from the penalty spot. This time, his mind is whirring with the significance of this single kick.

'You know what? It didn't look like we were going to score,' remembers Henry. He drops his voice, and implores what he felt at the time. '*Oh, come on. Not now* . . . In my mind I was thinking, *If I score the penalty now, we win. And if I miss?* You know when things start to go wrong. It's true. I felt a bit of pressure. Knew I'd better score this one. At least we would be drawing the game and I didn't see Leicester scoring another one.' He places the ball on the spot, winds back like a coil for his run-up, springs forward and drives in the equalizer. It is a mighty moment.

Scowcroft retains an image of how Henry's effort levels had a big impact on the game's flow. 'When we were leading, as a Leicester player you are thinking, *This is going to change any minute.* I can remember Arsène Wenger standing up and saying to Henry, "Come on Thierry! We need more!" And he just went from first gear to fifth gear and I have never, ever, seen a player do this before. One minute he was just strolling around in the sunshine, nice touches, and he sped through his gears to a level where he changed the game off the top of his head in the space of ten minutes.'

Arsenal up their game, and then Bergkamp works his magic once again. In possession in the middle of the pitch, he spots Vieira motoring forward and measures his pass to perfection. The ball pierces between five Leicester defenders, as if being guided by a laser beam. Vieira powers onto it, dinks the ball past the goal-keeper, and slips a crowning goal into an empty net. 'I remember that pass to Patrick,' smiles Bergkamp. 'Every goal he scored was from my pass, I keep telling him.' Vieira knows the joke oh so well by now. 'Dennis always tells me that he's the one who made my career. Because of that goal!' He breaks into nostalgic laughter.

For Henry, the identity of the scorer of that goal is meaningful. 'He was instrumental that year, and what I love about that year is that he scored the last goal,' he smiles. 'That sums it up for me. It couldn't have gone better than that.'

There is only one piece of unfinished business, and that is to get Keown onto the pitch as he needs one more appearance to reach the ten required to qualify for a championship medal. Keown is anxious. Although Wenger has promised he will make the substi-tution, he has a habit of forgetting these things. 'I could never rely on his eyes,' he grimaces. 'When we played at Portsmouth, they had an electronic scoreboard and it was saying eighty-eight and he thought it was eighty-three or something and I was saying, "Boss, there's only two minutes to go, for Christ's sake get me on." He said, "No it's not." That was how it was. I actually said to the ref-eree before the Leicester game, "I'm going to be coming on before the end of this game, don't bloody blow for time before, because the gaffer keeps forgetting."'

For Parlour, the situation is simply irresistible. 'It was only a little bit of fun,' he says, face creased up with mischief. 'I sat with Sylvain Wiltord and Edu and it was just a wind-up, really. Five minutes to go, I always remember Martin saying, "Do you think the boss'll put me on?" So, I said, "Martin, warm up in front of him. Go and warm up." So he takes his bottoms down, warms up right in front of Arsène Wenger. The boss is going, "Get out the way, Martin." So, he starts running up and down the line, they're all singing his name in the North Bank. I think to myself, *This will be the best wind-up I have ever done.*'

Parlour then takes off his track-suit as if he is preparing to be sent on as the final substitution. He tells Keown Wenger has told him to get ready to go on. 'I thought he was going to kill me,' he says. 'I've never seen Martin sprint so fast down the line, and Martin has got Wenger round the neck. He's strangling the manager and I always remember him saying, "Get off, Martin! Get off!" I thought I'd gone too far with this one. After the game, Wenger pulled me over and said, "What did you say to Martin? He tried to kill me on the side of the pitch." I told him what I did and he said, "That's the funniest thing I've ever heard." But Martin was a great character and he did go on for his tenth appearance and he deserved it.'

ARSENAL 2–1 LEICESTER CITY, 15 MAY 2004

While his immortals can-canned in the sun, Arsène Wenger stood awkwardly in front of his dugout and didn't know where to look. The mastermind behind one of the most remarkable feats in English football couldn't take it in at all. 'I was shocked,' he said. 'My dream was always to go through a whole season unbeaten. It's beyond belief. Not many managers can say they did that.' The last in this country, Preston's Major William Sudell, is long dead.

Arsenal's achievement may not make them 'great' in everyone's opinion – those who define greatness only by European Cups, back-to-back titles, and triple cartwheels on the way to every goal – but it is staggering in its own right. Won 26 drawn 12 lost 0. Not once in 38 games of high tempo, highly charged Premiership football did Arsenal lose their nerve, their quality, and most astonishingly of all they didn't even have a moment when they were crushed by a bad bounce or a bad decision throughout nine months of competition. 'We are unbeatable,' chorused the North Bank to the Clock End as the Premiership trophy was carried on to the turf.

Some 1,060,444 fortunate souls who have clicked through the Highbury turnstiles will not easily forget the procession that was 2003–04. Nor will a squad of players who were written off nine months ago as broken, bruised, bottlers.

They might have even lost their first game of the campaign when they trailed to Everton and found themselves down to 10 men early on. The resolve they summoned that August afternoon spurred them on once more yesterday when Leicester overturned all the expectancy 115 years of history drenched over Highbury. A penalty from the season's outstanding performer, Thierry Henry, and a match-winner from the team's heartbeat, Patrick Vieira, saw them through.

The Champions were alarmed to find themselves behind after a moment of genius from Frank Sinclair (it's not often those words appear in the same sentence) ripped up the form book 26 minutes in. The burly defender cantered over the halfway line and floated a Bergkampesque cross on to Paul Dickov's head. The little Scot was presented with the simple task (helped by another lesson from the Jens Lehmann school of eccentric goalkeeping) of nodding one of the season's unlikeliest goals into an empty net. Champions Arsenal 0 Relegated Leicester 1. As a wag piped up: 'Invincible, my Arse!'

In keeping with recent performances since the title was clinched at White Hart Lane, Arsenal found it difficult to raise themselves. Ian Walker was called into action only twice in the opening half, tipping Henry's whooshed free-kick over the crossbar and bravely smothering Robert Pirès's rasping drive before the onrushing Henry and Freddie Ljungberg could pounce on the rebound.

Would you believe Paul Durkin's half-time whistle interrupted the sound of Leicester fans ole-ing as they passed the ball merrily around?

Arsenal asked some stern questions of themselves in the dressing room. Now was not the time to throw away the best part of 3,500 minutes of undefeated football. Wenger described the atmosphere as a 'revolt' and Arsenal emerged invigorated . . .

Wenger is already wondering how to follow such a distinguished Premiership campaign. Is this as good as it gets? 'Well, to improve on this in the championship is nearly impossible, but we can win new trophies. I still have problems to realise what we have achieved. I can only say how proud I am of my players.'

Yesterday, as Campbell and Henry took some time out from the celebrations and lay in the centre circle, chatting, they looked as if they didn't have a care in the world.

Even Wenger began to let himself go a little during the lap of honour, when he was joined by his seven-year-old daughter Lea, who danced around the pitch with Daddy's medal on and hurled plastic trophies joyfully into the crowd. 'At that age, to win trophies is easy,' smiled Wenger.

Observer

Nowadays it is routine for players to bring their children onto the pitch for an end-of-season lap of honour. Then it was less commonplace. For Bergkamp, who was always keen to keep his life away from the pitch private, the moment symbolized a perfect synergy between his professional life and family life. It was a thank you of sorts for the sacrifice he felt his wife and children had to make for him.

'The combination with family there, with my eldest one Estelle there, was amazing,' he says. 'I think there was some talks about whether we would put children on the pitch or not. Then suddenly the daughter of the coach was there, so somewhere Estelle got pushed forward. *You can go now too.* That's a great feeling. People forget what happens behind the scenes. A little example, when I played on the weekend, the day before, after training in the afternoon I would like to rest, take a few hours' sleep, but that's fairly difficult when you've got two or three little children in the house. So my wife would take them to Monkey Town to play in those hours. It shows that in a way you're all working for the same thing. Why are the kids in school in England? Because Daddy is working in England. Somehow, it's my life, and they drag along. And then in those moments when you win trophies, you realize it is not only for me, it is for them as well. My wife compliments me that I could always separate those two while in the car, driving home, with some music on. But as soon as I walk in the door at home, I would leave the victory or the loss behind, I would be a dad not a footballer.'

During that hour or so of Highbury celebrating in the early summer's evening, the colours around the place seemed somehow more vibrant than ever. Grass the richest green, red and white glowing in the sun, the cream of the stadium's facade, the deepening blue sky above, and of course the shiny silver of the trophy.

Henry sat in the centre circle, looking all around to record this scene in his mind. Campbell joined him. The speed of the season slowed down. They seemed to be relaxing in a state of the calmest contentment. 'I was taking it all in,' says Campbell. 'Because it's just a magical moment. These scenarios or situations, they don't come round, you know? In any business, any line of work, any sport, there's always going to be a moment when you say: *Wow*. On the top of the mountain . . . You treasure it and you'll remember it for ever.'

Henry feels these moments can be abruptly cut short because of the relentlessness of the football calendar. He felt compelled to try to pause to remember, to really soak up the feeling. 'When you finish the season you have to go and play in a Euro, or the World Cup, or sometimes you have the Confederations Cup or go to play some friendly with your national team,' he explains. 'After the summer people are not going to care if you are champion or not when you return, back to business, and the league starts again. So that's why I sat down there, Sol came, and I said, "Let's look, let's enjoy it." We don't have time to enjoy anything when we play. It is kind of weird. You go around, you have some interactions with the fans – it was a lot that day. I wanted to take everything in. I wanted to see everything. We stayed there five minutes or so, it seemed like an eternity . . .'

Even the Leicester contingent took a moment to observe the atmosphere. 'We came back in, and a couple of bottles of champagne found their way into our dressing room,' remembers Scowcroft. 'I had a shower and got dressed in my Leicester tracksuit and came back out to sit on the mini-wall by the dugout to watch the celebrations. Those couple of minutes after Arsène Wenger lifted the trophy were as good an atmosphere as I had ever seen.

'I've got a really good friend who is an Arsenal fan and Barclays made these identical medals but made out of chocolate so I grabbed one for him as a souvenir. I'd arranged to go back with my parents after the game. Normally you would get a couple of hundred people outside by the time you leave an hour after the game and the streets would be pretty deserted but we couldn't get a taxi as the streets were packed. We had to walk to Highbury and Islington tube. I still had my Leicester tracksuit on and my kit bag and this stupid chocolate medal around my neck. Everyone was happy and drunk in the street and looked at me. It was such a long walk. The longest walk ever.'

North London was unmistakably red.

When he explains how Arsène Wenger foretold it all, Henry sounds awestruck. 'I always remember he came in the dressing room and I said, "Boss, why did you have to say that? At least wait until there is five games to go . . ." He called it, though. There is a phrase I love. I saw it on the internet, so I'm not going to claim it. "Amateurs call it genius. Masters call it practice." It's nothing to do with genius. He worked with that team, he knew what that team could do more than what the team knew about itself. For him, seeing it in practice and working with us, he knew we could do it. That's not a vision. It's not like he woke up one morning and he said, "Hey, that team can stay unbeaten." If someone else who didn't work with us, see us every day in training, know our full potential, came out with it I would say "That guy is crazy." But Arsène saw it and he knew.'

12

Reflections

Some years after the Invincibles, Patrick Vieira was approached to take part in an advert for a beer company built around a collection of crème de la crème footballers. During the negotiations, they felt obliged to broach a delicate subject. Would Vieira have a problem with the concept of him jumping for a ball with Ruud van Nistelrooy? He was relaxed about it, so set off for Prague where the advert would be shot. They were the only two footballers there that day. The pair shook hands, and during one of the breaks in filming conversation turned to that momentous collision at Old Trafford in 2003. 'We talked and we laughed about it,' recalls Vieira. At the end of the day, they hugged and went their separate ways.

Lehmann: Sometimes there are times when something perfect is happening. Of course, the environment always determines if something like that could happen or not. We hadn't been favourites to be champions that season. There was Manchester United, there was Chelsea, stuffed with money. Then Arsenal ranked third, without any chance. And then not having made any signings apart from a mad goalkeeper. When I signed, the back page of *The Times* wrote that 'the mad German is coming'. That was probably the perception. But it turned out for me to be a fantastic move, I was playing in a fantastic team, fantastic coach, fantastic environment. I can't think of one player who was there who doesn't like to come back to watch games, to be there.

Lauren: The biggest thing was that we didn't think about being unbeaten. We just thought: *Win tomorrow, win tomorrow.* Win the next game – that's it. Wenger was the key because he managed to get people from different generations, ages, with different ambitions, and put them together to make it work. At that time we were all international players, all playing in a European Championship or African Cup of Nations, so we all wanted to play. To keep the balance between us was very difficult. There were many situations where Wenger had to keep calm. His manner, and the way he manages the club, was very important at the time. He knows what is going on all around the squad.

Touré: When we reached the end of the season, the celebration at Highbury was amazing after the Leicester game. It was a family, everyone inside the stadium, I will always remember that. Everyone was on the moon. Looking back, I thank God. I was young, fresh, powerful and enthusiastic. I felt like I could run and run every day. I heard I have the record of trainings without missing a single day. I was so happy and the condition was so great. Everything came naturally. But I did feel I was in the right place at the right moment with the right people. That's God again.

Campbell: Not many players in the world can actually say: *We beat a record*. Preston North End had done it, but when those records began, there were only twelve teams in the league. You say to yourself: *It just doesn't happen all the time*. We all wanted to give our all. You know, that's the beautiful thing about sport. You do find out who's around you when you are up against it. I started this routine before games where we would high-five, hug, bang. *Let's be together today*. We were together.

Cole: None of us can grasp the scale of what we've done, how mentally strong we've had to be. Football don't get much better than this: stood on this pitch, at home, in front of this family of teammates, staff, and fans. There is no better time to be an Arsenal player, no better time to be an Arsenal fan. It was an incredible season where we clicked like the slickest machine. Our belief was the twelfth man running around in a red and white shirt.

Pirès: The mission was finished. The first goal was to win the league, and then there was another goal, to finish without losing.

For us it was the perfect season. If you win without losing the slightest match, above all in England, you have done something very strong. That's why we were able to make an impression everywhere in Europe. Even today people talk about the Invincibles. It's great that we entered into the history of the club.

Vieira: That final day was perfect. We won, we were unbeaten, it was a lovely day, you just want to enjoy it. Now I am retired I realize how important and big it was. You look around and see how difficult it will be for someone else to do it. It is not a normal thing. Everything you go through, so long, so hard, so difficult, with injuries and sendings off and suspensions . . . Anything can happen. It never crossed my mind we would go through the season unbeaten. We didn't plan it. I didn't think once we could do it. Luck can be part of it, but everything – the connection of the players, our togetherness – was perfect.

Gilberto: It's difficult to find the exact words. The best word that describes it is the phrase *We were invincible*. It was marvellous the way we performed that season, the way we respected the game, the way we could look into the eyes of each other with the feeling we were going to win. There is nothing better for a Brazilian than to win the World Cup. This was the same feeling. Especially when you talk about English football, how hard it is to play in England, to understand the way the game is played. I am very happy, when I look back on my career and my life, to have these achievements. Arsenal for me was like big school. When I see something in football I always turn back to Arsenal and the impact the club made on my life, my way of thinking about football. You can see in my eyes how I feel. I don't need to say a word – my feeling comes across in my eyes and this is the feeling I will have for the rest of my life.

Ljungberg: It's been more since I retired that I notice how big it is. People say what is it like to do that? For me it's all about the trophies, so I was a bit surprised. So now I would say I'm more proud of it than I was when I played. No question about it. People bring it up often. Pat Rice said it was about a trophy every year. A trophy, a trophy, a trophy. It wasn't about being invincible. I was just so proud to be with my teammates, and I felt we had a fantastic team.

Bergkamp: Now every season you look back and you see all the other teams struggle to go unbeaten, in every competition, in every league, and then you realize. Wow. With all respect in Scotland or Spain there are only two or three teams who could be champions. But in England there are probably five or six teams every season who could win the league, so if you can do that, go unbeaten, it makes it more special. I truly believe that with each year that passes you realize even more how special it was. It's not like all the other teams were rubbish. It's really a big achievement. Definitely. I'm proud of it.

Henry: We were all on the same page. Whatever it was – whether it was football, when we had to argue, when we didn't have to argue, whatever we had to do – we were always on the same page at the same time. You need to have the guys like we had. Great players. Winners. Men. You need to have a great boss around also. You need to have the right combination. Definitely, it does help if you have born winners around you. We all know that obviously we didn't win everything, but that year in the league, we had that. Everybody knew exactly what we had to do going on the field. We all trusted each other, and still do now by the way. You need to have that togetherness, that commitment. The boss didn't have to tell us much sometimes because we were all competitive and all winners. You could feel that nothing was going to happen to us. The thing that I said after the Leicester game – and I maintain it – is *When you're first, you're first*. The first team who did it in the modern game was us. Whoever does it now, they'll only be second.

Edu: When time passes you feel things are more important. People remember that time and appreciate that time we had. For me to be part of it, I don't have the words to explain what it means. To know the people I got to know so well, it was so nice. Maybe you have to live that experience to know how amazing and enjoyable it was.

Parlour: We had a lot of adulation afterwards. People were still talking about it for weeks. Even now, I'm very proud of being involved in that sort of team. And I certainly don't think it will get beaten. We had a load of off-days, I promise you now, where we could have lost. I don't know what it was in the make-up of the team but we always knew we could get a goal, we could get back in the game. I mean some of the games were awful, seriously. But we always had that belief we could get through and I think that's so important. Winning is a habit. You get used to that winning habit and you love it so much that when you go a goal down, you stick together.

Keown: I wanted to get on in the last game so I could get that medal. As I look back, I was thirty-six going on thirty-seven. That wasn't a bad effort to get ten games in a team that achieved that. I know I was involved. And I enjoyed every minute of it. Everybody had their moment, everybody had this belief. I remember Arsène saying he could go to war with this group.

Dein: We've been blessed at Arsenal, especially since Arsène's arrival. People take for granted being in the Champions League, playing some of the best football in the world, with some of the most gifted players. So we've been spoilt in many respects. Seeing our own team, the team that we love, the team that we support, going the whole season unbeaten was nothing other than sublime.

Rice: It's immense, you wonder will it ever be done again. Because there are so many players coming into the game from abroad because of the money situation. All the teams now have all got big players, it's such a pressurized thing, that I just can't see anybody else doing it. The feeling at the end was relief. Someone said to me the other day, how many FA Cup finals have you played in? I said I've played in five. They asked which one I enjoyed the best. I hated every one of them. When we won, after the game you felt great, absolutely terrific, but during the actual match I hated every bloody one of them. I just felt relief at the end of the final game against Leicester. It was immense. You think that you've made history. This will go down for my children, for my grandchildren. There was such a respect for each and every one of those guys. And it wasn't just from each other, it was from the staff and the supporters. Everybody loved them.

Wenger: It was my dream. No matter what happens now I have achieved one of my dreams.

13

Bulldozed

The image that most often comes to Thierry Henry's mind when he thinks about Arsenal has nothing to do with the Invincibles. He drifts back often to the summer of 2006, an end-of-season game against Wigan Athletic, with Champions League qualification on the line and the situation intensified because Arsenal had to win and hope Tottenham didn't if they were to hurdle their rivals for a top four finish. An afternoon dripping with emotion saw Wigan take the lead only for Henry to reply with a hat-trick. He bent down to kiss his sacred turf. Tottenham duly wobbled, and Arsenal were able to celebrate on a day which made their hearts soar and break simultaneously. They soared to overtake Tottenham. They broke to bid farewell to Highbury. 'That's something I will say comes in my mind once every two weeks,' says Henry. 'When I was sitting with Ashley on that little podium, I knew that I was not going to see that stadium any more. It was a sad day, to be honest. I'm not going to pretend to know more than the guy that was born and raised an Arsenal fan, that went there more than me, saw more games than me. But I felt like I became an Arsenal fan. I understood what it was. I loved Highbury. And, that day, a little part of me died, because I loved that place.'

When Nick Hornby recalls how he felt as Arsenal's Invincible achievement became enshrined, that paradise snapshot of Highbury ablaze in sunshine and success. He was struck by the notion that perhaps this would go on and on. 'I thought, I wonder if this will happen all the time, and it will be like we are Liverpool of the seventies and eighties,' he says. 'How extraordinary to be watching them at this time when they're going to win trophy after trophy. As an Arsenal fan we've won trophies, but we're used to long gaps between them. That was the third league title in six years, and the second in three years. Keeping the same players, and knowing that everyone wanted to play for us because of this amazing manager, and because of Thierry Henry, this could keep going and going. This is fantastic . . .'

It couldn't keep going.

Trying to establish a context for the Invincibles that frames the experience in that particular moment in time, it makes sense to return to the end of the previous season. On 7 May 2003, having floundered over the final furlong of the league campaign, Arsenal returned to Highbury for their last home match of the season. Southampton were the visitors, and they were unfortunate to find themselves in the firing line of some of Arsenal's unleashed frustration. That was followed up with a final away outing at Sunderland, which was similarly emphatic. Arsenal won those two games by an aggregate scoreline of 10–1, just ahead of the FA Cup final. It was as if in some way they were trying to shake some disappointment out of their system and make a point about how hungry they were to reclaim the title they frittered away even before the next assault began. Although those two league games didn't mean much other than in terms of professional pride, they would gain relevance in time. They began the sequence still celebrated today with the chant 'forty-nine undefeated', in honour of the record unbeaten stretch in the annals of the English game.

Wenger was asked after that Sunderland match about the ephemeral nature of success. 'It's always extremely fragile,' he replied. 'Especially so in football.'

At the exact moment Arsenal were smashing Sunderland, Chelsea and Liverpool met for a winner-takes-all affair with a fourth-placed finish and spot in the Champions League at stake. Little could anybody guess how the future of English football hinged on that result. The name Roman Abramovich meant absolutely nothing at that point to the English football fraternity.

Nobody bar a handful of businessmen and takeover executives had a clue that a thirty-six-year-old Russian oligarch had been casting his eye over four Premier League clubs with a view to a purchase. He looked at Manchester United, Arsenal, Tottenham and Chelsea. The latter were in debt to the tune of around £80 million, and days away from a serious financial crisis when Abramovich and Chelsea's long-time owner Ken Bates struck a deal. Chelsea making it into the Champions League was an essential requirement, and in beating Liverpool they opened the lid to a treasure chest that transformed the English game for everyone.

Perhaps the Invincible season could only have happened for Arsenal when it did. A graph of Arsenal's fortunes would pinpoint the peak moment. The upward curve of improvements inspired by Wenger, who had always seemed ahead of the game, spiked. The downward curve, with the combined pressures of building a new stadium and absorbing the heavy moving costs, alongside the influx of petro-dollars that enriched the competition, commenced. The 2003–04 season is the point where those two opposing trends meet.

The instant this mega-wealth piled into one club radically transformed the landscape. Chelsea embarked upon a money-no-object spree to upgrade the playing staff and the club's status over a dynamic few weeks. Wenger's choice description was 'financial doping', a reflection of the fact he has always valued pure sporting endeavour as a matter of principle – something precious which is stained by being artificially propped up by external investment. It wasn't long before Chelsea were emboldened enough to try to pluck Arsenal's finest players from them. They made a play for Henry and Vieira. David Dein rejected it and famously retorted, 'Roman Abramovich has parked his Russian tanks on our lawn and is firing £50 notes at us.'

There is a yin-and-yang contrast between what was happening to these two London clubs during that summer of 2003. Arsenal were feeling the pinch in anticipation of the move to the Emirates

Stadium. Although there were still numerous complexities to overcome before any foundations were laid, the club were committed to the project. Arsenal had to try to compete for a few years on the cheap. Wenger began Project Youth.

The plan was to pre-empt a period of belt tightening by recruiting the best young talent around, in the hope that they would develop a togetherness and loyalty to grow into a successful group until Arsenal were settled enough financially to push on again. Amongst the more intriguing transfers was the recruitment of a boy from Barcelona by the name of Cesc Fàbregas, and a teenager from France called Gaël Clichy. Meanwhile, Chelsea lavished Abramovich's millions on international stars with massive reputations: Claude Makélélé, Hernán Crespo, Adrian Mutu, Juan Sebastián Verón. They spent round about £100 million in the summer of 2003. Arsenal's outlay was a little over £1.5 million on Jens Lehmann.

Wenger tried to analyse the situation as logically as he could. 'We have never been big spenders but this season we'll be smaller spenders than ever,' he said at the time. 'At the moment the financing of the stadium hasn't been sorted out and, as a result, we have to be more cautious. Of course, it's not all down to money. But if you want to be successful it's better you have it.'

Picking up after the Invincible season, Arsenal continued where they left off. They won eight and drew one of their first nine league matches, scoring an average of more than three goals a game. Also undefeated in Europe, they were very much in the groove as they headed to Old Trafford on 24 October. Avoid defeat and they would reach the magic half century mark. Another unprecedented milestone for this awe-inspiring team was in their sights.

They ran into a couple of old foes. A typically close encounter tilted when Wayne Rooney took a theatrical tumble over Sol Campbell and the referee bought it. Arsenal were fuming with injustice again as Ruud van Nistelrooy stood over another Old

Trafford penalty. This time, he was unerring. Rooney scored again as Arsenal chased the all-important equalizer, and another inferno raged. For some of the players involved, that sore still niggles today. 'I still have that here,' says Touré, banging on his heart with his fist years later. 'That decision wasn't right. That shows how hard it was for us to lose a game. Most of the players still have that feeling.'

Chelsea went on to win the league in the season that followed the Invincibles. As far as Lehmann was concerned there was no immediate worry that their capacity to splurge would change things so intensely. 'I wasn't that impressed by the signings,' he says. 'Because we knew that we had the best players. We knew that they would become stronger and stronger. But at the beginning we thought if Abramovich failed to win something in the next two or three years probably he would leave. We realized quite soon that this wasn't an option. To a certain extent it was good for English football that Abramovich came in. He lifted it, it wasn't only Arsenal and Man U. All of a sudden there was the third power. I'm telling you it's about competition. If only Arsenal or Manchester United had become champions for the last ten years? How boring. Now English football has Manchester City too. Of course we don't really like that approach. It's too drastic. Clubs like that and Chelsea are stuffed now with money from a single guy.'

From the supporting perspective, Nick Hornby was with Wenger in interpreting all the new money as financial doping which damaged football's fundamental sense of possibility. It turned into more of a probability. 'At first I thought that it couldn't be done,' he says, of the brash ambition to buy a shortcut to success. 'It's all right, you know, because most footballers would rather play for a good team than a rich team. Then of course you saw what started happening. Manchester City is a good example in that as long as you can tempt a couple of idiots which builds you a platform, then suddenly other players are looking at Man City and thinking, *Maybe*. Like Robinho. He was an idiot for going there, but they threw so much money at him, I don't think he knew what he was getting himself in for. Then they were a team with Robinho in it, and then they were a team with Adebayor in it, and they've got a sort of undercurrent which changes the old Man City towards a new Man City. You see how it starts to work. Then within a year of course it's the next wave of players. And the third year you go *OK, this is over*. Of course it's disappointing.

'I think long term they will have to look at how American sport tries to keep competitive. We can't do draft picks because the whole world plays football. But the best way of making money, which is what they all want to do as a league, and advertising and so on, is if there are twenty teams who are as good as each other. And if it goes on like this I think there will be a loss of interest. If my kids only ever see Chelsea, Man City and maybe Man United win the league over the next ten or fifteen years, they will not be watching football when they're forty. Why would you? Why would you bother?'

Project Youth became one of Wenger's greatest disappointments. When he felt he was getting close to being fully competitive, the best players were plucked away by richer rivals. Fàbregas and Clichy left. Samir Nasri, too. Then Robin van Persie. For Wenger these were devastating, hammering, blows.

Arsenal were unfortunate that all the carefully constructed plans to become self-sustainably wealthy were made before the splurge of oil dollars moved all the goalposts.

The success crystallized by the Invincibles could not have been sustained on the pitch without the move from Highbury. 'We couldn't have done it for much longer, no,' assesses Ken Friar. 'We were starting to compete on an uneven basis. There is no question, we cannot compete with people supported by oligarchs or outside financial interests. We know we can't. To do that we needed a bigger stadium than one that held 38,000.'

Coming towards the end of Highbury's lifespan, it was

poignant that such vibrant, vivid, memories should be created as some kind of send-off. The lasting impressions evoke the purest happiness.

For Dennis Bergkamp, Highbury stirs up something romantic and absolutely fundamental about his vision of football. 'For me, as a child I was always looking at English football as my idea of how football is supposed to be. When I think of my time at Arsenal I always have that on my mind: a full stadium, the atmosphere, and a perfect pitch. That's English football. That's Arsenal for me. That pitch was unbelievable. So much care that people put in there. The groundsmen were playing their own game to prepare it. With the fans so close it was beautiful.'

Pat Rice loved the smell of Highbury. He had been around it for decades, since he bunked in as an eight-year-old in 1958 to watch the last game the Busby Babes played before they perished in the Munich air disaster. 'I just loved Highbury, absolutely loved it,' he says. 'It was like an old theatre, but to me it was a second home. I knew all the little nooks and crannies, everybody knew everybody, and the memories were everywhere.'

Highbury meant so much to people. Individuals reacted to leaving in their own way. Robert Pirès bought one of the flats on the redeveloped site as he wanted to prolong the connection. Thierry Henry, who always called Highbury his garden, refuses to go back and see what has been erected in its place. He needs to keep the memories he cherishes unspoiled. For Gilberto Silva, merely thinking about that place years later when he is thousands of miles away in Brazil makes his heart thump so fast he gets a little overwhelmed.

'The team and the ground were the same thing,' reflects Alan Davies. 'The ground had a lot of character. It was beautiful. Amazing. When I started going people were still talking about Alex James and Cliff Bastin. Those were the names that you heard. It seemed to me they were from another lifetime but it was forty years previously, and only recently I was posting a tweet about winning the Littlewoods Cup in 1987 with Charlie Nicholas and Tony Adams and that was twenty-five years ago. So you can feel that lineage in the place. It's in there. The Arsenal team that beat Italy in 1934, even though you weren't born, you feel attached to that. England didn't enter the World Cup and they sent Arsenal out with seven internationals to beat the World Cup holders. You feel the lineage to other games you have heard about that you couldn't go to. The Busby Babes 5–4. Anderlecht in 1970. For me it's things like beating Everton in the Littlewoods Cup in 1988 with 57,000 there. The West Upper was singing! You are so familiar with every bit of the ground. You've been around it. You've grown up with it. You are almost part of it. You feel like you are part of the ground. It was a hell of a thing to lose.'

Arsenal suffered afterwards. Wenger suffered too, which was ironic as the expansion of the club was inextricably linked with the success he brought and the vision for future prizes he hoped to secure.

Midway through the Invincible season, bulldozers began chomping into the earth just around the corner from Highbury. The Arsenal Stadium, to give it its formal title, was the place where the club's present and past were fused together on a daily basis. Local myth told that the footsteps of Herbert Chapman, the iconic manager whose bust adorned the grandiose entrance, could sometimes be heard in the East Stand corridors, which summed up how modern visitors were able to walk in and sense the old days. The future, just a few hundred yards away along Gillespie Road and round onto Islington's old rubbish dump and the industrial estate which backed onto Drayton Park, was beginning to take shape.

Something else happened around that time which made Nick Hornby wonder about another way that the nature of supporting Arsenal changed. 'When I think back to that time I think back to supporting a team that was really capable of crushing anyone else. So as an Arsenal fan I don't think that feeling will ever, ever be bettered. The Invincibles were so good, there weren't that many enthralling games at Highbury. There were games where you thought, *This is nice*, and you'd end up having a chat with the person sitting next to you because it was easy most of the time.

'I think it probably did something in terms of the relationship between the crowd and the team, that they're probably still recovering from. Which is that it turns it into theatre. Because if you're not going to a game wondering about the outcome, which most of the time that season we weren't, then you are going to admire. You want to see a great Thierry goal or two. And you want to see Dennis and it becomes a sort of *this is gonna be great* feeling, which is exactly what you'd do if you went to see a band or a big West End show. The sort of urgent connection between the crowd and the players maybe got damaged a little bit that year and I think possibly the level of anger there has been since is a consequence of that as well. Because you just kind of expected results in a very unhelpful way, I think. But that was the pleasure of the Invincibles season. It wasn't a drama of uncertainty. It was admiration for amazing individuals playing in a fantastic team.'

During the difficult years, as Arsenal's sightlines dropped from aiming for the title to what became universally mocked as the fourth place trophy, and cup competitions slipped down the list of priorities such was the pressure to retain Champions League stature, there were times when the atmosphere at the Emirates became very strained.

Barren spells have always been a part of Arsenal's history. The in-between years. Enduring them naturally makes success sweeter, but they are not fun. There was a seventeen-year wait in between 1953 and 1970, a cluster of mediocrity in the mid-seventies and mid-eighties, and in the post-Invincibles years the trail of silverware began to dry up again. It ended, perhaps symbolically, with Patrick Vieira's last ever kick in an Arsenal shirt to win the 2005 FA Cup. He was the first of the core XI to leave.

The break up of the Invincibles, in certain cases, happened with unwelcome haste. Vieira was sold to Juventus when he had remained loyal for almost a decade. He was twenty-nine, and Wenger wanted to promote Fàbregas.

A year later, Arsenal made it to their first ever Champions League final. Getting there had been a miraculous journey, and it seemed even more outlandish when they led Barcelona with only ten men after an early red card for Jens Lehmann. Barcelona scored two late goals to devastate the dream. The list of Invincibles who left in the immediate aftermath was ominous. Bergkamp retired, Pirès moved to Spain, Campbell, Lauren and Cole cleared their lockers. The latter departure was particularly disturbing, accompanied as it was by a tapping-up scandal involving Chelsea. That was the razor-sharp indicator of quite how challenging the battle against heavyweight salaries and promises of glory would be.

So that was more than half the main Invincible XI gone within two years. Within two more, the only one left was Touré. By 2009, he too had exited London Colney.

★

A decade after the Invincibles, and nine years after the last trophy hoisted by Vieira, Wenger finally watched an Arsenal team once again dance joyously and kiss a cup. In that moment, when Aaron Ramsey and his teammates summoned a burst of unbeatable spirit to recover from 2–0 down against Hull City to win the FA Cup – they simply refused to be vanquished on the day – it was as if the entire club had emerged from a tortuously long tunnel and into the light. Wenger visibly loosened up as he took off his tie and found himself soaked in alcohol and catharsis as the next generation celebrated. The years fell off his face. The albatross unhooked its claws.

It is fascinating that Wenger reflects on that trying period between victories as something bizarrely fulfilling. 'I believe that when one day I look back, certainly I will be very proud of what I have done,' he mused. 'It was a trophy-less period but certainly a much more difficult and sensitive period, and we needed much more commitment and strength than in the first part of my stay here. I went for a challenge that I knew would be difficult because we had to fight with clubs who lose £150 million per year when we had to make £30 million per year.'

So how do you measure success? For some it is only counted in trophies. Others cannot see beyond balance sheets. For the board at Arsenal, though, bridging that evolutionary gap between Highbury and the Emirates, and hanging on in there as they trod as steadily as possible, was perceived as a success of its own. Many in football would never agree with that, and Wenger has faced a repeated criticism that at other clubs, or in other leagues, he would not have been indulged. But within Arsenal's walls, they don't view it as an indulgence.

There has always been a bigger picture when it came to the relationship between Arsenal and Wenger. He had a vision, they backed it unconditionally, and if there were some bumps and bruises along the way so be it. 'Somebody else used the term incorrectly for Mourinho. But if there is any special one, it is Arsène,' says Friar, one member of the staff who straddled the old board at Highbury and the new one at the Emirates. 'He is a very special man and I don't think you will see the like of him again. He played an intimate part in the design of a new training ground and the stadium. He bought a lot of young players who matured like a good wine. The amount he has spent on transfer fees is amazing. He used to come and ask what he would be allowed to spend, and whether that figure was five million or fifty million he would say, "Fine, I know what I have to spend." He was content. He never once screamed and shouted and said, "How can I buy players with that?" He understood the ethos of Arsenal. He has taken ownership in terms of the overall project. He has total freedom, enormous support from the board, he is not under pressure all the time. It has been a unique job.'

Friar steps up from his desk at Highbury House, the club offices just across the concourse from the Emirates Stadium, and walks towards the broad window. Across the skyline, the exterior of Highbury's art deco West Stand dominates the panorama. It is still vivid and beautiful. He sees it every day. It always gives him the shivers.

How dearly Arsenal needed a trophy to display at the Emirates. Wenger looked more contented, more motivated, stronger and more determined than he had in years as he stood on the platform erected for the players to show off the 2014 FA Cup to the masses. For perhaps the first time since leaving Highbury, the Emirates was able to feel properly lived in. It felt like a big deal to the manager who had overseen this transformative decade. 'For a while I thought it was a curse,' he said to the crowd of the Emirates trophy drought. 'Now we have started, we don't want to stop.'

14
The Composer

Arsène Wenger was in his car, making his way out of Highbury after a game that had not gone to plan. A boy saw him, pointed his finger, and shouted, 'Hey, Wenger, I could play for Arsenal!' The manager looked at the boy and replied drily, 'Yes, I am sure you could. But the question is: How well?'

A decade on from the summer of 2004, Wenger sits on the sofa of his office at London Colney and looks back. Generally speaking, it is not his favourite direction. His instinct is to glance ahead. But try as he might, a flush of nostalgia is inescapable. Throughout the conversation about the Invincibles, his warmth for that time and those players shines through.

Arsène, in the Invincibles season the only change to a settled squad you made was a new goalkeeper. Why did you choose Jens?

I watched him in Dortmund. I liked his attitude, his intelligence, his personality. Then it was quite simple because this was a deal that was made between him and me directly on the phone. He without any agent, without meeting him directly. We had some interesting conversations. [He begins to laugh] You know Jens! Every detail becomes important. So I thought this guy will either be a complete flop or a complete success because he is special in the way he is intense, argumentative, and speaks his opinion. I was really interested. After two conversations I thought, *This is the right guy for this team because he is at the same level of motivation and personality as the rest of the team.*

The other strategic move came in deciding that Kolo could play centre back. Is it a sudden idea to try something like that?

Yes. I played him in a pre-season game in Austria. We played against Beşiktaş, and I said to the coach, Mircea Lucescu, who I knew, 'Can you observe my team and can I observe your team?' Before the game I asked, 'Are you good up front?' He said yes. I said, 'OK, give me your impression on my two centre backs after the game.' I played Kolo and Sol in that game. Afterwards he said he was impressed with our power. That is what I wanted to create. I had two turbo trains at the back with immense power. I thought Kolo, guided by Sol's experience, can work. That was a major move.

It's an example of your penchant for remoulding players into new positions. There were several in the Invincibles.

I had big fights with Lauren, who came many times to convince me he is not a right back. [He smiles at the memory] I said, 'Look, trust me, you are a right back.' He said, 'No, I am not a right back. I am a right midfielder, and I can even play central midfield.' I said, 'But you can make a magnificent right back.' After a while he accepted it.

Do you enjoy those challenges, overcoming that kind of resistance?

I like it very much because it really tests the personality of the guy as well. It is my job sometimes to find the right position for the players – it is a case of adapting to his physical potential, his physiological potential and his tactical level.

What is it about you and your coaching ideas that makes reinventing players such a key aspect of your work?

I was involved like that for a long time. For example, with Lilian Thuram, he was a right-sided midfielder when I took him and I put him at centre back. Emmanuel Petit was a centre back and he played midfield for us. When you make those kind of decisions you have analysed the player in detail, or you are not completely comfortable with the position he plays in. I bought Lukas Podolski to be a centre forward or a wide player but after a while I could see he is only a wide player, not a centre forward. He can play behind the striker but not completely at the top. Sometimes you have to revise your judgement.

That team seemed like a particularly intelligent group, as if this place was some kind of hothouse, a university of football where the smartest came to learn and develop and get smarter?

Yes. I must say I have worked at the top level for thirty years and always when you look back with successful teams you always come to the same conclusion: the guys were intelligent. You have players with talent every year, but to achieve something special, first of all you win it by little margins that at some stage of the season become very tight, and you need your players to respond with intelligence to get through these difficulties. You look back and the only thing that strikes you – you can take Henry, Bergkamp, Vieira, Lauren, Kolo, Cole, anybody from that team – they are all intelligent.

Did you enjoy watching the sparks fly between them when there was an atmosphere of tension and creativity?

Yes. They were demanding of each other. They were really strong personalities. In the dressing room it was not always easy. But there was a global positiveness about them, and competitiveness as well. Guys like Sol are demanding personalities.

If you go in the club shop today you can buy an Invincibles scarf or key-ring with the names of the first eleven who began the most games. How do you manage the bigger squad aspect, and keep everyone happy and ready?

First of all you give hope always to the players they can play the next game, and the next game is an important one. The most important thing is not to lose communication. To communicate with them, to explain they are part of it. Maybe a bit less of a part than they would want, but more than they think they are. That's down to the confidence in your honesty, and the distance between them and you. With time you learn to know when a guy needs a talk. It's the same in everybody's life. You have an idea of how close or far away you are in the distance of communication with people. Sometimes you think in your daily life, *At the moment we are not close enough*. It is the same with a player. Sometimes you think, *I am losing him at the moment, he is a bit out, let's get him back again*. You learn that in time. It demands patience, and making yourself available to do it.

Do you have to create a boundary in terms of your relationship with players?

You cannot be a friend. You have to make tough decisions. When you play in a cup final and you have to leave players out, if you are a friend, you cannot do it. You need above all comprehensive respect. That means you have empathy for people and you can't be scared to show it to them, but they have to know at some stage you will make the decision that can hurt them. They have to respect that, but you have to do that in a way that shows them respect as well. You cannot always explain everything, but they must know when you make a decision it is with honesty and respect.

Considering the cliché in the modern game regarding how you motivate millionaires, was that an irrelevance with this team in that they were self-motivating?

I think it's the other way round. These guys are millionaires because they are motivated. They are motivated because they want to be excellent. There are three kinds of motivation: the intrinsic motivation which means the guy is naturally demanding of himself that he wants to be the best, and he has always that inner dissatisfaction with what he has achieved. Then you have the extrinsic motivation, and that's the guy who wants to show others that he is the best in there and he will show them. The other extrinsic motivation is the guy who wants to be respected by others for his quality and what he is doing and he wants to show that quality. Too much money can be a problem sometimes but I don't think that affects the basics of what makes a player. He can lose his way a little bit. But most of the biggest champions have an intrinsic motivation and money doesn't change anything.

Of the most pivotal games during the Invincible season, the draw at Old Trafford was the closest to a defeat. Given the heat of the situation, what happened afterwards is interesting. How do you react and encourage the players to cope with such a situation?

It was especially intense for Martin Keown, who was treated like a gangster. Even his children said, "What's happening with my dad?" He was touched by that. Not a lot happened really but it was such news. I tried to minimize it with the group. Let them talk. Let us focus. For us what is important is our next game. I must say this was a team that was in some ways difficult because they had strong personalities, but on that front, it was a very easy team to lead because they were all mature, intelligent; they knew what was important and what was less important. Things like that were not difficult to deal with. OK, they had a go at Martin, had some jokes, but overall they were not distracted by that.

Is there a part of you that admired how they stuck up for one another even though you couldn't come out publicly and say that at the time?

Of course. I was very proud to see that. They were guys who were ready for a fight. Sometimes when you want to see the solidity of someone, you think, *Could I go for a street fight with this guy?* In this team I tell you we had some. That was their strength, the kind of charisma they had. They gave you the feeling: *I have the quality and I know I have it.* Charisma comes from the second part – *I know* I have the quality and I am ready to stand up for it.

When you talk about getting the maximum from your team over a season, although you did in the league, did you feel that didn't happen in the other competitions?

Yes, because that year we could have won the Champions League. Three days before we played Chelsea in the Champions League we played Man United in the FA Cup. I did not want to sacrifice the FA Cup, so I thought I would play a team I thought could beat Man United. The game was at Villa Park and I remember Man United on the day kicked us. Reyes got kicked, we lost some players, we lost some mental strength, and three days later we lost against Chelsea in the final minutes of the game. I could see we were jaded. So I think if I made a mistake that season, that was not to sacrifice the game against Man United. Many times the Champions League conflicts with the FA Cup and you sit there and think, *What do I do?* [He exhales deeply] That season we could have won everything. I tried to do it. We had the squad to do it. We had sixteen or seventeen players of top, top level.

That week segued into the Liverpool game, which went badly to begin with. In such circumstances, watching a situation like that unfold, do you feel powerless?

You are sitting there. The whole season you didn't lose a game, and suddenly in a week you think you can lose everything. Chelsea were not far behind us in the league at that stage. What was very worrying was at half-time, when you go in the dressing room, I could sense there was no response. The guys were absolutely speechless. You take one disappointment, two disappointments, and you sit there 2–1 down . . . I was really worried. I tried to mobilize the energy. *Come on guys, let's respond, let's go for it. We cannot accept this.* One of the things you need in our job is the special talent, and the special talent turned up with Thierry Henry. Suddenly it was 4–2 in minutes. Thierry made the difference.

Can you describe how that feels?

It is such a relief. The problem when you have experience is you anticipate well what can happen next. When it's not going well, you anticipate the disaster which is behind that. It's scary. So when it doesn't turn out that way it is a huge relief. When we won that game that was when I knew we would win the championship. The team was convinced of that. Very good managers minimize the time of crisis. Where one manager can lose five or six games, a very good one can lose two or three. The more you lose, the more you are in danger to lose the next one. To stop a crisis quickly is one of the most important qualities. The longer it lasts, the more you swim against the stream. The confidence goes, the questions rise. You have to respond quickly as a manager.

How strange was it that winning the league at White Hart Lane turned out to be such a mixture of emotions?

Because Chelsea lost, we knew that if we didn't lose we would be champions. We were cruising, amazing, and suddenly we were back to 2–2. I thought the referee was a bit unfair with Jens. He pushed Keane on a corner when Keane tried to tread on his foot. He gives a penalty and I still don't understand how he did it. We were champions, but there was nearly a fight between Sol and Jens! It shows you how much these guys were winners. We had to calm them down in the dressing room. It was not euphoria. It was really amazing. 'Guys, we have won the championship, come on!'

Why was it such a struggle in the final four games to stay unbeaten?

It was one of the hardest challenges. Most of the time when you are champions the concentration goes, everybody relaxes, and you lose the next game. As simple as that.

Did you give them a big speech to guard against that?

Yes. We played just enough in every game not to lose. But everything had gone! I was more stressed in those games after winning the league. Even the final game against Leicester we were down at half-time. I told them, 'Look, we have won the championship, now I want you to become immortal.' They were thinking, *This guy is completely mad. What does he want from us? What is he talking about?* But somewhere, they started to believe. In the games, even though the games were not convincing as there was no real urgency, we did just enough. We didn't lose. When we were down against Leicester you could see the response was strong. I had no worry any more.

Could it have only happened when it did? Before the Abramovich money really took hold, the move from Highbury, and then more external investment strengthening your rivals?

It was just in time. Everybody speaks of the Chelsea team that went on to win the championship afterwards but in 2004 they already had a super team. Abramovich came in and injected more money, they brought Didier Drogba and Ricardo Carvalho into a team who already finished second. They took over after that. We had Chelsea coming in, Man City later. Look what happened next – now you have

Man United not even in the Europa League. You make one or two average decisions and you are out of it.

Was there something that resonated with the money coming in – albeit legally – that reminded you of your experience in fighting the financial doping of Bernard Tapie's Olympique de Marseille when you were with Monaco?

You feel like you have stones against machine guns. People don't want to know that. They just want you to win the championship. It was a very difficult period but as well a very exciting one.

Recreating the identity of this football club, and the Arsenal style, was a major development. Were you surprised how quickly that change took hold?

What I like about Arsenal, and what I am very proud of, is that the club is a mixture of respecting traditional values while also being not scared to move forward. I believe in the last fifteen to twenty years you have all of that. You had Highbury, the move forward to the Emirates, fantastic periods, difficult periods, the strength that is underlying every decision at the club. I stayed here more for the respect I have for all that. There is something special here that coincides with how I feel a football club should behave. I still believe, even if we have frustrated our fans in recent years by not winning the championship or the Champions League or the FA Cup, that somewhere people respect that deeply. When we went the other day through Islington with the FA Cup you could feel the immense support behind the club. It's about a trophy but also about history and values. The club is respected all over the world for that.

How was it to observe the aesthetics evolve too?

That happened over a period of years through the quality of work we do. Sometimes when I speak to foreign coaches and ask about a player and they say, 'This is not an Arsenal player,' that is the best compliment you can get. It means two things: first, that Arsenal has a style of play, and, secondly, that the players have the characteristics needed to play for the club. That is a slow process we have created. Of course we want to keep that for the future.

Was there anything you learned about management from that group?

I learned you can achieve things that you think are not achievable, and you have not to be scared. People tried to make me look ridiculous when I said that we could win the championship without losing a game. I didn't say it like that. I said the ideal target would be that, but they turned it around and turned it against me.

Is that frustrating?

They make you look the way you are not and nobody likes that. But even if they turned it around it helped me to achieve it. It convinced me. Many times I had problems with that – not to be scared to come out with your ambition. But the way you speak out is seeds in the brains of your players. Because you speak to your players when you speak to the press. In its subconscious, it is interesting. I am very interested in the mental subconscious force of the memory of a team. For example, we have just come out of the Champions League final with Atlético Madrid against Real Madrid. Forty years ago they played in the final against Bayern Munich. I have seen the game, it's a game they deserved to win. In the last minute of the game Schwarzenbeck equalizes against Atlético Madrid; they replay two days later and lose, conceding four goals. This time, they play against Real

Madrid, in the last minute of the game they concede an equalizer and in extra time they lose 4–1. It is an exact repetition of the story that happened forty years ago. I am sure before the game they have spoken so much about that. And at that time, Luis Aragonés was the symbol of Atlético and they had his name embroidered on their shirt in 2014. During the game it is a really nice gesture to remember Aragonés, who was a man I loved. But I hope it was not a subconscious thing for the team to repeat the history. That is what you discover – the huge importance of the subconscious language is in people's minds, with the strength of that mental aspect.

So even though you suffered, and the team suffered, by mentioning an unbeaten season the year before, the seed needed planting?

I think it needed that to push the players to think it can be done. It is the seeds you put in the brain that sometimes flower later.

Reflecting on those players, can you express what was special about them in your eyes, starting with Jens?

To have such huge desire was his quality. He was a player who was ready to die to win.

Lauren?

Fantastic personality, underestimated player for me. Top quality and a real fighter as well.

Kolo?

Massive passion for the game, technically much better than everybody thought he was, and a happy boy as well. He brought such enthusiasm to the team.

Sol?

A deep thinker. When you get to war you can stand next to him. All these players were very intelligent, but as well Sol was a strong personality.

Ashley?

Ashley Cole was a regret of my career. He left on a misunderstanding between his agent and the club. A fantastic fighter as well. I recall I played him the first time against Bayern Munich in the Champions League and he showed straight away he would never get out of the team again. The rest of his career has shown how big a player he is. It should have been here, though.

Freddie?

Another strong personality, very focused to win. He came to see me the other day and I said to him, 'I remember coming to see you when you lost with Sweden against Portugal in the European Championship.' Two days later the guy at the hotel said he has not moved yet, he was so disappointed. He was an unbelievable fighter. Even in the Champions League final against Barcelona he was immense. He could find resources even when he was dead, because of his fighting spirit.

Patrick?

Patrick is one of the legends of the club. I think I owe him personally a lot because he was the first player I brought here and he gave me a lot of credibility. He had all you needed. The charisma, the class, the fighting spirit. He is just Patrick. Since he came to England every year people say, 'We have found the new Patrick Vieira,' and yet nobody found him! He was amazing because he could turn the game forward with two guys against him. I've seen Patrick having a go at the central defenders: 'Give me the ball.' 'But you are marked.' 'I don't care!' He still always managed to turn the game forward. An amazing football player.

Gilberto?

Gilberto is, for me, class. Modesty, humility, on a human front a top-class person. He was ready to sacrifice himself for the team. When you analyse it well, all these players were talented and intelligent, but when you look at the success of the team, you need that screen player in front of the defence who is ready to do the dark and dirty work for other people. Gilberto was that kind of player. I bought him when I saw him with Brazil at the World Cup in 2002 and I thought here is the piece who will give us something special. He was a good football player. After that World Cup, I walked in the dressing room and the way he behaved and the discretion he showed meant you would never for a second think this is the guy who has just won the World Cup.

Robert?

Robert is as well one of the legends of the club. A top-class football player, and the smiley killer. He killed you with a smile – but he killed you. Give him a football, you have him on your side the whole day. He loves the game, passionate, and such a great finisher, an unbelievable finisher. He was so intelligent in his movement he was always free. I still curse myself even today about the day he got injured in 2002. We played Newcastle and I said to myself, *I overplayed Robert.* I wanted to rest him. I always said, *OK, the next game.* Before the Newcastle game I thought, *This time I really have to rest him.* In the end I played him and thought, *I will take him off before the end.* We started the game and he was world class. Suddenly he hurt his cruciate. Honestly, after that he was never the same player; he lost just a fraction physically, even if he was the same with a football. Before he was injured he was the best player in the world in his position. When we won the championship you could see the way people reacted in the ceremony.

Dennis?

Dennis is the science, the intelligence, the charisma. A strong character, very determined, super professional. I have seen Dennis from the first to the last day of his career focusing on every single pass. Dennis was the intelligent perfectionist. Dennis needed to control the world through his perfection. When he missed something he was always unhappy. He had an intrinsic desire to be perfect in what he did. His teammates admired him, which was very important at that time. When your big players create a good understanding, and they respect each other, it makes your team stronger. For a while there was a big competition between Thierry and Dennis, but because of the age difference, it made them work together. When they got to that stage we became unstoppable.

Thierry?

Thierry was a super, super talent. This guy could do absolutely everything. What symbolizes Thierry are those special goals – the goal he scored against Liverpool, or the goal he scored against Real Madrid in the Bernabéu. That showed you how immense this player was. He was Usain Bolt with a top football talent. He had everything you dream to have as centre forward – pace, super intelligent, analyses very quickly everything, calm in his finishing. Even in France he is underrated. Sometimes he was perceived behind Zidane, but for me he was a dream striker. He was one who when we were being dominated could create a goal on his own from nothing. That gives a team such strength. Just find him once, he will do it.

★

When you make me go through this team it makes me realize how everybody was a special talent and a special personality.

Do you remember what you did after the Leicester game to commemorate this fulfilled dream?

No.

Really?

I am talking to you about the past, but it's painful for me to look back, because I am always so much focused on thinking forwards. It was one of my dreams, to win the championship without losing a game. [He pauses, breaks into a huge smile and his eyes light up as the next thought occurs to him] And I want to do it again.

Epilogue

Ten years on from the Invincible season, the strength of connection felt by the majority of the players for that time is profound. Nowadays, they are spread all over the world, but talking about their memories seems to transport them back to the fields of London Colney and the lush, trimmed pitch at Highbury. The same strength of feeling emerged from all of them, whether it was Jens Lehmann speaking as he ate a cream cake over breakfast in Munich, Lauren in the carpeted corridor of the Emirates Stadium, Kolo Touré fresh from the training ground in Liverpool, Sol Campbell settled on one of the deluxe sofas of his wife's interior design shop in Pimlico, Martin Keown drinking a coffee in Soho before hopping on the tube for a leaving do of an old friend at Arsenal, Freddie Ljungberg in a private room within a chic Mayfair tailors, Ray Parlour in his local pub in Essex, Patrick Vieira recommending the cheesecake in his favourite café in Cheshire, Gilberto Silva with the gentle breeze making the curtain behind him waft at home in Belo Horizonte, Edu in his office at Corinthians, Robert Pirès over lunch in Hampstead, Dennis Bergkamp in his favourite spot tucked away in the corner of the Ajax restaurant, Thierry Henry in New York City. Wherever they are, whatever they are doing, they still feel the bonds to the club, to each other, and to that extraordinary season they shared.

Their monument lives on in the minds of Arsenal supporters, who look forward to the day on the football calendar each year when every other team has lost a match, meaning the immaculate Premier League season cannot be equalled.

Here's to Arsenal's enduring Invincibles, as of May 2014:

Jens Lehmann, who returned for a second spell in 2011 and then did some of his sessions for his coaching badges at London Colney, still loves to visit when he can. He is looking to get into management as a main man rather than a goalkeeping coach.

Lauren, who lives back in Spain, came to the launch of the 100 club (formed by Arsenal to keep retired players who made more than a century of league appearances in touch with the club and each other). He tries to attend several matches a season. He is still a keen amateur boxer.

Sol Campbell returned to play in 2010. Another who made his way to the Emirates to don a club tie as a founder member of the 100 club, he enjoys his life outside football but still likes to drop in at the training ground.

Kolo Touré is still playing, and having ended the 2013–14 season at Anfield he went to the World Cup as part of the Ivory Coast squad. He keeps Arsenal in his heart and still calls his old teammates whenever he needs some friendly advice.

Ashley Cole has struggled to continue ties with the club since he left for Chelsea. Perhaps attitudes will soften in future.

Freddie Ljungberg is an Arsenal ambassador, who works with the supporters' clubs and has travelled to Asia on the club's behalf. He lives in London with his young family, and has opened a sports bar called Freddie's in his native Sweden.

Patrick Vieira works for Manchester City but keeps Arsenal in his heart. Ten years to the day after the final Invincible game against Leicester he posted the message, accompanied by a photograph of him on the Highbury pitch holding the Premier League trophy: 'I will never lose my pride being captain of such a special team.'

Gilberto Silva retired from football at the age of thirty-seven. In 2014 he returned to London, popped in to see some old friends, and was delighted when Arsène Wenger invited him to train with the current team. 'It was amazing,' he says. 'I just went to say hello. When I was there all the memories came flooding back.'

Robert Pirès, who has made his home in North London, goes to the training ground on a regular basis and is usually seen at the

Emirates on match days. 'It's important for Arsène, and for the youngsters, to show that you have to work to succeed. If I train with them, it's to give an example, and it's a great pleasure,' he says. He is an Arsenal ambassador who enjoys making official trips on club duty, and was on the pitch at Wembley when today's team celebrated with the 2014 FA Cup.

Dennis Bergkamp journeyed by car from Amsterdam to North London with his family in 2014 to commemorate the unveiling of his statue at the Emirates. His wish is to return to Arsenal in a coaching capacity some day.

Thierry Henry returned to Arsenal with a slightly different role in 2012 as a self-confessed fan who happened to have the chance to play for his team. When the hero of old scored a goal against Leeds the crowd in the Emirates Stadium experienced something akin to an out-of-body experience. While playing in the USA his heart beats in a red and white rhythm. When he is on the pitch for the New York Red Bulls fans yell at him, 'Thierry, your team has just scored,' or whatever the news from Arsenal might be, from the sidelines. It is expected he will return to London and be welcomed back to the club in a new capacity when he finishes playing.

Three other Invincibles are still playing – José Antonio Reyes at Sevilla, Gaël Clichy at Manchester City and Jérémie Aliadière, who joined Umm Salal in Qatar. Since hanging up their boots in their late thirties Pascal Cygan, Sylvain Wiltord and Nwankwo Kanu are enjoying life post-retirement. Edu continues to work in football with Corinthians and travelled to London to visit his old club during the 2013–14 season. Martin Keown and Ray Parlour are prominent Arsenal experts in media circles and remain close to the club. They are both members of the 100 club (with more than 300 appearances each) and Keown is an Arsenal ambassador.

Arsène Wenger ended the season with some important club business to attend to before heading to the 2014 World Cup, including signing a certain contract extension to take his tenure as Arsenal manager into a third decade.

Appendix: Arsenal FC statistics, Premier League, season 2003–2004

Player appearances and nationalities★

Squad No.	Name	Appearances	Nationality
1	Jens Lehmann	38 (0)	GER
3	Ashley Cole	32 (0)	ENG
4	Patrick Vieira	29 (0)	FRA
5	Martin Keown	3 (7)	ENG
7	Robert Pirès	33 (3)	FRA
8	Fredrik Ljungberg	27 (3)	SWE
9	José Antonio Reyes	7 (6)	ESP
10	Dennis Bergkamp	21 (7)	NED
11	Sylvain Wiltord	8 (4)	FRA
12	Lauren	30 (2)	CMR
14	Thierry Henry	37 (0)	FRA
15	Ray Parlour	19 (6)	ENG
17	Edu	13 (17)	BRA
18	Pascal Cygan	10 (8)	FRA
19	Gilberto Silva	29 (3)	BRA
22	Gaël Clichy	7 (5)	FRA
23	Sol Campbell	35 (0)	ENG
25	Nwankwo Kanu	3 (7)	NGA
28	Kolo Touré	36 (1)	CIV
30	Jérémie Aliadière	3 (7)	FRA

★ Players with the minimum ten Premier League appearances to earn a winners' medal. Brackets indicate substitute appearances.

The Games

| 16 Aug. 2003 | **Arsenal** Henry 35 pen., Pirès 58 | 2–1 | **Everton** Radzinski 84 | W |

16 Aug. 2003 — **Arsenal** 2–1 **Everton** — W
Henry 35 pen., Pirès 58 — Radzinski 84

24 Aug. 2003 — **Middlesbrough** 0–4 **Arsenal** — W
Henry 5, Gilberto 13, Wiltord 22, 60

27 Aug. 2003 — **Arsenal** 2–0 **Aston Villa** — W
Campbell 57, Henry 90

31 Aug. 2003 — **Manchester City** 1–2 **Arsenal** — W
Lauren 10 o.g. — Wiltord 48, Ljungberg 72

13 Sept. 2003 — **Arsenal** 1–1 **Portsmouth** — D
Henry 40 pen. — Sheringham 26

21 Sept. 2003 — **Man United** 0–0 **Arsenal** — D

26 Sept. 2003 — **Arsenal** 3–2 **Newcastle** — W
Henry 18, 80 pen., Gilberto 67 — Robert 26, Bernard 71

4 Oct. 2003 — **Liverpool** 1–2 **Arsenal** — W
Kewell 14 — Hyypiä 31 o.g., Pirès 68

18 Oct. 2003 — **Arsenal** 2–1 **Chelsea** — W
Edu 5, Henry 75 — Crespo 8

26 Oct. 2003 — **Charlton** 1–1 **Arsenal** — D
Di Canio 28 pen. — Henry 39

1 Nov. 2003 — **Leeds United** 1–4 **Arsenal** — W
Smith 64 — Henry 8, 33, Pirès 18, Gilberto 50

8 Nov. 2003 — **Arsenal** 2–1 **Spurs** — W
Pirès 69, Ljungberg 79 — Anderton 5

22 Nov. 2003 — **Birmingham** 0–3 **Arsenal** — W
Ljungberg 4, Bergkamp 80, Pirès 88

30 Nov. 2003	**Arsenal**	0–0	**Fulham**	D
6 Dec. 2003	**Leicester City** Hignett 90	1–1	**Arsenal** Gilberto 60	D
14 Dec. 2003	**Arsenal** Bergkamp 11	1–0	**Blackburn**	W
20 Dec. 2003	**Bolton** Pedersen 83	1–1	**Arsenal** Pirès 57	D
26 Dec. 2003	**Arsenal** Craddock 13 o.g., Henry 20, 89	3–0	**Wolverhampton**	W
29 Dec. 2003	**Southampton**	0–1	**Arsenal** Pirès 35	W
7 Jan. 2004	**Everton** Radzinski 75	1–1	**Arsenal** Kanu 29	D
10 Jan. 2004	**Arsenal** Henry 38 pen., Queudrue 45 o.g., Pirès 57, Ljungberg 68	4–1	**Middlesbrough** Maccarone 86 pen.	W
18 Jan. 2004	**Aston Villa**	0–2	**Arsenal** Henry 29, 53 pen.	W
1 Feb. 2004	**Arsenal** Tarnat 7 o.g., Henry 83	2–1	**Manchester City** Anelka 89	W
7 Feb. 2004	**Wolverhampton** Ganea 26	1–3	**Arsenal** Bergkamp 9, Henry 58, Touré 63	W
10 Feb. 2004	**Arsenal** Henry 31, 90	2–0	**Southampton**	W
21 Feb. 2004	**Chelsea** Guðjohnsen 1	1–2	**Arsenal** Vieira 15, Edu 21	W
28 Feb. 2004	**Arsenal** Pirès 2, Henry 4	2–1	**Charlton** Jensen 59	W

13 March 2004	**Blackburn**	0–2	**Arsenal** Henry 57, Pirès 87	W
20 March 2004	**Arsenal** Pirès 16, Bergkamp 24	2–1	**Bolton** Campo 41	W
28 March 2004	**Arsenal** Henry 50	1–1	**Man United** Saha 86	D
9 April 2004	**Arsenal** Henry 31, 50, 78, Pirès 49	4–2	**Liverpool** Hyypiä 5, Owen 42	W
11 April 2004	**Newcastle**	0–0	**Arsenal**	D
16 April 2004	**Arsenal** Pirès 6, Henry 27, 33 pen., 50, 67	5–0	**Leeds United**	W
25 April 2004	**Spurs** Redknapp 62, Keane 90+4 pen.	2–2	**Arsenal** Vieira 3, Pirès 35	D
1 May 2004	**Arsenal**	0–0	**Birmingham**	D
4 May 2004	**Portsmouth** Yakubu 30	1–1	**Arsenal** Reyes 50	D
9 May 2004	**Fulham**	0–1	**Arsenal** Reyes 9	W
15 May 2004	**Arsenal** Henry 47 pen., Vieira 66	2–1	**Leicester City** Dickov 26	W

Acknowledgements

I was blown away by the goodwill, ready co-operation, and fascinating story-telling from all these Invincibles: heartfelt thanks to Jens Lehmann, Lauren, Kolo Touré, Sol Campbell, Martin Keown, Freddie Ljungberg, Ray Parlour, Patrick Vieira, Gilberto Silva, Edu, Robert Pirès, Dennis Bergkamp, Thierry Henry, Arsène Wenger and Pat Rice.

I will always be grateful to David Dein, not only for his help, but also for miraculously arranging a ticket to White Hart Lane at the last minute in 2004. Thanks also to Ian Wright, Lee Dixon and Ken Friar for sharing their Arsenal wisdom and passion, to Nick Hornby for nodding in my direction to make this possible and sharing his perspective, to Alan Davies, whose memory for detail is as extraordinary as his humour, to James Scowcroft for an insight into what it was like to play against the Arsenal of 2003–04, and to Dave Woods for remembering that infamous press conference in 2002.

Thank you to an army of capable fixers. Katie and Dan at Arsenal fielded countless calls with patience beyond the call of duty, also Miel at Ajax, Steve at Liverpool, Jamie Jarvis, Walid Bouzid, Darren Dein, Stuart Peters and Adrian Philpott. For his Arsenal insight, expert photographic eye and generosity with the pictures, thank you to Stuart MacFarlane, who was a phenomenal help. For his in-depth knowledge, thank you to Iain Cook. For their superb expertise with the nuts and bolts and useful gems, thank you to Toby Moses, Ross Martinovic, James Copnall, Andrew Mangan, Paddy Barclay and Ian Hawkey. Thanks to Philippe Auclair for knowing how it feels to wear the same two hats, Tom Watt for the Highbury desk, and Mark, Rob, Ashley, Jo and Eugene for making me laugh along the way.

I cannot thank David Luxton enough for his rock solid support and endless calm. Also Ben Brusey for editing with such an enthusiastic and smart touch, and Penguin for choosing me to try to do this subject justice. Thanks to Marcus at the *Guardian* and *Observer*, Jamie at Fox Soccer and Paul at *Champions* for indulging my distraction.

And crucially, love to my wonderful family – to all four parents, who lend unfailing support, and to my superhero sons, Luca and Nico, who bring me endless sunshine. Thanks for understanding when I was more absent-minded – and just plain absent – than usual over a period of months. On that front, eternal gratitude to Justine Walker, the best nanny in the world, for holding the fort.

A word, too, for the Arsenal Foundation, who do such good work. www.arsenal.com/thearsenalfoundation

Sources

Books
Tony Adams, *Addicted* (Collins Willow, 1998)
Philippe Auclair, *Thierry Henry: Lonely at the Top* (Macmillan, 2012)
Dennis Bergkamp, *Stillness and Speed* (Simon and Schuster, 2013)
Sol Campbell, *The Authorised Autobiography* (Spellbinding Media, 2014)
Ashley Cole, *My Defence* (Headline, 2006)
Amy Lawrence, *Proud to Say that Name* (Mainstream, 1997)
Robert Pirès, *Les canards ne savent pas tacler* (Editions Prolongations, 2011)
Robert Pirès, *Footballeur* (Yellow Press, 2003)
Christov Rühn (ed.), *Le Foot: The Legends of French Football* (Abacus, 2000)

Film and TV
Arsenal Legends: Thierry Henry (Arsenal Media, 2013)
Keane and Vieira: Best of Enemies (ITV, 2013)

News articles and press releases
'Amazing Kolo Touré story', TalkSport, 20 March 2014
'Arsenal chief blasts "stupid" players', *Sun* (via Agence France-Presse), 23 September 2003
'Arsène Wenger's 1,000th game', *Daily Mail*, 20 March 2014
David Conn, 'Arsène Wenger's 1,000th match at Arsenal set to usher in his third era', *Guardian*, 15 March 2014
Sir Alex Ferguson quoted in League Managers Association, 'Statement regarding Arsène Wenger', 21 March 2014
John Giles, 'The impossible dream?', *Daily Mail*, 5 October 2002
Amy Lawrence, various *Observer* articles, reports and interviews
Steve Stammers, 'Wenger: I'm sorry', *London Evening Standard*, 25 September 2003

Jeremy Wilson, 'David Dein on the sliding doors moment that transformed Arsenal', *Daily Telegraph*, 21 March 2014

David Woods, 'Treble-talking Weng taunts rival bosses: You lot are too scared', *Daily Star*, 21 September 2002

Brian Woolnough, 'Arsenal chairman admits he's losing fight to clean up act', *Daily Star*, 23 September 2003

Index

and Ajax Academy 133

appointment as Arsenal manager 27–9, 65

and Arsenal's transformation 31–40, 132–3, 147–8; and evolution of intuitive playing style 133–46, 215–16

and the Battle of Old Trafford 7, 13–14, 15–17, 211–12

and Bergkamp 149–50, 220

and Campbell 157, 217–18

and the Champions League 104, 212

coaching methodology and management 29, 63, 77–80, 85, 97–8, 147, 148–52, 189–90, 208–12, 216; flexibility and improvisation 59–63, 68–80; health and fitness regimes 34–9; training system 139–45

on Cole 218

and Dein 21, 23–7, 39, 45, 46–7, 50, 100–101, 141, 146

developing and maintaining Arsenal's identity and success 42–58

Dixon on 151–2

and Edu 62–3, 152

and Ferguson 7, 13–14, 15–16, 173

and 'financial doping' 197, 199

first visit to Highbury 22–3

forecast of an unbeaten season 172–5, 187, 217

on Gilberto 219

and Henry 44, 67, 68–9, 103, 187–8, 220

interview about the Invincibles 207–21

and Keown 182–3

and Lauren 208, 217

and Lehmann 150–51, 164, 169, 207

vs Leicester City, 2004 182–3, 185

and Ljungberg 72–4, 218

on Pirès 219–20

post-Invincible season 196, 197, 198, 199, 200, 202, 204–5, 206, 225

press conference (autumn 2002) 172–5

Project Youth 198, 200

recruiting new players 42, 43–5, 47, 48–51, 53–4, 62, 75–7, 122, 198

and Touré 59, 75–7, 208, 217

and Vieira 122, 126, 148, 218–19

vision for Arsenal 41, 47, 146, 172–5, 202, 205

and Weah 21

and Wright 94n

Wenger, Lea 171, 185

White, Johnny 156

White Hart Lane 155–69

Wigan Athletic 195

Wilson, Bob 102

Wiltord, Sylvain 20, 60, 62, 89, 145, 225

Winterburn, Nigel 22

Woods, Dave 172–3

World Cup
1998 67, 70, 121
2002 44, 219
2010 99
2014 225

Wright, Ian 28–9, 33, 35, 38, 118, 119, 122, 131, 148

on Bergkamp 132

and Henry 93–4

and Wenger 94n